I0138779

It's Been a Wild Ride
Jim Warvell

Paperback ISBN: 978-1-62660-148-2
Hardcover ISBN: 978-1-62660-149-9

For more information email warvellfamilycollection@aol.com

Cover photo: Jan Warvell as Princess Kachina atop White Feather
Book and cover design by Michael Campbell, MC Writing Services

IT'S BEEN A WILD RIDE

JIM WARVELL

To Jan:

It's been a wild ride

CONTENTS

FOREWORD

This is the story of a *real* American Cowboy.

It is not the story of a man who wears a cowboy hat and rides a horse. No, this is a man who has been recognized for his work and his achievements and because of those things he has been inducted into the Texas Cowboy Hall of Fame.

He is also a showman.

This is not a man who sings and dances but one who really entertains and has often been called the man who raised the 'entertainment' value of rodeos to an entirely new level. If you have ever been to a rodeo and have seen the horse and novelty acts entertaining the crowds while the stadium gets ready for the next event, then you have an idea of what Mr. Jim Warvell and his family created.

They were showmen of the first degree!

I was writing articles for a newspaper when the editor asked me to meet and interview someone who had grown up in the local area. The man, I was told, had carved out a career on the rodeo and entertainment circuit. He was being honored for his achievements and I was to write the story about his induction into the Texas Cowboy Hall of Fame.

Having never met a "real" cowboy, I was anxious to do the story. We met at a local restaurant and over lunch he told me about his life and, as an added bonus, he told me some of the best stories I have ever heard!

The man was Jim Warvell and he was 75 years old when I met him! He lived on a ranch in Texas and had done more throughout his life than I even think he or the editor realized! When we were through eating, I knew I was having a meal with someone who had a story to tell. What this man had done in his life was more than a front-page interview. It was a book! Jim did not realize it, but I did!

This man had a fascinating story to tell about real cowboys and real entertainment. He just needed to know there were people interested in what he had to say. Once we established that he had a great story to tell, Jim started writing things down and the more he wrote, the more he remembered and the more he remembered the better the story became!

Jim started on a farm in Darke County, Ohio. He went from riding horses on a farm to riding rough stock in rodeos. He soon expanded to developing horse riding acts. He improved on those acts and was soon entertaining fans across America. His showmanship did not go unnoticed and he began entertaining the people of Europe, Asia and South America.

He tells this story in his own way, his own words and his own cowboy lingo. It is a fascinating story of "how the west was entertained" by one man and his family.

We meet thousands of people during our lifetime. Many of them are relatives and you have no choice but to accept them. Most of the people you meet are "here today and gone tomorrow." A few, however, are very special and can change your life and the perception you have about things.

Jim Warvell is one of those people.

Jim Warvell is a true cowboy and I am proud to say he is a friend of mine!

Bill Stevens

INTRODUCTION

I went to a little country school with no thoughts of what I would accomplish in life. When I graduated from high school, in the year book, one of my quotations was:

WHATEVER I DO,
I WOULD LIKE TO BE SUCCESSFUL

Not entirely knowing what that meant, I started on my life journey with young ambitions in mind. I had thoughts about professional baseball, but by having ponies and horses all my younger days, I gravitated to competing in local horse shows. This led to many adventures and future accomplishments of which I had no thoughts or dreams, one of them being that someday I would marry, and my wife and two girls would be inducted into the Texas Cowboy Hall of Fame!

Leading up to this induction point, I realized I crossed roads with people that I could never have imagined. It made me reflect on meeting and working with lifelong famous stars such as a man that I had seen in grade school. His name was Gabby Hayes. We worked a show that Gabby was featured in with the "Warvell Family." This trend seemed to follow us throughout the United States, Canada, Mexico, Brazil, Puerto Rico, Kuwait, Singapore, Japan, England and France.

There was also Glenn Randall, Sr., one of Hollywood's most famous horse trainers for the movies. He trained Roy Roger's horse "Trigger" and for the Ben Hur movie starring Charleton Heston. Glenn went on to perform with the Ben Hur Chariots at the same locations and venues where the "Warvell Family" was performing.

Show business led us to work with such people as Lucille Ball, Chuck Connors *(The Rifleman),* famous singers such as Charlie Pride, Wayne Newton and a number of other stars.

When we were inducted into the Texas Cowboy Hall of Fame, we were acknowledged alongside:

Tommy Lee Jones
Nolan Ryan
Lyle Lovett
Larry Mahan
Debbie Garrison
Pam and Billy Minick

Crossing our family's path in the past were other stars such as:

James Garner
Lucille Ball
Gabby Hayes
Wayne Newton
John and Bill Paxton
Irene Ryan (Granny from *The Beverly Hillbillies)*
Stars from the *Bonanza* TV series.
Antonio Aguilar
Montie Montana Sr.
Montie Montana Jr.
Edith Head (costume designer of Hollywood Fame who designed costumes for us on one of our shows)
Jones Benally, Navajo Hoop Dancing Champion and healer
The Wallenda Family (Circus legends)
Willie Nelson
Canadian Mounties
Queen of England's Troops
Presidential performance for Richard Nixon

Reflecting on my life the evening of the induction into the Texas Cowboy Hall of Fame, I had never imagined that I, my wife, and two girls would be awarded in this way. I thought about my words written long ago in my high school year book and felt that I had indeed accomplished them!

Jim Warvell

WHAT IS A COWBOY?

In the early days, the reference to a cowboy was not flattering at all. It started with the people in the eastern part of the United States. Each of them had specific jobs. Some of these people moved out west and brought their professions with them. They would move, set up their business and be immediately self-employed.

When the population of America increased and the need for more food (especially meat) became apparent, the western part of the country, with its open land and ability to raise huge herds of cattle, was the obvious choice for providing the food. Ranchers let their herds fatten on the abundant grass and seed before taking their stock to market. Moving the herds was called a "cattle drive" and when they started, the people who were hired to ride horses alongside the herds were usually the ones who were out of work or had trouble finding work. This work was low paying and very difficult, especially for those doing it for the very first time. It was also a dangerous job and it took a special individual to go out on these cattle drives for weeks or months at a time.

Cowboys on cattle drives would sleep under the stars. They were subject to whatever the weather threw at them. There were dust storms, drought and horrible, uneven terrain they needed to conquer. It might be exceptionally hot during the day and miserably cold at night. It was not a job for the faint of heart. As if the weather was not bad enough, a cowboy also had to deal with the natural aspects of the outdoors. The snakes, scorpions, coyotes, mountain lions and other predators were everywhere.

Because of the job, cowboys often wore the same clothes for days or weeks on end. Personal hygiene was often neglected since they often worked from dawn until dusk. There were a lot of yellow teeth and a lot of smelly bodies. The only friends and acquaintances they had were other cowboys. There wasn't any female companionship on the cattle drive and if anyone on the trail broke an arm or a leg, they had to fix it themselves and do what they could until the injury healed. The motto on the trail was, "no work, no pay" and they meant it!

When they came close to a town, these men were often paid so they could "blow off some steam." The cowboys would go into the town where they (and their money) would be greeted by the merchants of the town. The "saloons" got most of their business, but the brothels would also get some of it too! After spending their hard-earned cash, the cowboys might get into trouble before they were sent back to their camp. With no more money to spend, the townspeople were very happy to see them go!

This is when they were referred to as "cowboys" meaning they were a lower member of society. This moniker lasted for several long years until the image began to change.

William Frederick Cody, known as "Buffalo Bill," had a pivotal and an important impact on the image of the cowboy. He had been a Pony Express rider, stage coach driver, army scout and buffalo hunter. [1]

Buffalo Bill went east and, while he was there, started to change the reality and perception of the west and of cowboys in general. A writer named Ned Buntline wrote some fascinating stories about Buffalo Bill and the frontier in the western part of the country. The stories became hugely popular and the residents of the east coast could not get enough of them. Buntline depicted the cowboy as a prince on the western plains who was battling the elements, fighting the Indians, taming the land and taming the wild horses. According to Buntline, cowboys were the American heroes of the west!

Buffalo Bill was a showman and he did a few small theater shows regaling his stories to a captive audience, who, once again, could not get enough! From these enthusiastic crowds Cody got the idea to form

---

1 Some say buffalo hunters were despised because of their poor hygiene and strong smell from months of handling buffalo hides and not washing or changing their clothes!

a show called "Buffalo Bill's Wild West and Congress of Rough Riders of the World." It was a gamble and it paid off handsomely!

Several years later, a man looking for a catch name (to attract some attention for future political aspirations) would take the name Rough Riders[2] and turn it into a successful run for the presidency. His name was Teddy Roosevelt and the Rough Riders were very active in the battle of San Juan Hill!

The list of characters in this original show included real cowboys, Native Americans (Indians to eastern folks!), Mexican Charros, Russian Cossacks and a few more thrown in for good measure. All of the people he used in his show were real and authentic to their heritage as were their costumes.

Two of the biggest names in his show were Chief Sitting Bull and a young female sharpshooter from Greenville, Ohio, named Annie Oakley.

Chief Sitting Bull had surrendered after being instrumental in the famous massacre of the 7th U.S. Cavalry at the Battle of the Little Big Horn. He was a very impressive sight in his Indian regalia with the big feathered headdress worn only by the chiefs of the tribe.

Annie Oakley, known as "Little Miss Sure Shot," was famous for her precision shooting. She held several shooting records and some of them still stand today. Her target shooting act mesmerized the audience. Men were supposed to be the best marksmen of the era, but here was this little lady who was shooting at everything and hitting everything she shot at! Annie was with the show for 17 years.

For almost 20 years, Buffalo Bill took his troupe of several hundred all over the country. He brought all his livestock with him as well. He often went to Europe and performed for some of the biggest dignitaries of the day. In 1905, Buffalo Bill's show performed at the base of the Eiffel Tower in Paris, France to more than 3 million spectators!

People all over were totally enthralled by the reenactments of the scenes from the Wild West. Some had never seen a real, honest to

---

2 The name Rough Riders, however, was first used by Buffalo Bill!

goodness Native American in person. Others were even more enchanted by the artistry of the men and women who were riding wild horses, roping and wrestling steers, shooting firearms and performing acts that seemed to go beyond the capabilities of an ordinary person.

All walks of life saw this highly successful show, from the common man on the street all the way to Kings and Queens of Europe. Adults and children were beginning to yearn for more information about the west. Children began playing cowboys and Indians with toy guns, bows and arrows. The success of the Buffalo Bill show inspired other Wild West shows such as "Pawnee Bill's and the 101." Everyone was soon making money on this new form of entertainment.

Then came the real breakthrough! Short films and movies suddenly grabbed the attention of the public. It was soon obvious to Hollywood and the film industry the best moneymakers were westerns! The cowboy was soon immortalized on film and even more people got to see what was happening in the west. Great actors like John Wayne, Tex Ritter and Gene Autry became legends and stars of the silver screen. Later, television perpetuated the image of the cowboy with great shows like 'The Lone Ranger,' 'Wagon Train,' and 'The Roy Rogers Show.' Westerns took over the Saturday morning time slots and then they took over the evening time slots as well with shows like 'Maverick,' 'Cheyenne,' 'Have Gun Will Travel' and many, many more.

The public wanted more and soon they got more romanticism in the cowboy characters. Gene Autry and Roy Rogers were soon riding "dancing" horses adorned with silver saddles and shiny bridles. As they rode down the dusty trails they would sing a song (often a love song) and sometimes they would even play the guitar.

For generations, the public was shown images written by script writers. Soon, these images were ingrained in the viewing public's mind. They took this type of "cowboy living" to be fact and believed this was how the cowboys out west really lived.

With more and more people clambering to see more of the cowboy world (and to be a part of it) opportunities began to spring up everywhere! Wild West shows began to diversify into different sports. An exhibition show became an event and later a contest, where cowboys would compete for money and the audience would pay to see them do it.

In addition, big cattle drives were now a thing of the past. Big ranches had sprung up and cowboys worked for a ranch on a seasonal basis. Instead of spending months and months on cattle drives, they worked the cattle on a daily basis until they were trucked off to market or loaded directly onto freight cars. As everything became more and more professional, so did the cowboy. Good money and a steady income could be made for those who knew what they were doing.

Soon, more acts came along at these "contests" (rodeos). These acts included Roman Riding (standing bareback on two or more horses), trick riding (acrobatics on a running horse) and jumping over a car while Roman Riding, just to name a few of the incredible daredevil acts of the era.

Only the best were hired and only the best could achieve these feats.

New ideas for spectacular acts were a guarded secret because of the high competition for getting jobs at the very best venues.

This same secrecy also applied to the rodeo cowboy and ranch hands. The old methods of training were fading away but these talents were still coveted by the ranchers. Knowledge had become power and this power was the ticket to being the very best and getting paid the most money. Ranchers knew this and kept only the ranch hands who knew their jobs. The rodeo promoters applied the same principle. They knew who were the best performers and those were the cowboys who were asked to compete in front of the huge paying crowds.

So, for the public, the word "cowboy" had become loosely used and thrown around. If a person put on a pair of boots and a "cowboy" hat, he was called a cowboy. If he owned an acre of land, had a horse and some hamburger in the freezer, he would call himself a rancher.

However, in the ranching and rodeo world, the word "cowboy" was used humbly and with all reverence. Often, someone would say, 'You are a hell of a ranch hand and a good "cowboy" This would be the ultimate compliment and signify that the recipient had reached the pinnacle of success in his chosen profession.

You can call anyone a "cowboy" but a true cowboy is one who has worked hard and earned his name![3]

3 Jim Warvell is one of those cowboys. He was inducted into the Texas Cowboy Hall of Fame in 2010. Known for his specialty acts and shows, Jim knows what it takes to be a true cowboy. He grew up on a farm, rode in the rodeos and then expanded to specialty acts. In doing this book, Jim had a particularly good quote about the men in this book and how he felt about them. "This is what went through my head when my family and I were inducted into the Texas Cowboy Hall of Fame. I felt honored and guilty. Guilty because of the old cowboys who worked all their lives as cowboys. Men like Wiley and Bill who are long forgotten and have never been recognized with an honor like this. That is why I think the word 'cowboy' is sometimes used without merit."

CHAPTER 1

THE YEAR WAS 1936. The great depression had wreaked havoc on the country. World War II was still five years away (for most Americans, at least) and life in western Ohio, Darke County to be exact, was still laid back and easy going.

This area of Ohio is known for many things. Annie Oakley was born here, only three miles from the farm where my grandparents lived and where I was born. Lowell Thomas the great radio and newspaper personality was also born in the county. Anybody from the 30s, 40s and 50s should know his name for sure!

The biggest attraction is 'The Great Darke County Fair,' one of the biggest and arguably the best county fair in the country (certainly in the state!) In 2018, The Great Darke County Fair attracted almost a quarter of a million people and this is just a county fair! Darke County is also known for its agricultural community and having some of the best soil in the state of Ohio. Corn, bean and wheat crops are the mainstay of the farmers and the quality of the crops is second to none!

THE FAMILY

My grandparents were two of those farmers. They lived on a small farm (75-80 acres) near a town called Ansonia, about 10 miles north of Greenville, the county seat for Darke County.

Their house was typical of the small family farms that dotted the entire country. My grandparents cooked over open flames in a large 'fireplace' type oven. There was no electricity and no running water (all the water had to be pumped by hand) and, of course, there was the proverbial outhouse. The doctor and veterinarian were miles away and because the only mode of transportation was a horse drawn carriage it meant they were at least two hours away (one hour to go get the doc and one hour to bring him to the house!).

Grandpa was called 'Red' and besides being a farmer, he was also the blacksmith of the area. He worked out of the barn and all the locals brought their horses and equipment to him for repairs and upkeep. Between that and farming he was kept pretty busy.

With no doctor or veterinarian nearby, my grandparents quickly learned to be self-reliant and that meant grandpa had to learn all about their animals. He was the vet of the family and grandma was the doctor! When necessary, grandma also became a midwife and on May 2, 1936, she had to use those skills as she delivered her first grandchild, a bouncing baby boy: *me!*

I was given another name, but one day my grandfather looked at me and said, "I'm going to call him Jim." Not James, not Jimmy and not Jimbo. From that day on, I was Jim to him and to everyone else as well. It is the only thing I will answer to.

Goldie Warvel (c. 1930s): Grandma Goldie cooking at the family farm where I was born

My mother was one of six children and she was very active in sports when she was in high school. She would have two more children in the years to come. Jack, born two years later, and Joe, the youngest who would come along 12 years after me. My father was about 5'8" and very strong. He went by the name of 'Lefty' (for obvious reasons) and did whatever it took to keep food on the table. He played professional baseball with the St. Louis organization, sold sporting goods in Greenville at Skillman's Department Store and he managed semi-professional baseball teams. He also worked and bred horses. He did anything to make a dollar and put food on the table and clothes on our back.

Growing up in this type of environment may seem harsh to some (hearth cooking and outhouses) but it was normal to us. We were not the only ones who lived like this because our friends were in the same boat as we were! We just made the most of it!

Dad loved baseball and he groomed me to be a baseball player from a very young age. I loved the game and I was decent at it, too. I could pitch and play the field, something my high school team would later use to their full advantage.

GROWING UP

I went to Butler Township school for grades 1-8. We had a basketball team but you had to be in the 7th or 8th grade to be on the team. During lunch those of us in the lower grades (1-6) would all hit the basketball courts in the gym and play. One day, the coach of the school's team saw us play and he wondered why I was not on the basketball team.

"Would you like to be on the basketball team?" he asked.

"Sure," I told him, "But I'm only a sixth grader so I can't be on the team."

He was surprised but he recognized I had talent so he went to the principal and asked if he would make an exception. They contacted my parents and when all was said and done, they allowed me to be on the team as long as it did not affect my grades. I got to play basketball for three years instead of two!

When you graduated junior high school, and were ready for high school, there was a choice to be made. Because of where we lived, we could pick our high school. We could go to Arcanum High School (the biggest school in the biggest local town) or we could go to New Madison High School (now called Tri-Village High School). It was up to the student as to which school they would attend.

I chose New Madison High School and it was here that my athleticism allowed me to play varsity baseball, basketball and track from my freshman year on.

In the 10th grade, my brother Jack and I, like many farm kids, had our own horses. We used to race them at county fairs. We eventually sold our racehorses and bought two quarter horses from Texas. The quarter horse is reputed to be the fastest breed of horse over a distance of a quarter of a mile. They were bred for speed and we raced these horses as well.

In 1954, I set the county record for the pole vault! It lasted for several years until the new fiberglass poles came into common use and allowed pole vaulters to jump much higher. I set the pole vault record with a stiff, one piece metal pole. With these solid, non-bending poles, you had to have a spring in your step and power in your jump because that was all you had to get over that bar! (The fiberglass poles would bend and the 'spring' of the pole as it straightened out would send the pole vaulter soaring through the air.)

I tried one of these new fiberglass poles but my timing was thrown off and I never did figure out how to use it properly. I was playing four different sports. Other pole vaulters started using the fiberglass poles but I stuck with my trusty metal pole, set a record and when I left high school my record was still standing.

The family moved to Savona, Ohio, a small town with a maximum population of 55 people, provided you counted the transients and the visiting relatives. It was only three miles from New Madison where the high school was located. The railroad tracks were less than 150 feet from our house and since this was one of the major forms of transportation, we got a lot of trains running near our home. The big, modern steam engines would come flying down those tracks and when they did our beds would shake a few inches across the floor.

THE OUTHOUSE

Our home was just like the other homes in the neighborhood. Again, we had no running water and we had to use an outhouse. Our neighbors were in the same situation as we were and, once again, we just made the most of it. To us, it was how people lived.

We should pay a little tribute to the beloved outhouse! Believe it or not, the outhouses of this era were as much a status symbol as anything else. This may sound strange but it is true!

If you had a brick or concrete outhouse, you were considered 'affluent.' Most folks (including my family) had the old wooden outhouse with spaces between the boards and knotholes in the wood. These 'facilities' usually had two holes in them, one large and one small.

Since most families were not 'affluent,' they tried to save money any way they could. So, instead of toilet paper, every outhouse had a large catalog in them. These were usually from one of the larger retail stores because their books were bigger and had more stuff to look at!

These catalogs served two purposes. You always had reading material and you always had 'toilet paper.' Unfortunately, the catalog pages were not very 'comfortable' to use so, while you were sitting there reading the books (or looking at the pictures), you tore out a few pages and crumpled them over and over again to soften them and make them usable for the task at hand.

Lime was scattered over the contents to keep the smell and flies away (it didn't always work but we tried!) When the outhouse needed cleaning, there were people who went around and did that, just like the people of today who go around and do odd jobs like mowing the yard.

On the back of the outhouse was a trap door exposing the waste. These traveling outhouse cleaners could shovel it out and make cleaning easier. This cleaning would usually cost around $2.00.

I remember the outhouse had a wooden door and in the middle of the door was a knothole that you could see through while you did your business. On the outside, under the roof and around the building there were usually several wasp nests. One day, I was sitting there (reading the Sears catalog) and my brother Jack was near the outhouse. He had his BB gun with him and he decided to take a shot at the hole in the door. He did and it was a 'perfect' shot. The BB went through the hole and hit me in the shoulder! Thinking I was being stung by wasps, I jumped up and ran out of the outhouse screaming and hollering with my pants still down around my ankles.

To this day, Jack has never let me forget that story!

THE PONIES THAT AGED VERY FAST

The farmers were not rich enough to own tractors so they had to use horses and mules to plow their land and haul wood to the house. These animals were a necessity and we learned at an early age how to take care of them since they were some of the most important things we owned.

There was a big barn on our property. Dad fixed up two stalls in this barn and got us two ponies, one for me and one for my brother Jack. The ponies were not the best by any means but my brother Jack and I took great care of these ponies. We brushed them, walked them, fed them and made sure they could be ridden with ease. Jack and I would often ride them and play cowboys and Indians.

One day, dad came and told us the ponies were getting old and would soon disappear. Jack and I did not know what he meant until about a month later, we went out to the barn and the ponies had disappeared! We were stunned but remembering what dad had told us, we understood.

Two more ponies showed up before long so we took good care of them too. After a few weeks of grooming, riding and nurturing these ponies, dad came to us and said that these ponies were getting old. A month later, these ponies were also gone!

It did not take long before two more ponies arrived and the process repeated itself once more. Dad informed us that ponies got old quickly and disappeared because of their old age. This continued on and on over the course of the year.

Ponies would arrive, they would be given to us and then Jack and I would take care of them. After a month, they would get old and *poof,* they would disappear! I tell you this story because there is a happy ending to it!

About 25 years later, I was visiting a horse barn in Greenville, Ohio, when I was introduced to a man who trained race horses. We talked for a few minutes and then he made a statement that took me by surprise.

"I knew your father," he told me, "and I knew you and your brother Jack, too!" I smiled and tried to remember him but there was no memory of him.

"Sorry," I said sheepishly, "but I don't remember you. How did you know the family?"

"Well," he explained, "I ran several carnival rides and one of them was a horse ride for young kids. I had to have gentle ponies that were used to having kids ride them. I always bought my ponies from your dad because he used to tell me that he had two boys who brushed the horses, fed them, rode them and took great care of them. I never had to worry when I bought ponies from your dad. They were always gentle and well taken care of by your family." I laughed and told him what happened and how dad told us the ponies were getting old right before they would disappear from the barn.

He laughed and told me the rest of the story.

"I once asked if you boys cried when he took the ponies away from you. He said he told you boys the ponies were getting old and going to disappear so you boys would not feel sorry for the ponies and not cry in front of them!"

"He told me you boys thought 3-year old ponies died of old age. It was easy for him to sell those nice ponies to me and then take some 'unbroken' ponies and give them to you for training. You guys did a nice job of training them, too!"

It was nice to know that ponies don't disappear when they get old. You learn something new every day!

PASSING THE TIME

I learned quickly that horses on a farm are a necessity. When they are seven or eight years old, the work horses are usually sold. The ones that have a lot of cow experience usually stay a little longer. They can be used to rope, cut the herd and other important things necessary to keep a farm or cattle ranch in business.

Although the work was hard, farmers also learned to have fun, too. I used to love it when the farmers would put on horse shows to 'show off' their horses and contests to see who had the best horse and rider combination. I participated in most of them and my friends and I became pretty good at them, too!

One of these contests was the 'scoop shovel' race. A shovel would have a long rope tied to the handle. The end of the rope would be put around the saddle horn and while one rode the horse, his partner in the race would grab the shovel's handle, sit on the metal part and 'ride the shovel'! The object was to have the horse and rider pull the shovel across the arena, around a barrel and back to the finish line. The fastest one would win, provided they crossed the finish line with their partner still 'riding the shovel.' If you fell off, there was nothing for you except a disqualification and a lot of bruises! Our scoop shovel partner was Danny, our travelling buddy. Danny was so good at this event, he earned the nickname 'Scoop Shovel'!!!

We also had a 'pick-up' race. Again, it was a race involving two contestants. One would be riding a horse at the start-finish line. The other contestant would be waiting at the far end of the arena. The horse and rider would take off as fast as they could, race to the waiting partner and the partner had to grab either the rider's arm or the saddle horn and pull himself onto the horse. Then the two of them had to race back to the start-finish line. Again, the fastest time would be the winner but if the partner missed the 'grab' he was in for a nasty fall!

The tire race, however, was by far one of the funniest to watch and one of the toughest to do. Tires were laid out in the arena and a contestant had to ride as fast as he could to them. Once there, he would dismount and his horse would (hopefully!) stand perfectly still while the contestant got off the horse, ran to the tires and then crawled through them while not letting the tire leave the ground! (Try it sometime!) Once through the tires, the contestant ran back to his horse, turned him to the finish line and while the horse was now running at full speed, the contestant would hang onto the saddle horn, let his feet hit the ground and then 'jump' onto the saddle, similar to what the Pony Express riders used to do.

These were fun and very competitive. I enjoyed them immensely but had no idea I was preparing myself for my future! Heck, I was not even out of high school yet!

When I did get out of high school, I had a chance to play professional baseball. I knew if I signed a contract my time would probably be spent in the minor leagues and I was not very interested in that. By now I had spent four years playing baseball, basketball and track. The senior yearbook staff listed my future in the world of coaching but that did not interest me, either.

It was time for a change!

CHAPTER 2

THE YEARS FLEW BY and before I knew it, I was in the last two years of school. These years would be filled with studying and sports since, during the winter school months, these were the things that interested me the most.

Of course, I always kept my eyes open for rodeos and horse shows and because I did, my brother and I got the chance to go to the biggest horse show and contest in the state of Ohio. It was called 'The Congress' and all you had to do was mention it to anyone who knew anything about horses and they knew exactly what you were talking about!

Jack and I went to 'The Congress' and we both entered the events we enjoyed the most and both of us won ribbons! We might have won some money, too, but all I can remember is showing off our ribbons because we were so very proud of them! 'The Congress' also had some rodeo events like calf roping, saddle bronc riding, steer wrestling and more. We stayed and watched the rodeo and decided that was what we wanted to do next. We wanted to be rodeo cowboys!

Our horses were with us and we kept them in the same barns as the horses used by the well-known cowboys. We were young kids and we talked to many of these cowboys. After listening to what they had to say, we went out and bought the same type of rope used by the famous calf ropers. Jack and I set a bucket in front of our horse stalls and started throwing the rope around the bucket.

Luckily, there was a professional calf roper from Tracy, California, who had his horse next to ours. He watched us for a few minutes and then told us he would be willing to show us how to 'calf rope.' He was a true and great professional calf roper and he taught us how to hold the rope, to twirl it and then to throw it. He also showed us how to rope one end of a bale of hay. We wore out several pieces of rope in those days, not to mention the fact we also got to 'tenderize' the hay before the horses got to eat it (and they never even thanked us!).

Jack and I must have made a good impression because our new cowboy friend invited us to his ranch in California. He said ranchers always needed good ranch hands who knew their way around horses and farm animals. He told us we could work in the daytime and at night we could rope calves until our arms hurt! We could not do it that year but we were hoping to do it the next year.

Unfortunately, we never saw him again. Many years later, I thought of him as I worked a rodeo in the area near Tracy, California. He was nice enough to help us and I wish we could have met up just one more time.

It was at 'The Congress' that Jack and I turned from contest horse show riders to rodeo cowboys.

A LOT TO LEARN

We entered a lot of events even though I did not know the rules! For instance, we thought if you were riding rodeo rough stock all you had to do was stay on the horse to win. We did not know you needed to have the most points to win! We also did not have the right kind of spurs for riding the bulls. We had to buy the special rigging used for bareback riding and since it was new to us, we had to figure out how to use it!

A *rigging* is a piece of leather that fastens to the bucking horse (sort of like a saddle) but you have to sit on the bare back of the horse (hence the name). This rigging has a hand hold that looks like a suitcase handle but is always in an upright position.

As if all of this was not enough, we also had to purchase special spurs to ride the horses. The rowels of these specific spurs were round and would spin like a wheel. We definitely had a lot to learn but we were willing to learn and willing to take a shot at every event they had!

We thought bareback riding would be simple. The bucking horse (with the equipment we did not know we needed but had to buy) was in a chute, unable to escape. You then climbed down onto the horse, got yourself settled and grabbed the leather hand hold. Then you motioned for the gate man to open the gate. Once that happened, the horse would tear out of the gate and begin to 'buck, twist and turn' as it tried to throw the rider off.

While the horse is doing its part, you, the rider, have to do your part. To get the most points possible, you need a horse that will buck and while the horse is turning and twisting the rider is trying to bring his spurs over his shoulders, waving his free arm in the air for balance so he can stay on the horse. All this at the same time! It was extremely tough on your tail bone because every time the horse moved, the rider felt it!

Again, these were all new rules to us and we had to learn them quickly or not make any money on the rodeo circuit. I can remember those first few rodeos with fond memories now, but back then, oh, boy!

The other contestants and the fans loved watching us ride. Our knees would go every which way, our arms would be flailing and there would be a lot of daylight between us and the horse. All this happened before there was a 'SPLAT,' and we were on the ground! Being enthusiastic young rodeo cowboys, we would pick ourselves up off the hard arena dirt, brush ourselves off and say, "That was fun but I can ride him next time!"

Back in those days, Robert Mitchum was a big movie star. He starred in a movie called "The Lusty Men" and it excited me to no end when I saw the movie!

Mitchum played a rodeo cowboy. His character is old and out of shape. He wants to stay on the rodeo circuit but his friends and fellow cowboys advise him not to ride anymore because of his age. Mitchum tells them, "There never was a bronc that couldn't be rode and there never was a cowboy that couldn't be throwed!" Mitchum's character enters that rodeo and is killed when he is thrown from the horse. It was a sad ending but he died doing what he wanted to do.

It was his movie that made me realize I wanted to do what I wanted to do and that was to be a rodeo cowboy!

Jack and I still had not made any money and we definitely needed some. While on the road, we heard about a man who was putting on horse shows at state fairs, carnivals and anywhere else he could earn a few dollars. He called it a "Wild West Show." The riders who worked for him got $5 a head every time they rode one of the horses out of the chute.

We thought about it and it sounded like easy money. We knew how to ride horses and bulls were not that hard to ride (were they?), so Jack and I decided it was time to switch over and make a little money. A fellow rider named Dave joined us and the three of us were soon on the phone talking to a man named Cherokee Hammond who had the little family Wild West Show. He asked us a bunch of questions and before long he hired all three of us. All we had to do was make it to his next stop, a little town in the Great Smoky Mountains. We knew this was a great deal! We were now Wild West rodeo hands going to the Smoky Mountains!

When the three of us arrived, we were a little stunned. The fairgrounds certainly had seen better days (probably 60 years ago!) but this was our new home, for a few days anyway, and we looked up 'Larry,' the man we needed to meet. Larry told us this was where we would be riding and as we stood there, we looked around and saw nothing but dirt, dirt and more dirt. There were a few campers but no chutes, no arena, no grandstand, no nothing!

Our eyes soon landed on two big trucks with horses tied to the side of the truck.

"Where are all the other horses, bulls and cowboys?" I asked.

"They will all be here in a couple of days," we were told.

Since it had been a long trip, we decided to call it a day and get some sleep. Back then, I had a Chevrolet pickup truck with a homemade camper shell made with four posts. There was one at each corner and some masonite nailed to the top and sides. Rain could creep down the sides of the 'shell' but the middle of the truck always stayed dry so that is where we put our sleeping bags. Often, however, we would just sleep outside and use the stars as our roof!

OUR FIRST 'RODEO'

The next morning, we got up to find a few changes to the surroundings. There was a new addition to the neighborhood in the form of an old truck that looked like it was loaded with junk. When we went over to look at it, we discovered the 'junk' was a disassembled rodeo arena including chutes, chute gates, calf pens and the other items we would need to have a rodeo! There was also another truck next to it that contained the bleacher seats for approximately 75-100 spectators. This was a true mobile rodeo if there ever was one! This was the rodeo arena we would be working in but first, we had to put it together.

Usually, when we worked other arenas, they were already built and stayed in place year-round. When you were 'on the road,' however, you learned to bring your arena with you. It had to be disassembled, moved, reassembled, used and then the process would start all over again.

Since it was still early in the morning, we got in the pickup, headed out and found a local grocery store. Although there were diners and cafes in the town, we decided it would be cheaper to live off of crackers and bologna until we started earning some money. The cafes wanted a nickel for a cup of coffee and around a dollar for eggs, ham and toast. That was just for one meal! We knew we could eat for days on that kind of money as long as we bought groceries instead and that is exactly what we did! We got our supplies and headed back to camp. Our 'breakfast nook' was on the grass beside our pickup truck. It was here we ate our breakfast, lunch and dinners! For kids like us, how could life get any better!

It wasn't long before Larry "The Wild West Man" came to our truck.

"Good Morning," he said to us.

"Good Morning," we replied. He proceeded to tell us that a couple of his cowboys had been hurt riding at the last stop. When he said that, we thought there might not be enough of us to have a show and therefore, we would not get paid!

Our fears were put to rest when he added that he had a son and son-in-law who were good hands and willing to help. In addition, he also had found a couple of local boys who wanted to try their hand at the rodeo circuit and ride some of the wild stock. That put our mind at ease and we were suddenly getting excited about the day.

"Now," he told us, "We have to put the arena together. I need some extra hands so if you want to earn another $10, you can help. I also have some kids from town to help so what do you say? Will you do it?"

Wow! Ten dollars was $10 and that was several days' worth of gas for the truck and food for us! Plus, we did not have anything else to do that day so we readily agreed.

As we built the arena, we met his son and son-in-law. We discovered his son took care of the bulls and the horses. He also ran the chutes where the horses and bulls were put before they were turned loose into the arena. The son-in-law was the pickup man. He was the one who made sure the bulls and horses were taken out of the arena after they had been ridden. This would free up the arena for the next rider. He was also a trick and fancy roper (twirling the rope in various loops, like the famous Will Rogers) and he was a bullwhip specialist. His wife was a trick rider. They were definitely a big part of this 'Wild West Show' and we realized this was actually a family show and family business!

We finished building the arena and took the rest of the day off. Tomorrow would be the big day for us! As we were about to go back to the pickup, we heard a voice calling us. It was Larry, the head man.

"Hey, boys! You did a good job today in setting things up. Tomorrow we are going to be short a couple of cowboys but we still have to buck 10 to 12 head for the crowd. That means each of you will have to ride four horses instead of one."

We knew he needed help. The crowd would pay for the opportunity to be entertained but to do that we would have to put on a show and ride a certain number of wild animals to keep them happy. We were here for a couple of days and if the first day was a rip-off to the fans then word would get around and no one would show up for the second day.

"So," he continued, "How about it? You willing to ride four animals a piece?" One horse was $5. Four horses were $20.

"Yes," we told him, "No problem."

"I also have a mule that we have been advertising," he continued. "Anybody that can ride that mule will receive $1,000 from me!"

This was the first time we had heard about this but it was his 'calling card' and drew a lot of people into the show. Locals would try to ride the mule. Their friends and town folk would turn out in droves to watch them. The thrill of someone earning a quick $1,000 or getting thrown from a bucking mule was a magnet to a town that rolled up the sidewalks every night at 7PM!

THE MULE

These townspeople thought this was the chance of a lifetime to earn that money. All they had to do was ride a mule for 10 seconds. For many, they had been riding horses and mules all their life. How hard could this be? Larry's mule, however, was very special!

I remember the first time I saw that mule. He would be led out for people to see. He seemed calm enough but then, what did we know! They took the mule to the chute. He was still calm enough. The rider climbed up on the chute and then sat bareback on the mule. There were no reins so the rider had to hang on to the mule's mane (the hair on the back of the mule's neck). Even then the mule was still calm and sedate.

No problem, right?

Wrong! Then they opened the chute and all hell broke loose!

The mule jumped out of the chute! He did not walk out, he jumped out! Next, the mule went into a spin and not just any spin. This mule would spin so fast it was almost impossible to count the spins! After only a few seconds, the rider would be flying through the air only to land hard on the ground.

The mule would stop turning, give out a, "Heeee Hawww," and then become the calm, mild-mannered mule that people had seen being led into the arena! This would happen over and over again. All of us thought about riding the mule (or trying to) but I wanted to ride the other stock (broncs and bulls). The money would have been nice but watching more experienced riders get tossed like a fruit salad was disheartening, so I politely declined.

HOW SO FEW CAN BECOME SO MANY

Later in the day, Larry asked all of us about taking extra turns and riding extra events. As Larry was short on riders for this event, he said to us.

"The fans like to see a variety of cowboys, especially from the western states. They don't want to see the same ones over and over again. You three are going to be my 'different' cowboys from the western states."

"They will recognize us," we told him.

He shook his head and laughed.

"When you ride as yourself," he explained, "We give out your name and where you are from. Then, after you are done with that ride, we take you back and put a different colored shirt and hat on you. When you ride the next time, we will give you another name and a different state. We can even let you wear a bandana so they can't see much of your face. Well, what do you say?"

It sounded odd to us but apparently Larry had done this before and had it all figured out! Sure enough, the three of us were made to look like ten different cowboys throughout the course of the show. The best part was we got paid $5 for every time we rode and we got in a lot of practice.

I remember that first day when we were 'different' cowboys. Somebody in the grandstand hunted me down and called me by one of the 'other' names Larry had given me when I was riding. He had told the crowd I was from Billings, Montana.

"Excuse me," said the stranger, "I went to school in Billings, Montana. Do you know so and so?" I had no answer for him so I tried desperately to get out of the situation.

"Uh, can you look me up later?" I replied, "As you can see, I'm kinda busy right now and can't visit with you."

For the rest of the day I tried to stay clear of that guy and kept a low profile.

We learned really quick that Larry's family members who made up the rest of the show (specialty acts and trick riding) were really good at what they did. After the acts were done, Larry and is family sold popcorn, cotton candy, peanuts and drinks in the grandstands. If you worked for this "Wild West Show" you learned to do a lot of different jobs!

Later in life, I had time to reflect on Larry and his "Wild West Show." This family had talent, a lot of talent! Under different circumstances, they could have been great, really great! All they had to do was take one of their many acts, get new gear, (saddles, ropes, costumes, good music, good announcer, etc.) and then do some advertising. I think they would have been sought after by the best circus, rodeo and entertainment companies in the world! Larry and his family loved their way of life and even though it was hard work and a lot of 'what ifs' they managed to live good, happy lives.

Hey, "What is Life" anyway?

Our first day as Wild West hands soon came to an end. We were tired and exhausted beyond our expectations but we were somewhat amused too. The three of us slept in the pickup truck, again. Unfortunately, it had rained all night. This had created mud holes everywhere and a lot of slippery and sliding conditions. It had also leaked in the truck.

Come morning, we had a problem. After the previous two days of work, we were in dire need of a shower but there was none to be found. We ended up washing ourselves by using a garden hose.

Our buddy, Dave, decided to go into town and get a cup of coffee but we knew he probably was going after cigarettes. Since the town was more than a morning walk away, I let him drive my pickup truck.

MY STUCK TRUCK

When Dave came back, he drove through a deep mud hole. Lo and behold, he got my truck stuck in the mud hole all the way up to the axles! We tried but the three of us could not get it out and we were thankful that somebody volunteered to use their truck to pull my truck out of the hole.

Unfortunately, his truck could not get enough traction (did I mention it had rained the whole night?) and we got nowhere with his truck. Somebody who was watching all this suggested we should ask a local farmer and see if we could get his tractor to pull the truck out of the hole. It was a good idea but it would have taken two to three hours to find a farmer, get a tractor there and pull the truck out.

We did not have a lot of time (show time was only a few hours away) and we were about to leave the truck there.

"I can get your truck out," a man said.

I looked at the man and he looked very familiar. It turned out he was in the show and had an 1800 to 2000-pound steer that was used in the show. The ox (steer) would actually do simple tricks like standing on a pedestal on all four of his feet. The man would put a harness on the ox and tell people how he would use him to pull huge tree timbers out of the forest.

Once the crowd was in awe of these feats, the man would invite a bunch of kids (12-13 years old) to come into the arena and hold onto a rope that was about 50-60 feet long and attached to the harness on the ox. Soon, there would be a long line of kids holding the rope and ready to prove how strong they were. Hah!

The tug of war would easily be won by the ox. Then there would be 20-25 kids on the rope and that was a losing effort for them as well. This was all very entertaining to the crowd and once he had them all in the palm of his hand, the man would send the kids back to their parents. This would be accompanied by a huge round of applause and cheers from the crowd.

Remembering his act with the ox, I thought, sure, he can bring his ox over here and hook it up to the truck. If he could pull out the truck, fine! If not, we would have to try something else but I was willing to give it a try.

The man left and since we were now only about an hour away from starting the show, a crowd of people (men, women and children) were now arriving. Most of them were big, strong men who were willing to try and ride a mule for $1,000!

For the moment, these future customers were now watching the 'how do we get the truck out of the mud hole?' show for free!

The ox owner soon returned. He returned, but the ox was not with him.

"Where is the ox?" I asked.

"Oh," he explained dryly, "The ox would have a hard time pulling that truck out of that mud hole. I did bring a long rope though."

I was confused but he smiled at me and then tied one end of the rope to the front of the pickup truck. He took the other end and walked the rope until it was laying flat on the ground in a straight line.

"Okay," I asked as I walked up to him, "What now?"

"Watch this," he said. "I am going to ask those kids over there to come over here and pick up this rope and pull that truck out of the mud."

"Uh-huh, sure," I muttered.

I watched as this man who had a way of communicating with an audience went over to the crowd. He talked to everyone and soon he was recruiting the kids. Before long he had 40 or so kids hanging on to that rope. All of them were eager and ready but he had to give them a pep talk first. As he did this, the people gathered around to watch and see if these kids (who could not stop an ox from moving) would be able to move a pickup truck.

On his order, the 40 kids pulled all at the same time. The people began to cheer and encourage the kids to pull their hardest. They clapped, yelled out their children's names and kept up the momentum. I was stunned as I watched the truck jerk forward once, twice and then out of the ground it came! It was, to me, amazing. My truck was back on solid earth.

All the adults cheered and clapped. The children were heroes and soon reunited with their parents. The excitement and happiness for all of them was a lesson I have never forgotten.

"How did you know all those kids could pull out the truck?" I asked the man.

He laughed.

"I knew the kids could do it," he told me. "All those little feet on the ground are like caterpillar feet and that power is enormous."

"But they could not move the ox," I said, still slightly confused.

"They CAN move a 2000-pound ox with all its power," he continued explaining, "When there are enough of them and it looks like they might come close to stopping my ox, I stop the show and tell all of them to try again later. It's all part of the show."

It was obvious he was a showman. Here was a pickup truck in a mud hole and this man had turned it into a full-blown act that entertained dozens of people. Plus, the parents and the children now had something to brag about for years to come!

I had learned another lesson about showmanship and entertainment. It made me realize that half the act is in the presentation and the other half is in the execution.

CHAPTER 3

THE FIRST OF MAYS

The leaves started to turn and the 'old' members of the show started to make comments. We knew Memorial Day (May) was the beginning of the season. School was out and the entire family was available to attend the shows. We also knew that Labor Day (the beginning of September) was when school started and our patrons would be busy with winter preparations.

These old-timers were soon talking about the 'First of Mays' and we had no clue what that meant especially since we were at the end of the season (August/September).

Next year, after I was a 'one-year' 'seasoned' veteran it became apparent what the term 'First of Mays' was referring to! We were all at the arena when a bunch of boys came around looking for work. We were calling them rookies but the old hands were calling them 'First of Mays' because that was the time of year they showed up looking for a job.

My friends and I thought we were the working 'heart and soul' of the Wild West Shows but we soon discovered we were the 'First of Mays' the old hands were referring to back when we started on the circuit. It was just another lesson learned in my life! Sometimes the things you learn humble you and make you a better man.

With this 'Wild West' experience under our belts and money in our pockets, we decided to look around and see if we could get a job somewhere else until May came around and we could get back to the 'show' circuit. We picked up some work and the winter months could not go by fast enough. I even worked two jobs because I wanted to be financially ready for the next season.

It was during this time we heard about another 'show' that was based in Illinois. It was said to be the best one out there. The show we were interested in was called "McKinley's Wild West Show" and it was going to be our next stop! They had great bulls and some of the best bucking horses. The Wild West hands came from all over, including Oklahoma, Texas and Colorado. The show also had a good variety of specialty acts like Roman Riding where a rider stands on the backs of two horses that are side by side while racing them around the arena. (The name depicts the image of Roman Chariot races from the Roman Empire.) Some Roman riders had three horses side by side and stood on the backs of the outside two horses. They also had trick roping and trick riders. Among these acts was the best dog and clown show I have ever seen in my life!

One of the cowboys that rode in the arena was a veteran of these shows, or should I say he was an 'expert' in the field! He went back to the '101 Wild West Show' which was an equal to the 'Buffalo Bill's Wild West Show.'

When May rolled around, Jack, Dave and I found ourselves at the fairgrounds near the headquarters for McKinley's show. Like the other shows of this type, they had a portable arena and, since they were always looking for help, we were given $10 to help set up everything. When we were done, it actually looked like a western arena and we were proud of the job we did. The place was filled with banners, flags and a big tarp advertisement that said, "Welcome to the Wild West Show."

I had learned another lesson about showmanship and how to impress the people.

BROKEN BONE #1

We were also hired as riders. During our first performance, I got on a bull and rode it. As I was getting off the bull, I broke my wrist, the first of many 'breaks' I would get during my rodeo career. That night I could not sleep. The next morning, I went to the doctor. I don't know if he x-rayed it or not but I do remember he put a cast on my wrist and charged me $45 for the visit. That was a lot of money back then and it took a chunk out of my savings.

For the rest of my life I had a stiff wrist but I had also learned another valuable lesson. Whenever I broke anything I made sure the doctor was one of the best, and the break was set and cast properly. It was a lesson that would serve me well in later years.

In a couple of days, I was riding again. The cast did not make it any easier but you have to do what you have to do if you want to make the money you need to survive.

WILEY

The veteran cowboy named Wiley soon took an interest in my rodeo future. He was the pickup man in the arena. That means he would take riders off of the bucking horse when their riding time was up. Usually you had to stay on the animal 8 seconds to get a score. He would also clear the arena for the next event (riding or specialty act).

Wiley was soon teaching me how to rope correctly, to ride the Wild West horses and how to properly handle livestock of all kinds. He knew his stuff and I was very excited that he was helping me to become a really well-rounded hand.

His help was invaluable to me. I enjoyed riding saddle broncs which is a bucking horse with a saddle. This came from the early methods used by cowboys who were saddling a wild horse. It was the first step in training a ranch horse. The term bronc busting came from the early cowboys that rode and had the talent to ride the wild horse on their first saddling. Sometimes, this did not involve a lot of talent but a lot of boasting from a bottle! This is how the origin of saddle bronc riding began.

Although I really enjoyed it, there was always something that seemed to go wrong and keep me from being the best I could be. Wiley watched me on several occasions and soon he was teaching me how to do it properly.

First, he taught me how to measure the buck rein (rope). The buck rein is tied to the bronc's halter and then the cowboy holds onto it. I was doing it wrong and Wiley showed me how to 'measure' the rein so it was the right length for me. Each cowboy will have a different measure of the rope because of their difference in weight, height, etc. Some of the key factors in the length of the rein include how low the horse holds his head when he bucks indicating you need a longer grip, or a horse that holds his head up high, indicating you need a shorter grip on the rein. If your length was too short or too long, you could end up being pulled over the horse's head or being too far back in the saddle.

The actual measurement is made with the bronc standing saddled in the chute with his head in a normal position and the halter and rein attached. The rein is then brought back tightly to the base of the saddle horn. If someone knows the horse really well, they might say, "Take three fingers." This means you lay three fingers down from the saddle horn and that is the spot where you grab and hold the buck rein.

After the measurement has been made, the rider takes some hair from the horse's mane and sticks it into the buck rein as a marking spot.

The art and beauty of a saddle bronc ride is to stay balanced and in the middle of the saddle. I also seemed to have trouble with my saddle.

"You know," he told me during one of our training sessions, "There is an old saddle behind the chutes over there. It is not used by the other cowboys but you should actually start using it to ride the broncs."

I knew which saddle it was and it was an ugly thing to say the least!

"Why that saddle?" I asked him. He grinned and said, "That saddle has a broken tree in it."

I knew what he meant. A saddle is made of two main pieces. The first piece is a shaped wood contour and the second piece is rawhide that is pulled over the wood frame. When wet, the rawhide covers the wood and then it is all left to dry. After it dries, the saddle is now one complete unit. This particular saddle was broken 'crossways' in the middle of the seat.

When a horse would buck while a rider was using this particular saddle, the seat would move (remember it was broken in the middle) and the saddle would take the shock of the horse's moves and act like a shock absorber to the rider.

I did not know Wiley very well at the time but I soon learned to trust him. If I had a problem I needed to tell him about, Wiley would sit down with me and figure out a way to help me solve that problem. He became a very powerful mentor in my life. I took his advice and was soon using the 'broken' saddle. I now had a new saddle and a new way of holding the buck-rein (rope). I was ready for my next ride.

A group of horses used by the rodeos for bronc riding is called a 'string.' In our string of horses there was one named 'Beaver Dun' and he was the best bucking horse in the string. You have to understand that for a rider to win an event he needs a horse that will jump, buck, twist and turn. All of this will give the rider extra points and it is the total points scored that will win the event and the big money for the rider. Beaver Dun was the horse you wanted (if you could ride him) but since the horses were all drawn at random, you were taking pot luck at getting him.

Unfortunately, we all knew Beaver Dun usually won the battle! It was also the horse I decided to try and ride! Getting on him was easy but when the gate opened I learned why he was the best we had! Beaver Dun took about three jumps and I was on my back watching him go in the other direction!

Wiley was the pickup man and he was soon at my side.

"Okay, what now?" I asked Wiley when I got up and left the arena.

"Get back on him and do it again," he said calmly.

When the show was over the next day, I did exactly that! They brought him to the chutes and I got on him once more. Unfortunately, the results were exactly the same. Wham! I was on the ground.

This went on for about two weeks. It soon became an 'after hours' spectator sport as the other hands watched while I would get on Beaver Dun and then get bucked off of him after two or three jumps.

During this time, I received instructions and advice from everybody and I do mean everybody!

"Get on an easier horse."

"Have you thought about being the cotton candy vendor?"

"Do you know which horse that is?"

"Let me guess, you are from the East Coast, ain't you?" On and on it went. Comments, advice and lots of laughs, for them!

Wiley never said much during the first few attempts but then he very quietly started giving me little tips and some new ideas to try.

I listened to him but not too much to the other guys.

Finally, many, many days later and many, many 'lumps' later, it happened! Around 10 PM or so one night, I got on Beaver Dun and actually rode him! Wiley was the pickup man that night and rode up alongside me and got me off the horse. He was grinning from ear to ear and with his gold teeth there was no way mistaking that he was happy because I could see almost all of those bright, shiny teeth sparkling in the bright lights of the arena! He was not the only one who was smiling, either!

Wiley never bragged about himself or others for that matter but on this night, this very special night, he paid me the ultimate compliment. "Now," he said calmly and proudly, "you can ride all the rest of them without much trouble."

It was one of my proudest moments.

CHAPTER 4

I WORKED WITH WILEY for the next year. My knowledge of how to handle wild horses, cows and other livestock was an education no man could buy even if he went to college for years and years. This man had his ways and to some they might seem crude or rough but they were the best ways and I learned more and more from him each day.

Watching him was a learning experience in itself. I may do things one way but watching Wiley would show me another way of doing it. Sometimes I would start doing things his way and other times I would try and 'meld' the two together. Either way, things always seemed to work out for the better.

As I said before, Wiley would never brag on you but if you did something good he would always give you that big smile of his and that was good enough for me! I quickly learned never to say, "I can't do that," because those words were not in Wiley's vocabulary. It may be one of the many reasons why he and I got along so well.

"Have you ever been married, Wiley?"

He paused and looked at me with a thoughtful expression.

"Yes," he answered with a soft smile, "I was. My first wife was named Opal and she rode saddle broncs."

That was all he ever said about her and that was all I ever asked about her.

Several years later I was looking through some old rodeo magazines when I came across the story of some specialty rodeo acts. One of them was about a woman named Opal who was a saddle bronc rider. As I read on, the article said Opal was killed after being thrown while riding a saddle bronc in Madison Square Garden. Her husband was in the crowd and had seen the whole thing.

It soon became evident that she was Wiley's wife.

During the course of our friendship, Wiley mentioned he was now married to a woman named Betty. She was a professional trick rider. Betty and her best friend were currently working the circuit doing their act and the two of them would meet up later after the season was over.

WHEN THE SEASON IS OVER

Labor Day soon came and went. The rodeos were closing for the winter and I was sitting around one day when Wiley walked over.

"So, what you gonna do for the winter?" he asked.

I had an idea of what I wanted to do but was not really sure of anything.

"I don't really know," I answered slowly as I thought of a good answer. "I think I'm gonna buy and sell some horses and try to make enough money to get through until next season."

I knew that after the rodeo season, many of the rodeo riders and workers would head down to Florida or some other southern state. They would make extra money working on ranches until the next rodeo season came around. Of course, the warmer climate was also an attraction.

Wiley was no exception. In the fall of 1956, he had taken a liking to a 19-year-old youngster on the circuit and, being that youngster, he wanted to know if I wanted to go with him to his winter retreat. I could be one of the ranch hands and earn enough money to enjoy life and have a few bucks left over. I readily agreed, knowing it would be another opportunity to learn from an experienced veteran. He told me when we would be leaving and I told him I would be ready to go whenever he was. I had some money and I invested it in a 'new' 1954 pickup truck and still had some left over to get a small house trailer so I had something to live in.

As I packed up to head down to Florida with Wiley, I reflected on the previous year. It had been a great year! I was around some of the best cowboys in the business and saw some of the best specialty acts there were. I would ask about the acts because they intrigued me.

"You should have been here last year," they would tell me." We had one of the very best horse acts performing for us. This woman had these beautiful pure black horses and she rode them full bore around the arena as fast as they could go. Then she would ride two horses bareback by standing up on them (Roman Riding) and while doing that she would jump them over hurdles. As if that was not enough, she would go Roman Riding around the arena on one horse and do it by standing on one leg!"

They could not remember her name and if they did, I did not remember it. This was my life now. My friends were going home but I was going to Florida and starting a new adventure.

BUZZARD'S ROOST

We finished the season and headed to the "Circle T Ranch" in Indiantown, Florida just south of Okeechobee. So, here I was, in my pickup truck pulling my camper trailer, following my friend and heading to Florida. Wiley led the way as we wound our way south. In Georgia, we pulled over for gas.

"How much farther do we have?" I asked him.

He looked at me and thought for a second.

"Oh, about 16 or 17 hours," he answered, "But we are not going directly to the ranch. We are going to make a stop in Quitman, Georgia for a few days first."

This was news to me.

"Why?" I asked.

"There is this place called 'The Buzzard's Roost' and we're gonna go there," he replied.

I waited, hoping for more information but Wiley said nothing.

"Okay," I countered curiously and trying to make conversation, "What is the Buzzard's Roost?"

He smiled and said, "It is a farm where some of the old cowboys and Wild West hands camp for the winter. Some of them just stop this time of the year to visit old friends and talk about the season. Most of us just drink beer and play cards. When spring comes around and the rodeos get going, they will all go their separate ways until the season is over and then we do it all over again."

Satisfied, I got back in my truck and continued to follow Wiley. We soon pulled into what I thought was a 'Hobo Jungle'! There were old trailers, house trailers, big and small trucks and animal carriers of all kinds. Several campfires were surrounded by groups of people who were standing, sitting and lying nearby. There was laughter, storytelling and reunions happening everywhere!

When we stopped and got out of our trucks, people came over and greeted Wiley, shaking his hand, joking and talking to him. No one said anything to me.

For a few minutes, I thought that if I was not with Wiley I would have been stoned and run out of the camp!

Wiley made a few introductions and I was soon just another 'camper.' That evening, we were all sitting by one of the campfires and enjoying ourselves. I was not much of a beer drinker (2 beers were my ultimate maximum!) but it was obvious Wiley and his companions were used to this social atmosphere and the beer and alcohol flowed freely.

All of a sudden, one of the gals began to sing western songs. Her name was Smokey and boy, did she have talent! Like many newcomers to Wild West Shows, she did many jobs. Her jobs included meter-maid, singing, riding broncs and even steer wrestling!

After years of honing her craft, she would eventually perform in the rodeos like Pendleton, Cheyenne and Calgary, Canada. These were some of the biggest venues in the west and she was doing things that people were not used to seeing women do! Her specialty was being a saddle bronc rider.

The group decided to have a rodeo of their own. It would be mostly made up of old-timers who had 'been there and done that.' To protect themselves and because they only had limited resources, they decided to forego the 'rough stuff' and settle for roping steers and calves. A few clowns would 'play' with the bulls and there would be some racing. There were also a set of twins that worked the big indoor eastern rodeos and they would be at this one. "Snake Horse Rogers" and his brother "Brahma," named after the Brahma Bull, were going to be there and so was I.

The night before the rodeo, all of the old-time cowboys went to one of the local night spots for dancing and drinking. I was with Wiley and thanks to him I was lucky enough to sit at a large table with 10-15 other cowboys who had some fantastic stories to tell! I will never forget some of the tales they told and the characters who told them!

The beer and mixed drinks flowed freely that night. Being a non-drinker, my senses stayed sharp but as the evening wore on, the senses of everyone else dulled! After a few hours, everyone but me was feeling exceptionally 'happy' and 'pretty good'!

As we sat and partied, two men, about 25 years old came sauntering over to our table. They knew cowboys and rodeo people were in the bar so they began making smart remarks about the Wild West people, what we did and how we did it. Each of these men weighed about 225 pounds and both were built to last. You could see a fight was in the air and it was coming soon, too! The first thing that went through my mind was, 'these old guys are drunk and won't feel any pain at all but I'm stone sober and this is going to hurt me bad!'

When they got to our table, an invitation was issued by the two 'fighters' who were now standing right next to our table. They wanted to go outside and settle a few things, like who was tougher.

"Oh, damn," I thought to myself, "This is gonna hurt really bad! Really bad!"

The 6′4″ thin, but not skinny, Wiley did not like that idea. He was tough and sitting next to him I knew he could take care of himself, but

I was a sober 19-year old and I knew this was gonna hurt me bad! Still, I had nowhere to go.

I watched as Wiley stood up and got face to face with one of the men.

"Here we go," I said to myself, "And, boy, is this gonna hurt!"

Wiley was six inches away from one of their faces when he spoke plainly and sternly to him.

"Listen, you potato ass," Wiley began, "We are not going outside but they are about to carry you outside. So, you better walk away while you can still walk."

"Oh man," I thought, "He called them a potato ass! Now I know this is really gonna hurt!"

Wiley stood still and did not move a muscle as the man looked at him. Two seconds later it happened. Much to my surprise, the two men turned and left the room.

Wiley sat down and things returned to normal and I didn't feel any pain at all!

Smokey was singing in the bar that night. She certainly knew how to carry a tune and her voice was a pleasant addition to the evening's entertainment. Near closing time, she came over to our table and started joking around with all of the old timers sitting at the table. It was late and Wiley said he was tired. Before long, everybody was headed back to the campground. I rode back with Wiley and he dropped me off near my camper. Wiley had a bed in his truck and I assumed he would sleep there but as I entered my camper, I turned and saw Wiley standing next to Smokey's trailer.

I went inside and was soon fast asleep, thinking nothing of what I had just seen. The next morning, we were once again on our way to the Circle T ranch in Florida.

The stop at the Buzzard's Roost was a fun part of my life and I have fond memories of the friendships I made and the stories I heard. I found it odd, but Wiley and I never talked about that first trip again.

About 16 years later, I was on the professional rodeo circuit when I spotted someone I remembered from a long time ago. It was Smokey!

We talked for a few minutes and during our conversation she introduced me to her daughter, a tall, thin girl who reminded me of someone I knew. A few minutes later, Smokey told me that her daughter was, indeed, Wiley's daughter. I guess Wiley was not very tired that night, after all. It took me 16 years to find out the truth!

THE CIRCLE T RANCH

We arrived at the Circle T Ranch just as the daylight began to fade. Wiley told me to park my truck and camper behind a 30-foot camper trailer. At the time, I did not know it was Wiley's. He would leave it there during the summer rodeo season and use it during the winter. I told Wiley I was beat and he said not to worry. It was not long before I was fast asleep, wondering what the future would bring.

The next morning, I awoke and got a look at my new home for the next few months. There was a large two-story colonial type house with two new pink Cadillacs parked under an open garage not too far from where I was parked. A large white, cinder block building containing showers and toilets was not far away, either. This was for the ranch hands and since I was here to work, it was now for me too!

Behind these buildings were five or six paddocks (corrals) and approximately 30 horse stalls. Scattered throughout were chickens walking around and picking up grain off the ground. This was definitely a working ranch with self-sustaining abilities.

The ranch manager was a cowboy from Montana named Mr. Bill Parks, who we called Mr. Bill. He and his wife were saddle bronc riders back in the day when the rodeos were just being organized. He was friendly but, at the same time, he was also mission oriented and his mission was to be sure this ranch operated like it should. It did not take long before I learned what that meant.

We were up early the next morning. Our job for the day was to round up 150 cows. There were three ranch hands that worked the ranch on a year-round basis and we were to help them.

We also had a ranch hand named Bill who did most of the welding on the ranch. Bill also shod the horses and did a lot of the blacksmith work as well as his cowboy work. Homer was a Florida native who was responsible for the fence work and helping Bill with the cowboy work. Harold was a full-blooded Seminole Native American Indian who drove the cattle trucks and did all the miscellaneous jobs around the ranch.

Bill and Homer had two or three horses they rode all the time, alternating them so they would not get tired. Since I had no horse and since they were certainly not going to give up one of theirs, Mr. Bill (the ranch manager) tried to figure out what to do.

"Look," he finally told me, "We got a horse in the back-pen area. You can ride him if you want but you got to bridle and saddle him yourself."

I figured they were testing me to see how this 19-year-old, first timer could handle himself. They did not know I had been around horses all my life. They thought I was just another 'wannabee.' It was a short walk to the back area and, sure enough, my new ride was in the back pen. As I began to saddle him it became apparent the horse was pretty green, a term we use for a young horse with little experience in the field. (Guess I was pretty green myself, now that I think about it!) The bridle and the saddle were put on with no problem but getting *in* that saddle might be a little more of a problem.

Here I was, behind the barn by myself with a green horse that I had to ride because there was no other horse available. To be sure I could get on him without harming either of us, I did what is known as 'cheeking.' Experienced riders know how to control a horse when getting in the saddle. To do this, you take the bridle and pull the horse's head to the side where you are putting your foot into the stirrup. If the horse decides to buck or move, it has no choice but to move in a tight circle with you in the middle. When the horse finally stops, you simply put your foot in the stirrup, and pull yourself into the saddle. Because the horse is moving in a circle, it will have a harder time getting away from you.

Once in the saddle, my new 'partner' and I joined the rest of the riders and as soon as we did, my horse settled down and became easy to ride. The group of us rode down one of the ranch roads for 45 minutes. Mr. Bill and Wiley were in the lead. They finally stopped, got off their horses and opened a wire gap. (A 'gap' is a cowboy's name for a gate). This usually consisted of barbed wire tied to a 5 foot-long, 3-inch thick post. We rode through the gate and found ourselves in a massive pasture area. Bill and Wiley closed the gap and were soon riding with us toward where the cattle were located.

It was time to go to work!

RANCH HAND

If you really want to know what a cow puncher does, well, here we go!

Mr. Bill was in charge and he told us to go to the far end of the pasture, make a half circle, round up the cattle and bring them back to the gap. All I could see were trees, palm plants and a lot of pasture. There were no cows in sight!

"Wiley," I said, looking for guidance, "I don't want to get lost out here in the middle of nowhere so what should I do?"

He laughed and looked at me.

"Ride at the back with the rest of the ranch hands. Make sure you keep one of them on your right and one of them on your left. That way you will always be in the middle and won't have to worry about getting lost."

"Oh, yea," he continued, "Here is the most important thing. You will hear the cowboys whooping and hollering as they round up the cattle so, if in doubt, just head for the noise and then yell and holler as loud as you can. One more thing and this is one of the most important: *Never, ever* get at the front of the herd!"

I did as I was told and much to my surprise, I managed to make it through the morning. As a group, we managed to get the herd out of the huge pasture, through the gap and down to the smaller pasture where the separating pens were located.

It was now midday. The horses were tired and so were we. Mr. Bill told us to take care of the horses and then get some food into our systems because we still had a lot of work to do. When lunch was over, we got fresh horses and moved the cattle from the small pasture to a fenced-in area that would hold them until the next day.

Early the following morning, we rode to the cow pens. Some of the cattle were now in a 75-foot square area. It was our job to move them in groups to a smaller corral that could hold 20 cows and calves. We would open a gate, let the right amount of cattle inside and then close the gate. At the other end of this corral was another gate that led to a long, thin lane where only one cow at a time could walk. When it was opened, one of the cows would enter and walk down the pathway. Several cowboys manned a series of gates and as the cows entered, they would be steered into one of the four available pens. These pens were designed for specific purposes.

The dry cows (cows that were barren and had not given birth and therefore had dry or empty udders) went in one of the pens. These cows were considered a burden and were sent to the market for sale. It sounds cruel but the purpose of a cattle ranch is to produce cattle and a barren cow is of no use to a cattle rancher.

The calves were sent to the 'calf chute.' Once inside, a cowboy would pull a handle and the sides of the pen would close in on the calf and hold it firmly so it could not jump forward or backwards. These sides would then flip over laying the calf down and exposing the calf's left side as though he were laying on a table. The calf would then receive all immunization shots, ear markings (notches in the ear to identify the calf as being yours) and last but not least, the calf was branded with the mark of the ranch. Once this was done, the calf was stood up and let loose into a small pasture area.

In this process, there would be 3 or 4 cowboys doing the work. One would do the branding, another would administer the shots and one would work the gate and put the ear markings on the calf. The man who runs the 'head chute' has a most critical job. He must trap the calf at just the right moment when the calf puts his head through the hole in the gate. In order to get this done, someone had to be behind the calf grabbing his tail and pushing him into the calf chute. Believe me, working on this end of the calf means you will never look at guacamole in the same way as you used to! That means the man who got this job was always the lowest and least experienced man on the ranch. Guess who that was? At the end of the day you could tell who your friends were!! Calves have a tendency to 'dump' when scared or pushed from behind.

Once all this was done, the calf was returned to a standing position and let loose into a small pasture area. The entire calf process would take anywhere from 5 to 8 minutes depending on the expertise of the cowboys doing the work. Once one calf was finished, it was pushed out while another one was being pushed in and the process would be repeated!

The third pen was for the mama cows. These mama cows would be held in this pen until their calves were finished being vaccinated and doctored. The fourth pen was for multiple uses depending on the herd and what the rancher wanted done with his cattle.

When we were done, the calves and their mothers would be reunited. They were left alone for an hour. This was enough time for them to calm down and get settled. Once they calmed down, these cows and calves would then be sprayed with a high pressurized flea and tick medication. Once they were sprayed, the entire herd would be sent to a pasture that had not been grazed in a long time so they could settle and graze. This pasture would be home to them until it was time to wean the calves from their mothers.

During this entire process, Mr. Bill was keeping a tally on the cattle and he informed us that in the coming days we would have to go back to the big pasture because we were 45 cows short.

Sure enough, a few days later, we were back in the saddle and back in the pasture trying to find a small number of cattle in a large number of acres! We started in the far corner, just as we had done the first time. We had to search this vast expanse and were soon in areas of the pasture that were filled with bushes and a swamp like mud and soil composition.

You had to be really careful in this area and if your horse started sinking, you immediately backed up and retraced your steps.

That is what happened to me. It took me a few minutes to get out of the predicament and when my horse and I finally got back on solid ground, I found myself separated from the rest of the riders. I could hear them whooping and hollering so, heeding the words of my mentor, I headed off in that direction. I was pissed off at myself! Here I was, a 'rookie' if you will, and I was being no help to them at all! I hauled ass and tried to catch up with them since they had found some of the cattle and were in the process of heading them toward the gap.

As I rode toward them, I heard a calf bawling and it made me stop to check it out. I pulled up and rode toward the noisy calf. Much to my surprise, I found 12-15 head of cattle hiding in the bushes and trying to stay out of the heat. I rode down behind them and started whooping and hollering. They were as shocked as I was and they began to head toward the open field.

Once cattle are out in the open, you can pretty much control their direction of travel and that is what I did. They eventually were headed toward the gap and as I got closer to my objective, Wiley heard the hollering and came back towards me. He spotted the cattle and then he spotted me. He rode up to me and the grin on his face said it all!

"So," he hollered at me, "What do you think you are doing Juuuuungle Jim?" I shrugged, he smiled and the two of us finished driving the cattle down to the gap.

Mr. Bill, the ranch manager, never said anything to me, even after he saw the cattle. I guess he felt bad that a greenhorn (a rookie) who got lost was able to find 15 head of cattle that the foreman of the ranch could not find. I thought he was just a tough old bird but I learned he had a softer side and maybe wanted to say 'thank you' in his own way.

A few days later we were riding back to the big house when Mr. Bill rode up next to me.

"Listen here," he began, "We got seven or eight 2-year old horses on the ranch. They are all unbroken but if you want to break them I will give you one of them and it will be your choice. It's up to you."

"Can I keep the horse here, on the ranch?" I asked hopefully.

He thought about it for a few seconds.

"Yea," he replied, "As long as you provide the feed and take care of it."

I had some money coming in but I needed more. I asked around and the ranch hands told me there was a lot of other work on local ranches. It was a tough but solid way to earn some extra money doing what you liked to do. It was also Mr. Bill's way of saying, "Thanks."

BETTY AND JAN

We had been on the ranch nine or ten days when Betty, Wiley's wife arrived. She was a very polished trick rider and had been on the rodeo and entertainment circuit but they had all closed down for the winter. I was not introduced to her for two days. We were busy and she was trying to get settled into her new life.

Finally, Wiley called me into his trailer and introduced me (formally) to his wife. We sat in their trailer and talked about many things but Betty had an ace up her sleeve.

"I have a new friend for you," Betty told me casually. "Her name is Jan and she will be here in a few days. She will make a great friend for you!"

"Does she ride horses?" I asked. Betty laughed.

"Jan is one of the best. She is a Roman Rider and she also does trick riding.

She has two black mares that she rides in her act and they are called 'The Flying Black Clouds.' She and I worked together last summer."

It sounded interesting especially since almost all the ranch hands were married with kids. I was the only single person of my age group and my entertainment at night was to go to my trailer and read a book or play solitaire with my trusty deck of cards. There were very few televisions so having a new friend to talk to sounded very, very interesting.

Three or four days later a truck pulling a horse van pulled into the compound. There was a large painting on the side of the horse trailer. Two beautiful black horses were surrounded by the words 'The Flying Black Clouds.' I watched as the truck stopped and a tall, long legged blonde got out of the driver's seat. Everyone except me apparently knew who she was because she was immediately greeted by those who were in the area. I was riding a colt in the yard at the time and as I rode by her I nodded and said, "Hi!" She gave me a wave. It was the first acknowledgement I ever got from the woman named Jan!

I got up early every morning as I had lots of broncs to ride. Usually, I rode each one for about two hours and it took up most of the day. With work keeping me busy and my finances low, my meals often consisted of a can of beans. Sometimes they were hot but often they were eaten right out of the can. There was a store about half a mile from the campgrounds. In the evening, I would go there and for 20-cents I would buy a pint of ice cream or ice milk as it was called. With my purchase in hand, I would go back to my trailer where I would sit at the 'kitchen' table by the window and eat my 'dinner' while reading a book or the newspaper. This was the life I had chosen and I liked it more and more each day!

One evening there was a knock on my trailer door. I opened the door and there stood a tall, beautiful, blond woman. "Hi," she said sweetly, "We haven't met yet but I am a fan of yours. I see you every morning as you leave on a colt and then I see you at night sitting by the window in your trailer."

Her name was Jan and she owned the beautiful black horses I had seen around the ranch. Needless to say, I was flattered and enthralled to meet her. She went on to tell me she had a propane tank that needed changing and would I mind taking out the empty one and putting in a full tank for her.

I was soon in the propane business and changing her tank. When I was done, we sat down and visited. Wow, I thought to myself, this girl is something special and here I am, just a cowboy trying to make enough money to get by! Jan said she had grown up in Indiana and I thought, "what a coincidence!" I grew up in Ohio right next door to Indiana." From what she told me, we grew up maybe 110 miles apart and now we meet in Florida. It seemed odd to me but I was not complaining!

Janice Wilkey "Flying Black Clouds" (c. 1950s)

Janice Wilkey outside her van (c. 1950s)

CHAPTER 5

JAN

Janice M. Wilkey was born in 1933 in Sullivan, Indiana. Jan's grandfather was William "Bill" Wilkey, a well-known man throughout Indiana, Illinois and Kentucky. He was a mule and horse trader but was best known for judging mule shows and mule contests, both which were very popular during the 1930s and 1940s. He also judged at the Kentucky State Fair.

Bill raised some of the best bulls and cows in the state of Indiana. They were so good he would show them at the Chicago Livestock Shows, The Kansas City Royal and the Kentucky State Fair, among others. He and his livestock always traveled by train using rail and stock cars.

If there was one thing for sure, you could always bet that Bill would have small ponies and horses on their farm. He may have been a livestock trader in cattle but he loved his horses! This was good news for Jan who was an only child. With the nearest neighbor miles away, she grew up with animals as her best friends!

One of her favorite memories occurred when no one was home except her and her grandfather. He got her to take her pony into the house and upstairs to one of the bedroom windows. It took some maneuvering but Jan got the horse to the second floor into the bedroom and over to the window. Here she got the horse to stick its head out of the window and when she leaned out the window as well, her grandpa Bill took a picture of them!

It was all in fun and games except that Grandma Wilkey was a woman of particular taste and kept a spotless house. She saw the picture and that was the end of taking ponies to the bedroom windows!

Jan's father was Wilbur Wilkey, a respected farmer and ranch manager. During World War II, Wilbur went to California because he saw an advertisement saying the shipyards needed workers. The pay was far more than he was making so he headed west. He had no shipbuilding skills but he learned quickly and was soon working as a welder.

After he had been there and established himself, he had his wife, Ruth, and his daughter, Jan, come to the west coast. Ruth was a good typist and found secretarial work right away. With both of them working, it left little time to supervise their young daughter, Jan.

Mr. Wilkey and Ruth decided it would be best to send Jan back to Indiana where she could stay with relatives. They decided to send her back by passenger train so she could live with her grandmother and grandfather. To do this, they took a name card and put her name, address and the stop where she would meet her grandparents. They tied the card to a string and then put the card around her neck.

Jan was around 9 years old at the time and she traveled from Salinas, California to Linton, Indiana… a trip of over a thousand miles!

Ruth told her if something happened she should look for a man in a red hat. (At the time, train employees and Porters wore red hats.) It may sound strange based on today's methods, but Jan made it back to Indiana and lived with her grandparents until the end of the war.

After the war and with money in his pocket, Wilbur and Ruth returned to the family residence in Indiana and began looking for work. His reputation was still intact and soon he was back in business. There was a wealthy land owner who owned a tract of land in Linton, Indiana. The land was, for all intent purposes, useless because it was more of a swamp than anything else. He knew Wilbur had a good grasp of basic engineering and construction so he asked if he would be interested in clearing the land and making it usable for something other than breeding mosquitoes!

Wilbur checked out the land and decided he could do something with it. Before long, he was knee deep in mud and silt but he stuck to it and worked a miracle! The owner was so impressed with the outcome that he hired Wilbur to run the new ranchland! The owner named this new ranch, 'The Goose Pond.'

To make the land profitable, Wilbur started by working the land and getting it ready for planting. He put crops of clover, blue grass and timothy (a plant used as a form of hay and feed) into the ground. These plants flourished and allowed the owner to expand even further, this time into the cattle industry.

To expand into the cattle business was risky but the owner wanted to give it a try. Wilbur was sent to Texas where he brought back several hundred head of Mexican Longhorn steers. When they arrived in Indiana, the steers were in bad shape. Most of them were thin and barely able to stand. With Wilbur's supervision and plenty of lush field grass planted in the pastures, the steers thrived and began to put on a lot of weight. After several months of good food and being taken care of, the steers were big enough to be sold at the Chicago markets.

This expansion took a lot of work and required a lot of ranch hands. Jan soon became one of those ranch hands and quickly learned how to handle herself around cattle and horses. It became second nature to her and she was good at it!

Her schedule meant working on the ranch before school, going to school and then working on the ranch after school and on the weekends. She did not have a lot of free time.

Jan had a black mare called 'Blackie' that she rode all the time. She and the mare were soon cutting cattle out of the herd so they could be branded. Her skills increased and soon she was roping the cattle, something even the men had a hard time doing!

When another black mare was born on the ranch, Jan claimed it and soon she had two black mares to work with. As soon as she was old enough to enter the local contests, Jan took her now well-trained horse and entered every contest she could at every county fair in the states of Indiana and Illinois.

In 1951, Jan and 'Blackie' won many events, including 'working cow horse,' an event that needed discipline by both the horse and rider. Their reputation and winning streaks were well known and as the year came to a close, Jan was named "Frontier Girl" of Illinois, an honor given to the best female cowgirl in the state!

Jan was definitely making a name for herself! It was around this time that 'Life' magazine wrote an article on 'The White Horse Troupe' from Naper, Nebraska. The story was about Ruth Thompson who had a specialty act consisting of nothing but pure white horses.

During the spring, Ruth would bring young girls to her ranch and train them in the art of 'Roman Riding.' This type of horsemanship is dangerous and involves a rider and two horses. The rider puts one foot on the back of each horse and rides standing up. To make this stunt even more exciting, some of the riders managed to learn Roman Riding with three barebacked horses. They would stand with one foot on each of the outside horses and hope the three horses were able to stay in stride!

Occasionally, Ruth would find a long-legged rider who was willing to try four horses but this was the most dangerous of all the Roman Riding stunts. Again, the rider would have one foot on each of the outside horses while standing up and trying to keep all four horses going at the same speed. All of these stunts were dangerous and required a lot of training for both the rider and the horses. Many of the girls managed to do the two-horse stunt but few ever managed to master the four-horse stunt!

The girls who were invited to Ruth's ranch in Nebraska learned the act while performing the duties of a typical ranch hand. Once the girls had mastered the act, Ruth and her show would be hired by state and county fairs, rodeos, circuses and other spectator sports. Her show was always popular and a real crowd pleaser!

Jan read the article and it got her imagination working overtime. She immediately began to teach herself this new type of horsemanship. Jan went to work and before long she was Roman Riding with her two black mares. There were bumps and bruises along the way but soon enough she could ride her horses with the best of them!

She wrote a letter to Ruth Thompson telling the Nebraskan about her horses and her own act. Ruth asked Jan to come to Nebraska to ride for her White Horse Troupe! It soon became obvious that Jan had a lot more experience around horses than most of the girls who attended Ruth's ranch. The girls worked for room and board and got paid very little (if anything) for doing the act. According to Ruth, their pay was in the learning experience they would get from traveling on the riding show circuit.

These beautiful horses and the beautiful women who rode them got plenty of attention both locally and nationally. When show time came, there were always 10 girls and 10 horses in the show and all 20 of them were top notch in every sense of the word!

"Queen Of The Range"

ighter of Mr. key of south ddaugher of ilkey of Sul- the highest Range, at the se Show last day. Besides amce copped noney awards r ability in about seven years ago. She graduated from Linton High School in May, 1951.

She commenced riding horses and ponies when she was about five years old, while living on her grandfather's farm. Even while a child, she taught the horses tricks and always loved riding. She has been in innumer-

IN HORSE SHOW SUNDAY — Miss Frontier Girl of 1951, shown, will be seen in both performances at the National Stock Horse show tomorrow night and Sunday afternoon at Aurora Downs. In real life she is Miss Janice Wilkey.

Miss Wilkey Wins Horse Show Honors

Miss Janice Wilkey of Linton collected new honors last weekend at the National Stock Horse Show at Aurora Downs, Aurora, Ill., when she was selected as "queen of the ring."

Miss Wilkey gave exhibition rides Saturday night and Sunday afternoon at the national show. She rides three horses Roman style, standing on the two outside horses and jumping hurdles with them.

She is the daughter of Mr. and Mrs. Wilbur Wiley of South Linton. She has won many honors in horse shows in the Middlewest in recent months.

Frontier Girl In Horse Show Over Weekend

Miss Frontier Girl of 1951 will be at both performances of the National Stock Horse Roundup at Aurora Downs this Saturday night at 8 o'clock and again Sunday afternoon. In addition to holding the title of Miss Frontier Girl, she is a very accomplished horsewoman and assists her father on their farm at Linton, Ind., where he feeds 5 to 10,000 head of cattle.

Miss Janice Wilkey, as she is known by her college classmates, is extremely popular at all western horse shows and has been featured at most of the big horse shows in the midwest. She accomplishes the difficult feat of jumping three horses over hurdles while riding Roman style standing upright on the two outside horses.

She will appear along with over 200 or 300 exhibitors at the first annual National Stock Horse Roundup at Aurora Downs Saturday night and Sunday afternoon, Sept. 22 and 23. Tickets are now on sale at your local merchant or Aurora Downs. Box reservations are now being filled.

Janice Wilkey, 1951

Jan was very long-legged and she soon mastered the very dangerous and tricky art of Roman Riding not three but four horses! She was one of the very few women who ever mastered this art and Jan was one of the best.

Even today, if you look up '4 horse Roman Riding' in some encyclopedias and horse magazines, you will see Jan's picture showing you how it is done!

Success breeds competition and if you are doing something that is working, others will try to do the same thing in order to emulate your success. The White Horse Troupe did not go unnoticed and soon there were others who were also doing 'specialty' acts for spectator events.

One of these individuals was named Jinx Hoaglan. He was putting together a specialty act of his own. Although he did not have any Roman Riders (yet!), he did have an act with several horses jumping over obstacles. His horses were well known for jumping over tables where two men were sitting and playing cards.

Jinx also had a mule that liked to play 'kickball.' The mule would kick a large rubber ball into the crowd and when the crowd member would throw the ball back, the mule would kick the ball back into the crowd once more. This would continue for as long as the mule felt like kicking the ball!

Jinx was a showman and his acts were polished and unique. He was also a businessman and Jinx was always on the lookout for a new act, something that would make his show even better and bring in the money.

One day he saw another act using Roman Riding and pure white horses. Immediately, he knew what he needed to make his shows stand out and be the best! Jinx went out and bought his own white horses, after which it was now known as, 'Jinx Hoaglan's White Horse Troupe of Franklin, Indiana.'

Jan finished out the year with Ruth Thompson and then went home for the winter. Since the ranch Jinx owned in Franklin, Indiana, was only 75 miles from where she had grown up, Jinx decided to see if his 'neighbor' was interested in switching teams. He called Jan and asked if she wanted to come and do some Roman riding for his shows. He explained that he had 10 white horses and would need 10 beautiful girls to go with them, similar to what Ruth had in her shows.

Jan thought about it, but this time she wanted to get paid better for her services. All of Ruth's girls worked for just room and board and that was not going to cut it anymore. She also wanted to bring along her black mares since she was already familiar with them and could Roman Ride them with no problem.

Jinx knew a good deal when he saw one. When spring arrived, Jan was riding her black mares and training the other girls in Roman Riding. She was clearly the best of the group and Jinx was happy to have her in his show.

Jinx Hoglan had a new act. It was advertised as 'The Flying Black Clouds.'

Jan worked for Jinx for one season. She learned and improved her act and before long she decided to take her act out on the road and try it on her own. It was a huge step but she had the act to do it!

Janice Wilkey (c. 1950s)

Janice Wilkey at Ruth Thompson's White Horse Ranch: White Horse Troupe in Naper, Nebraska (c. 1950s)

She left Jinx and began looking for new employment. She was soon hired by the 'McKinley Wild West Show' owned by a man named (what else!) McKinley. During her time with this show, Jan expanded her act by adding some trick riding and acquiring a new horse she named Frosty.

One day, a photographer saw Jan sitting on Frosty. He liked the scene so much he took a picture of her and soon Jan and Frosty were on the front of thousands of post cards all across the nation! The picture would have the caption, "Welcome to Nebraska," or Idaho or Oklahoma or whatever state you bought the postcard in. Some of those cards are still out there somewhere!

Jan worked with 'McKinley's Wild West Show' for one year and then went totally professional. She joined the R.C.A. or the Rodeo Cowboys Association. She listed herself as a specialty act performer. This allowed her to go after the really big rodeos and specialty shows. She started working smaller R.C.A. rodeos with hopes of working her way up to the bigger rodeos.

When the season was over and winter was beginning, Jan and her friend Betty (who was married to Wiley) left for Florida. They would all head to Florida until the next season began and that is where we would all finally meet.

Jan Wilkey was on her way to being the star attraction and getting paid for her services. In no time at all she would be driving a truck and pulling a horse van into the 'Circle T' compound. On the side of the horse van would be a large painting of two beautiful black horses surrounded by the words 'The Flying Black Clouds.'

Postcard of Janice Wilkey on Frosty (c. 1950s)

CHAPTER 6

HOW DID I MISS THAT ONE?
BACK AT THE CIRCLE T RANCH

For the next week Jan and I sat and visited every evening. On Saturday, she asked me a very interesting question.

"Do you like John Wayne?" she wanted to know.

"Yes, I do."

"Do you like western movies?" she continued.

"Yes, I do," I replied once more.

"Well," she replied coyly, "I only have that huge horse trailer but you have a pickup truck and there is a John Wayne movie playing in the next town."

What I said next was something that she would tease me about over and over again for the rest of our lives!

I looked at her, smiled and said, "Well, if you want to go you can borrow my pickup truck."

Her hopeful, happy face suddenly had a stunned look on it.

"Well" she said with a strange look, "Don't you want to go with me?"

"Why sure," I replied, "But I didn't know if I was invited!"

We both laughed about it afterwards. Thankfully, that was the beginning of many good times ahead for both of us!

Through those talks I got acquainted with Jan. She was only 22 years old and was already the reluctant victim of two failed marriages. I would often see her sitting on a step outside of her horse trailer and staring off into space. She would do this for hours. I never interrupted her because her thoughts, like mine, were private.

It was obvious that Jan was a fun-loving woman who had many friends. If you mentioned a 'party' she was right there, especially if it involved dancing and having fun. One day, a rodeo friend stopped by the ranch. He drove a semi and was hauling oranges from a warehouse. That evening he and Jan went to a nearby town where a local band was playing. When I got up the next morning, the semi was gone and when I came back at noon, there was a sheriff's car sitting beside Jan's horse trailer.

After lunch, I was riding one of the horses and I spotted Wiley. We stopped what we were doing. I told him about the sheriff's car and I asked him if there was some trouble back in the camp. Wiley said Jan and the truck driver had gone into town and were in one of the night clubs when the driver was shot in the leg. Wiley said Jan needed to be more careful or she might get shot herself or get in some sort of trouble. There were some rough customers in the local towns! That bothered me but we were each leading our own lives.

In the next 5 or 6 weeks Jan and I became good friends. In time, I noticed she did not sit on the step and stare into space anymore. The best times were when she would help me ride the colts. I would also help her with her two new black horses that she was trying to break into her act.

This was not a romantic attachment. It was not love at first sight but it was soon a solid friendship and we learned to rely on each other in times of need. Before long, the two of us were jointly planning what we were going to do the next day. To make extra money, I found work on other ranches in the area. When they had more work than I could do, Jan would often come with me and help out. We were a really good team!

CHAPTER 7

ONE OF THE BRIGHT SPOTS in any year was when the annual rodeo came to the ranch. Being in Florida, rodeos like this could start earlier in the year. The rodeo's arrival meant Jan soon had to go back to work. She was a performer and with her black horses she had a fabulous act!

The rodeo kept us all busy. Wiley and Mr. Bill, the ranch manager, worked the arena in pushing the bulls and bucking horses to the right pens. At the time, this was the biggest ranch rodeo in Florida. The grandstand was always full of people as West Palm Beach was not too far away. Other towns close by were Stuart, Okeechobee and Belle Glade. As far as the residents of these towns were concerned, it was time to head to the rodeo, eat barbeque, chow down on some hot dogs and have a good time!

Bill and Wiley both did rodeos 'back in the early days' with the Turtle Association. Later, this name was changed to R.C.A. or the Rodeo Cowboys Association. Every new member got an R.C.A. card with a number on it. The membership cards started at number one and went up from there. Jan joined the R.C.A. in 1958 and her membership card was in the 5,000 range. I got my R.C.A. card in 1960 and it was in the 7,000 range. I have only seen one or two cards that had single or double digits on them and Mr. Bill had one of them. The R.C.A. later became the P.R.C.A or the Professional Rodeo Cowboys Association. It is the same organization with an updated name. Membership card numbers now range in the hundreds of thousands.

Mr. Bill would often hire some of his old buddies to help work the new variety of jobs when the rodeo arrived. The Circle T Ranch hands were also helping with the rodeo jobs but he needed more people once the rodeo came to the ranch. I was one of the new hires and one of the jobs I ended up doing was to help round up 75 or so wild horses. These 'broncs' were used in the rodeo and came straight from the open range. We had to do that several days before the rodeo arrived. We also had to gather the bulls used by the rodeo.

It was a chance for me to see how good I was but disappointment soon saddened my hopeful attitude. I did not have an R.C.A. card so I could not compete in the events. Still, I hung around and tried to help out as much as I could. By watching and listening, it became a learning experience for me.

When the rodeo left, it was the end of February. We still had six more weeks before the summer rodeo circuit began. To pass the time, I continued riding and breaking horses for other ranches and cowboys in the area. Word got around quickly that there was a guy at the Circle T who could do the job and soon they were specifically asking for me!

Throughout my time at the ranch, Mr. Bill was never real friendly to me but he always treated me with respect. I got the feeling, however, that there was some sort of tension between him and Wiley. Mr. Bill was the boss of the ranch hands and Wiley was the hired hand. It seemed to me as if he thought Wiley was a threat to him especially since the owner of the ranch and Wiley were good friends.

Mr. Bill had approached me about training 6 or 7 two year old ranch horses. My agreement with Mr. Bill was simple. In payment I could choose one of them for my own and keep it on the ranch until I left. Since I would soon be off to the rodeos, I took my one horse and off I went.

Jan, however, had her horses and she needed somewhere that would allow them to have some fresh air. There was an empty corral on the ranch that we wanted to use. Wiley told us the empty corral was never used and as long as we furnished the grain and hay for the horses it would be okay to use the corral. Her black horses soon had a new home.

BROWNIE

There was a ranch near the Circle T that had six, unbroken horses. These four year olds were a challenge and I made a deal with the owner to ride them until they were ready to be ranch horses. My reputation was starting to pay off in the form of extra work and extra money. The foreman of this ranch, Bandie, brought the horses to the Circle T and I broke them there.

The owner of the ranch where Bandie worked had several ranch hands but none of them were 'savvy' when it came to breaking horses. Most of what these ranch hands did was done with a jeep and a feed sack. This was a form of 'modern' ranching. The ranch hands would feed cattle every day from a jeep while honking the horn. The cattle eventually learned to follow the jeep anywhere, including into the cow pens. It saved a lot of time and was easier on the ranch hands! (It was sort of like a cowboy's version of Pavlov's experiments!)

Bandie himself had a method to break horses that came out of the 1800s. He said it worked but I never tried it because I thought the horse could easily hurt himself. His process involved getting a big log or a railroad tie or something else that would not move easily but would still 'give' a little when pulled. Bandie would 'foreleg' the horse and bring the horse to his side. Two men would then get on the horse to keep it down. While doing this, a stout halter would be put on the horse. A soft 25-foot cotton rope was attached to the halter. The other end of the rope was attached to the log (railroad tie). Once everything was secure, the horse was allowed to get back on all four legs.

The horse would try to run away but as the rope tightened the log would give a little and the horse would be rewarded with an 'easy' stop. The horse would pull away again and once more it would be gently pulled to a stop. This would continue for the entire day. Sometimes the horse would get tangled in the rope but by the end of the first or second day it would untangle itself.

Over the course of the next few days, the horse would settle down. Soon, it would be gentle enough to be led away. This method had several advantages. The horse would become more and more calm without riding it and if the horse ever got caught in a fence or other obstacle, it would not fight and hurt itself because he was used to the tension.

Bandie brought two horses I really liked. One was a very nice spotted, 4-year old paint horse. He wanted someone to put in the time to train this horse because the boss man wanted to give the horse to his daughter. According to him, all the horses were not 'halter broke' which means you could not lead them or touch them without scaring them. I was happy to help him but there was another horse I wanted to train first. It was a big bay horse that showed a lot of white in his eyes and rollers in his nose.

If a horse is wild or 'spooky' (he scares easily) he will open his eyes very wide and expose a lot of white. This is similar to the 'Banjo Eyes' look of scared individuals. The horse will also have a tendency to lift his head higher and look down his face at the object that is scaring him. He will then blow his nose very hard and as the nose vibrates from the force, it will sound like he has rollers in his nose. Horses will do this in the pasture sometimes if they see a deer, bear or something strange that has scared them.

Since they had no names. I decided to call the big bay horse 'Brownie.' The first thing I did with him was what is called 'tying a hind leg up.'

There was always something special about my ropes. I would take a 1½-inch cotton rope (found in any hardware store) and 'untwist' the strands. These strands would then be 'combed' until it was fluffed out. When that was done, I would divide the fluffed rope into four different sections and 'braid them,' just like you would do if you were making a pigtail. I would use four strands (instead of the normal three strands) and this would make the rope very soft and increase its size to almost 2 inches in diameter. It was a lot of work but it was much better for the horses.

I would first tie the horse to a wall or stout safe fence. He should be halter broke by now even though he still has not been ridden. I would use one of my 25- to 30-foot soft cotton ropes and gently slide it around the horse's neck and tie it. I would then step away and get far behind him so he could not kick me. With the horse contained, I would take the cotton rope and swing it over both sides of the horse, flapping it over his entire body. At first, the touch of the rope would scare the horse. However, when the horse discovered that nothing was going to hurt him, he would stand and then we would go to the next step. The rope would be put on the ground and the horse would step over it. This put the rope between the horse's hind legs. I would then 'flap' the rope up and down. This would scare the horse since these are areas where the wild horses have never been touched. Before long, the horse would also get used to this and stand quietly once more.

When I thought it was the right time, I would let the soft cotton rope slip down his left hind leg and settle just above his hoof. The rope would go around this and the end of the rope would be fed through the loop around the horse's neck. Gradually and slowly the slack would be removed and the horse's left hind leg would soon be off the ground.

I would throw some half-hitches (a type of knot) around the horse's left hind foot and before the horse knew it he was tied to the wall with his left hind leg 6-12 inches off the ground.

All this has to be done very carefully. You have to work near the horse but still be far enough away that he will not be able to kick you. If you do it right, you are ready to continue. If not, you will need to seek immediate medical attention!

The horse is now standing on three legs and tied to a post or solid fence. With the horse secure, I could walk up beside him and get him used to having someone close to him. Normally, I would 'rub' a saddle pad over him (a soft pad used to protect the horse from the saddle) and then throw a saddle on him. If this went well, the bridle would be next. Sometimes they would try to kick you but with only three legs to stand on, they soon learned to concentrate on standing and not kicking!

In time, the horse would become used to everything you have done and just stand there with a saddle and bridle on him. As mentioned before, as long as you show a horse you are not going to hurt him, you would be amazed at how gentle and trusting they can become. Once you have established who is in charge (hopefully you!), the horse will let you do things like brush him, take the bridle on and off and take the saddle on and off.

After you have mastered the above, you can untie him from the wall and slowly walk him to the middle of the corral. Remember, he still has only three legs on which to walk so he cannot run, jump or kick. You can now climb into the saddle. Since he is on three legs, he learns to just stand there and get used to all these new experiences. You get out of the saddle and then you get back in the saddle. By doing this several times the horse will get used to the commotion and have no fear of someone being in the saddle and on his back.

It is important that you do not try to ride the horse! If you do, you run the risk of hurting both the horse and yourself!

By now, the horse has gotten used to the saddle, the bridle and someone getting on and off of his back. Once you are satisfied the horse is ready, the next thing to do is ride him. BEFORE you ride him… you take the soft cotton rope off of his leg. He is now standing quietly on all FOUR legs. Time to get on.

I always made sure the horse would be facing a wall or pole fence so he could not run off. I would gently and quietly sneak up into the saddle (a common saying among ol' timers, would be to say that you have to work around a wild colt "like a thief in the night"). Once I am in the saddle, the horse can only take one or two steps before I turn him into the wall or fence. Then we go back the other way and take four or five steps before he is turned once again into the wall or fence. If he tries to buck, you just turn him into the wall or fence and he has no choice but to stop.

This is not a 'one time and it is done process.' Brownie and I went through those steps for two or three days. I could soon trot him and take him in a small gallop. When I thought we were both on the same page, I decided it was time to take him for a longer ride and let him out of the corral (round-pen).

Wiley was standing next to the gate and he opened it for me. As I rode out, I passed Wiley and he had a really sneaky smile on his face. I did not know if that look meant I had done a good job or if he thought he was about to see me get thrown off a horse. Most cowboys just love to see other cowboys get thrown off of a bucking horse, especially under these circumstances!

Brownie looked down his nose and all that white showed in his eyes. I was sure glad that Wiley did not throw his hat under the horse or do something else to 'spook' him, a common trick that often gets a horse bucking and kicking.

We rode steady for about a quarter of a mile. Brownie had his head down and was relaxed, or so I thought. As we rode along, he suddenly stubbed his foot on something and that was more than enough to send him into a frenzy! He dropped his head, jumped in the air and turned back toward the ranch. I was totally taken by surprise and thrown to the ground! When I hit the ground I still had the reins in my hand. To my surprise, Brownie did not try to run off. Instead, he walked up to me and just looked at me. It was as if he was saying, "Well, you're the expert here, what are you going to do next?"

I realized it was a long walk back to camp and the thought of Brownie getting loose with my saddle and running all over creation was not appealing to me. Luckily, there was a spare tie rope on my saddle because I usually leave the halter on the broncs for two or three days while I am trying to break them in.

I got up off the ground, got my extra rope, led Brownie to a nearby tree and tied him to it. Knowing he could not get away from me, I climbed back into the saddle, undid the rope and tried it again.

The rest of the day was really good. As we rode along, I could tell he had what we cowboys call, 'a good, easy mouth.' He would respond to going right and left with no problem. He did not try to throw me and we spent another 3 hours on the range. When we returned, I took the saddle off of him and let him loose in the corral. I wanted him free and relaxed because we were going to do it again the next morning.

Things went well the next day. I started off by riding him around the corral a few times. When we were ready to hit the range and leave the corral, a feed truck went by our location. Brownie looked down and I just knew the whites of his eyes were big and bright! I could not see his eyes (I was sitting back in the saddle) but when the truck went by I could easily hear the 'rollers' coming from his nose. We stayed in the corral until he settled down. After several minutes, I decided to try it one more time.

We spent half the day in the countryside before we rode back to the ranch. He was riding nice but when a covey of quail suddenly flew out of the bushes near his face the ride was on again! Brownie put his head down and squealed like a wild horse would do. He went into his spin just like a rodeo bronc. I hit the ground once more! When I looked up, what do I see but Brownie standing there looking at me. I was curious to know what that horse was thinking at that time! Then again, maybe not! I tied him to a tree once more, got in the saddle and off we went. The rest of the day was easy riding. Before long, he was back in the corral and I was figuring out what to do next.

We went through this routine for the next four or five days. We would ride, he would get startled, down I would go. I'd look up and there was this big, brown bay staring down at me. (I could swear he was laughing!) Then I would tie him to a tree, get back on and away we would go. It seemed to be a pattern but it was working and you don't fix something that ain't broke!

At times, it seemed Brownie was leading me to a tree instead of me leading him. In about a week, he quit bucking me off but I still rode like I was on a piece of glass! He had developed a beautiful sliding stop and was able to turn on a dime, but I had to stay alert!

For the next 35-40 days, I tried something else. I would tie a rope to a log and then 'dally' the rope around the saddle horn. We would drag the log until I was ready to let it go. Brownie did not mind the rope on his rump as we pulled the log. He was used to a rope in that location from when I had tied his hind leg up and found out the rope would not hurt him. (Soft ropes do have their benefits!)

The next part of the training involved a section of the ranch where the sick cattle were put to pasture. Cows have a tendency when they are sick to go into the brush and lay down. These sick cattle will move slower and lay down more often than a cow that is in good health.

To get Brownie used to being around livestock, I would take him to the 'sick' pasture. We would walk up to the sick cows, stand next to them and watch them. Since they were slower and only moved when necessary, Brownie got used to them. We would follow the cows at a walking pace. Before long, Brownie would walk up to the cattle and just stand there.

When the horses had been broken, Bandie came and took them away. I told the foreman that Brownie would make a good ranch horse but at times he could be 'spooked' easily. He knew what I was talking about but the ranch where the horses would be used had a lot of cattle and he needed horses that were used to being around livestock. Brownie might be a good first-string horse but they just had to keep an eye on him. After he left with the horses, I never saw Bandie or any of the horses ever again. It was not because I didn't want to see them but my next stop was a ranch in Texas so we were miles and miles apart.

Brownie's story doesn't end there!

About 5 or 6 years later while I was at home in Texas, I got a call from a man in Houston, Texas. He said he wanted to talk to Mr. Jim Warvell. I said, "You got him!" At the time, I was in the business of buying and selling horses and I thought he wanted me to buy a horse, I was wrong!

It seemed a horse I had broken long ago was now part of the rodeo circuit. This man told me he roped steers with this horse and his son and daughter used the horse to rope steers as well.

"Well, do you want to sell him?" I asked.

What he said next made me proud of what I had done.

The man laughed and told me the horse was part of their family and no money in the world could buy him. His kids had learned to ride on this horse and now they were using him in the rodeo. No, the horse was definitely not for sale.

He then asked me if I had another good horse to sell like the one he bought from the man who recommended him to me.

I tried to remember what horse he could possibly be talking about. Having trained so many horses, there was no way to guess which one it was!

Finally, I told him that maybe he had me mixed up with somebody else. "I truly do not know which horse you are talking about," I told him.

He laughed and said, "I bought this horse from a man that recommended you to me."

"What was his name?" I asked.

"The man's name was Bandie and he was a foreman on a ranch in Florida.

He told me the horse's name was Brownie."

I could hardly believe it! Sometimes the truth is stranger than fiction!

THE PAINT

As I mentioned before, there was a very nice paint colt in this batch of horses. The owner of the ranch wanted it trained to be very gentle because he wanted to give it to his daughter.

When Bandie drove up with the horses I was to break, he backed up to a special corral. You see, when horses are born in the open lands and not handled by people they learn to fend for themselves like any wild animal. So, when you a take young horse like this and turn them loose, they will run around the corral protecting themselves and look for a way out. They will look for holes, broken fence lines, openings or anything that would set them free.

To make sure they were safe and stayed put, I had stalls along one side of the corral and by leaving the doors to the stalls open, the youngsters would run into the stalls on their own. They would also run out of the stalls. They got used to the stalls and were not afraid of them.

The first night they were fed hay in the corral. The second night they were fed hay in the stalls and they went in on their own. In only a couple of days they were going in and out of the stalls as if they owned the place. I could now shut the doors behind them, wait until they settled down and then get them ready for the training process. Each day I would work with one or two of the horses, usually the ones I had worked with the previous day.

The paint colt seemed fairly quiet but when I went in the stall with him he backed up into a corner. He raised his head, looked down his nose and showed a lot of white in his eyes! He took one of his front legs and struck at me. I had to back up quickly to avoid getting hit. I stood quietly for several seconds. When he calmed down, I slowly went back to him again but once more he struck out at me.

I did not take this personally. Horses are taught to do this in the wild. They use their front legs when they are striking at a coyote, a rattlesnake or other danger that is near them. This was a problem easily solved. I got a 6-foot rope and when he struck at me, I looped it around his striking foot. The rope would then go under his knee so I could control it. Once again, the 'three legged' stance worked wonders. I would hold his leg up and try to rub his nose. At first, he would not let me but, after several attempts, I managed to do it and make friends with him. He was not hurt and we created a friendship, of sorts.

We did this on a continual basis until he let me come to him and rub his nose without striking out at me. I ended the training process and I rode him for 30 straight days. He got real gentle. He had a nice, easy trot and with just a slight pull on the reins he would come to a sliding stop. I was proud of how gentle he was!

I knew this horse had to be extra gentle because he was going to be owned by a young girl. I thought he was gentle enough but something was bothering me. This horse had always been ridden by me either in the morning or at midday when no other person was around. I had to be sure this horse was gentle around other people.

One day I was finishing our daily ride and, at the time, was feeling really good about the way this horse was working out. As I got back to camp, I spotted Jan.

"Hey," I yelled out to her, "Could you please come over here and ride this paint? I want to see how he is around people and how he rides for you."

As Jan walked up to the paint, I was sitting in the saddle. I noticed the horse as it watched her. His head went a little bit higher as Jan got closer. His neck arched and as he looked down his nose at her, he struck his leg out at her!

Because she was used to horses and how they can react, Jan jumped back and the paint's kick missed her. She tried it again and the same thing happened.

Out of the corner of my eye, I saw Bill, the ranch hand, walk towards me. I asked him if he would walk up to the paint. He did and when the paint arched his neck I told Bill to be really careful. Sure enough, it did not take long before the paint had his ears pinned back to his head and he was showing his teeth. This horse was ready for anything!

Bill got closer and the paint struck out at him!

"What's the matter with that crazy son of a bitch?" Bill shouted as he jumped back out of the reach of the horse's hoof.

"Apparently, I am the only person he trusts." I replied. "I guess I am his only friend in the world!"

I knew there was another solution to this problem and it had to be done quickly! I asked Jan if she would go over to the fence and get in a position where she could get in the saddle. As she did, I moved the horse near the fence. When I had him in the right position, I settled him down and put a red bandana (kerchief) over his eyes. As I carefully slipped out of the saddle, Jan carefully slid into the saddle. The horse had no clue what had just happened.

We removed the bandana and Jan rode him for almost half an hour. There was no fear in the horse or in Jan. She trotted with him, made him do circles and figure eights, backed him up made him stop and anything else she could think of.

The two of them were fantastic together! The horse was gentle, responsive and quiet. Jan, the horsewoman that she was, handled him with firmness and in a manner that instilled confidence and cooperation in the horse.

When she brought him to me, she dismounted and I held the horse's head as she rubbed his nose. You could tell he was not completely sure about her but things went off without a hitch.

The next day, Jan came to ride him again. This time I was not in the saddle but standing next to him, holding his head and rubbing his nose. Jan put a foot in the stirrup. Nothing happened. She pulled herself into the saddle. Nothing happened. I let go of the bridle. Nothing happened. We nodded at each other and soon the two of them were off on another safe ride around the ranch. Having taken care of the problem, Jan and I alternated riding the horse for the next week. We were soon getting other people to come up to him. They would hold him and rub his nose. This seemed to take the fear out of the paint and with the fear gone, the other people could get into the saddle and ride him.

When we could do this on a continual basis, I thought he was ready for the boss's daughter. Mind you now, I was only 20 years old when all this happened. Having been around horses all my life and keeping my ears open and my mouth shut (except when asking questions) I had learned a lot. During this time, I had always heard about a 'one man horse' or a 'one woman horse,' meaning some horses only would respond to one individual and one individual only. I am not disputing this philosophy because I do know that some horses respond better to some people more so than others. They may relax more around men than women or vice versa. Like people, horses have personalities too!

Over the course of my life. I have been around thousands and thousands of horses. I have ridden them in Europe, England, South America, Japan, Canada, Mexico, Kuwait and a slew of other places. In all that time, I have NEVER been around a horse like this paint! When you rode this paint, it was like having a German Shepherd police dog for protection. That little horse was always on the guard for snakes, coyotes and anything else that might harm his friend who was sitting on his back! It was amazing!

Satisfied, I finally released the paint back to Bandie and I never saw him again. Before I left for Texas, however, I did ask one of their ranch hands how the paint was doing. He told me the paint was one of the gentlest horses on the ranch. I never said anything to him about the horse and what happened during the time I had him, but I knew the paint had a good home and I let it go at that!

CHAPTER 8

MILT "THE BRAGGART"

It was soon time to leave Florida. The nice winter weather was now spreading across the country and the rodeo circuit was calling me! April and May were close and that meant the real fun was about to start.

When I came to Florida with Wiley, Jack and Dave, my old camping and rodeo buddies, left and went to Arizona to work at a race track called Turf Paradise. Jack had a nice big horse that came off the King ranch in Texas. They used his horse to 'pony' or lead the racehorse and rider from the barns to the racetrack for a morning workout. In those days, you could earn two dollars for each racehorse you would accompany. Racehorse trainers were always on the lookout for people with nice big 'Pony' horses and good riders to help assist their valuable racehorses to and from the track and sometimes they would hire Jack to 'lead' the racehorse around the track at a gallop if the trainer did not want the exercise rider or jockey to work the horse. Jack and Dave would also clean the stalls and do odd jobs around the racetrack.

We were to meet in Florida during the month of May. At least that was the plan. Once we were together, our goal was to work the amateur rodeos throughout Tennessee, Arkansas and other states in the south. Wiley knew of our plans and he told me about an old acquaintance who was putting together a rodeo in North Carolina. I had never heard of the man but Wiley said his name was Milt Hinkle and he would treat us right.

Milt, it seems, had a colorful background! Wiley said we would recognize him right away because he was a big man (over 6-foot tall) and walked with a permanent limp that required a cane. Later we would discover that Milt had made a lot of promises during some of his earlier 'promotions.' He had been involved in a lot of 'shady' deals and often left town in the middle of the night without paying any of his debts.

I asked Wiley why Milt walked with a limp and he told me that Milt had bragged just once too often. It seems Milt had once been a good steer wrestler and had bragged about what he could do with a steer. One day a Mexican rodeo promoter was listening when Milt bragged about how he could jump out of an airplane, catch a steer and wrestle it to the ground. (Wrestling a steer is hard enough but to do it by jumping from a plane?)

Milt bragged about this and the Mexican promoter decided to take him up on the offer. He knew there was a bi-plane in the area. This bi-plane had two wings, one above the fuselage and one below the fuselage and, because of this configuration, it could fly very slowly. This was just the right kind of plane for a man who wanted to jump and wrestle a steer! Well, needless to say, the Mexican promoter leaped at the chance to see this act of bravery. He told Milt they could go to Mexico where he could get a big crowd of people together who would pay a lot of money to see this 'feat' of excellence!

As the story was told to me, they would build a small platform on the plane. Milt would stand on the platform while the plane went as slowly as it could. He would then jump off the platform (like he said he could!), catch a steer and wrestle it to the ground. Needless to say, the problem would be how to keep the steer going straight but the promoter also had that figured out too!

He would have people standing side by side forming a lane or pathway for the steer to run down. The plane would come down and Milt would jump from the stand on the plane, catch the steer, wrestle it to the ground and make a lot of money!

Apparently, Milt was stuck so he agreed to all this. The promoter went back to Mexico where he got several other partners to go in on the deal with him. They did a lot of advertising and this event soon became a big thing down there. When Milt arrived, he was treated like a king (he was a star, after all!) and he enjoyed every minute of it.

Time keeps moving, however, and when it was Milt's turn to do his amazing stunt, they ran into a snag. Milt was about to get on the platform when he suddenly decided he could not do it because if something went wrong it might be 'fatal' to him. He had enjoyed this 'amusement' and now it was time for him to leave.

Milt, however, had forgotten who he was dealing with! The promoter came up to him and he brought two of his friends with him. Both of these men had shotguns with them. Milt was told if he did not go through with the stunt the men would shoot him right then and there!

Milt knew there would be a lot of anger among the people who had paid their pesos to see this stunt. He also knew these Mexicans were serious and would have no problem shooting him right then and there.

After some careful consideration (probably about half a second's worth!), Milt decided he would get on the platform. Once he was onboard, the promoter told him that if he did not jump from that plane onto the steer, there would be someone at the other end who would be happy to shoot him off the plane!

Milt now had three choices. He could get shot right now or he could get shot if he decided not to jump or he could jump off a moving plane and try to wrestle a steer to the ground.

He was on the platform and the plane was soon in the air! The plane came around and the steer was let loose. The pilot got the plane in position and Milt tried to judge where the steer was going to be. He jumped off the platform (it was definitely better than being SHOT off the platform!) and soon discovered he had misjudged the steer's location.

Milt hit the ground and broke his leg and his hip. The fall did not kill him but it was close! His injuries healed and he was able to 'limp' out of Mexico. Milt ended up with a permanent limp that required the use of a cane for the rest of his life!

When the three of us finally caught up to him in North Carolina, Milt was almost 80 years old. This was probably going to be one of his last 'big' promotions and he wanted to go out with a bang! He was promoting a rodeo for the brand new indoor arena they had just built in Charlotte, North Carolina. He told them he wanted to put on a first-class rodeo. That sounded good to us but then we found out that the man promoting this first-class rodeo was using his broken-down Oldsmobile as his office! Truth was… Milt had nothing!

Through tough negotiation, he had managed to assemble some rough stock from the local area. This was stock that had never been in a rodeo arena before. He had lined up horses, bulls, calves and some other livestock to round out the entertainment. The feed for these animals came from the local feed store with a promise to pay for the feed from the 'big profits' of the event.

He had talked to most of the people that I met at the Buzzard's Roost and he convinced them to help or participate in this rodeo. He told them it would be a big success with their help. The riders and contestants were made up of young amateurs that wanted to be in a rodeo. The old cowboys (professionals) took care of the livestock just as they did 100 years ago. They had some feed boxes that were 10 feet long. They would ride their horses, rope the feed box and drag it to the feed lot for the animals to eat. This would be repeated until the animals were fed.

They would do the same thing for the bales of hay. The hay would be roped and dragged to wherever it was needed. Somebody would then cut the string on the bale and scatter it along the fence line or wherever it was going. Sacks of feed would be thrown across a saddle, opened and spilled into the feeder boxes. Today this would all be done with a pickup truck or tractor but back then horses were the major source of just about everything!

As I think about the way we did things back then, I am reminded of an old saying:

"If a cowboy can't do it on horseback or in bed, then he can't do it!"

Milt stuck it out and the rodeo went on as scheduled. Jack, Dave and I made some money but I made more than money at that event. I watched some really good cowboys having fun and being serious about their craft. It might even be the last rodeo for some of them but if it was, they were going out with a whoop and a holler!

Wiley roped about every bull and steer in the arena that day! Since the bulls had never been in a rodeo before, they were new to this game. The surroundings confused them and they would often go the wrong way or get scared and just run around trying to get out. Wiley ended up roping every one of the bulls (most of the steers too) and leading them out of the arena so no one, the bulls included, would get hurt.

The Charlotte rodeo lasted three days. During that time, Milt never got out of his Oldsmobile. He was very grumpy and not an easy man to talk to about anything. He would just sit there and write things down on paper.

I once asked Wiley what Milt was doing and he said he did not know but the Oldsmobile was full of coffee cups, scraps of paper, food wrappers, blankets, clothes and an assortment of other trash and personal items.

One day, I saw a man walk up to the Oldsmobile. He was smoking and when he got to the car window the man exhaled a big cloud of smoke into the car. Milt, who was sitting inside, as usual, just lost it! He began yelling at the man and telling him to get away from his car.

Two hours later, Milt decided to move the car but it would not start. Milt threw another fit and some of the old timers went to help and see if they could start the car. Milt, however, did not care about the car, he wanted to find the man who had blown smoke into his car. He kept screaming that the smoke had, "ruined his car" and now it probably would never run again!

We were beginning to think that old Milt was becoming senile and the past had caught up with him. Thankfully, the rodeo ended and we all went our separate ways. Although I would never get to see this fantastic group of old timers again, it was an honor to have had that adventure with them. It was a chance to work one time with the old promoter Milt Hinkle and be welcomed once more by the group from the Buzzard's Roost.

CHAPTER 9

BACK ON THE CIRCUIT

After the North Carolina rodeo, Wiley went to Arkansas to visit Betty because she and Jan were working a show there. After that, he was on his way to the McKinley Wild West Show where he worked every year. Jack, Dave and I were headed to a two-day amateur rodeo that was only 150 miles from Charlotte. We headed there and when we were done our goal was to head for Arkansas and find more work.

The only way to get into the elite club that allowed you to work any of the rodeos was to use your permit and keep working your way up through the ranks. Once you had earned enough money (I believe it was in the $2,000 to $2,500 range) you could then apply for and be accepted into the R.C.A. (Rodeo Cowboys Association) and that meant you could then enter any of their rodeos.

The three of us pulled into the rodeo and found it was taking place at a baseball park. We looked around and saw many familiar old trucks and vehicles. Suddenly, it dawned on us! We were with Larry the Wild West Man! We had worked some of his events the previous year.

Larry had promoted his rodeo and gotten the town council to hire him so he could put on an amateur rodeo in the ball park. He put up the fences, the chutes and everything else right on the baseball field. One part of the fence turned out to be the snow fence used by the city during the winter months. The fence went around 1st base, 2nd base, 3rd base and on to the grandstand.

The venue had $100 prize for each event. There was saddle bronc riding, bareback riding, steer wrestling and even a 2-man wild cow milking contest!

WILD COW MILKING

We signed up for our events and even signed up for the wild cow milking contest. The milking contest was always a fan favorite! The promoters would get a bunch of wild cows and turn them loose in the arena. Several 2-man teams were given one empty soda pop bottle per team and lined up against the fence inside the arena with the cows. When the signal was given, the time started.

Each team would race into the cow herd and try to catch a cow barehanded. One partner would grab the cow's head and slow her down so the other team member could get a few drops of milk (hence the name, wild cow milking) in the soda pop bottle. Both ends of the cow were mighty dangerous. She would have no problem head butting you, kicking you or doing whatever it took to get away from the maniacs who were hanging on to her!

Sometimes the cowboy trying to fill the bottle would have to grab her tail or leg while trying to milk her and get the squirt to go in the small bottle's opening. It was hilarious! Imagine the chaos in the arena with cowboys getting stomped on while trying to milk a very wild cow! When the 'milker' got a few drops in his bottle he would run as fast as he could to where a judge stood. The judge would turn the bottle upside down because he had to witness milk coming out of the bottle even if it was just a drop or two. When that happened, the judge would drop his flag and the time would stop. The fastest time would win the contest.

It was not only a fun contest to watch but it was also a lot of fun to participate in! You have to remember that the cows they used for this event were wild cows so the action in the arena was wild, crazy and dangerous most of the time.

THE DRAW

When a cowboy entered an event such as bull riding, the rodeo secretary wrote his name down on an entry list. After everyone had registered, a number would be drawn for each entry. This part of the rodeo is called (appropriately) 'The Draw.' It is the only fair way to match a rider with his animal. No one knows which animal they will get and there is no 'human' factor involved to taint the outcome of the event. Each animal is given a unique number and that number is 'branded' onto the animal's hide. The number drawn would now correspond to the number branded on the animal. This is how the rider and the animal are paired.

The horse I was to ride for the saddle bronc riding event was a pretty good horse. I had ridden him a few times the year before. I knew this horse did not turn back or twist but would buck and kick in a big circle, usually along the fence line. The problem I saw was not with the horse but with the arena!

They had not smoothed out the ball field. All they had done was take up the bases. It was safe in some areas and not so safe in others. When the time came, I climbed on the horse, grabbed the buck rein and got myself ready for anything! The chute was opened and my horse made a big jump. He began to kick high and turn. It was an easy ride up until we started toward the pitcher's mound (and they do not call it a pitcher's 'mound' for nothing!). He bucked over the mound without falling down (I breathed a lot easier once we cleared that mound) and then headed for the 4-foot snow fence. As he neared 2nd base, he circled back towards 3rd base, rounded it and headed for home plate.

By now I was not sure if I was playing baseball or riding a horse but a few more kicks and jumps brought me back to reality. Unfortunately, the dugout was too close to my path and we were headed right for it! The dugout was a 4-foot deep hole where the players would stay until it was time to bat or go into the field. We came within inches of the dugout's edge! All I could do was hang on. Thankfully, the horse turned and headed for home plate. We had missed the dugout but were now headed back to where the bucking chutes were located.

My time on the horse finally ended and the pickup man soon came alongside and pulled me off the saddle bronc. When I was safe on the ground, I felt like I had hit a home run and was more than thankful to get out of this dangerous place alive! I was ready to go to Arkansas and get involved with a professional rodeo in an old-fashioned rodeo arena!

DAVE AND A GOOD NIGHT'S SLEEP

We left the ballpark rodeo behind and were soon on our way to Arkansas. The plan was to meet Wiley, his wife, and Jan at one of the rodeos. To get there, we had to drive over some mountains. At that time, there were no Interstates. You had to use the back roads and what main roads that existed, regardless of their condition. We drove up, down and around curve after curve. Most of the time we were lucky to go 35 miles an hour.

At Milt's rodeo, I had traded my steer wrestling horse for a black mare that I could use as a calf roping horse. She was not good enough to use in the professional circuit but she was good enough to use when I wanted to practice my calf roping skills. I would often buy and sell horses depending on my needs and especially if I could make money on the deal.

I decided to bring her to Arkansas so I put her in the bed of the pickup truck and hauled her that way. Don't worry! I had a box built around her to keep the wind and rain out. She was protected the best I could. I also had my little camper trailer that was pulled behind the pickup truck. Jack, Dave and I sat in the front of the truck and down the road we went. I was driving and about 1:30 in the morning, I stopped for gas. There was not a lot of room for us in the front seat of that truck and it was not very comfortable, especially when you were trying to sleep like they were.

Jack and Dave knew there were two nice beds in the camper we were pulling. Dave decided that after we filled the truck with gas he would go into the camper and sleep on one of the beds. I agreed and told him that if he wanted us to stop for any reason all he had to do was open the window of the camper, stick his arm out and wave it around. I would see his arm in the mirror and stop the truck. He agreed and off we went once more.

It was early in the morning, very dark and we were still traveling through the hills. Jack was sleeping in the truck next to me and I was driving. There were no other cars at this time of the morning and the blackness of the night made it hard to see anything that was not in the vision of the headlights.

The sun came up and when I looked in the mirror I saw a bandana sticking out of the camper's window. An arm was attached to it and both of them were waving frantically!

I woke Jack and told him we were going to stop because Dave was giving me a signal. I drove until I found a safe place to pull off onto the side of the road. I had barely come to a stop when Dave jumped out of the camper. I thought he might have to go to the bathroom but instead he walked up to the driver's side of the truck. He looked rough and disheveled.

"Geez," I told him, "you look like you have been through a street mauling!" "What's wrong?" Jack asked him. "Didn't you get any sleep?"

Dave then went into his story and it was a pretty good one, too! He had gone into the camper and laid down on one of the beds. He was feeling comfortable and ready to enjoy a good sleep. All went well until we rounded a pretty sharp curve and he was completely thrown out of the bed! He decided to flag us down so he stood up and headed for the window. It was about that time we went around another hairy curve and he was thrown to the other side of the camper and slammed into the opposite wall!

The curtains, he told us, were standing straight out and it was becoming impossible to stand, much less give me the signal to stop. Sometimes the curtains would stand out one way and then they would stand out the other way. As long as he stood up he was thrown from one side to the other so he decided to get on his hands and knees and crawl to the center of the camper. My camper had a small hallway with a refrigerator on one side and a bathroom door on the other side.

Dave said he put his back against the bathroom door and ended up sitting down with his feet against the refrigerator. He stayed 'locked' in that position, trying to be as stable as possible so he would not get thrown around the camper. He sat there all night until we got out of the mountains and he could get up and signal me to stop. He had been waving and yelling for several miles but I never noticed. Next time he will think twice about taking a comfortable bed over the uncomfortable front seat of my pickup!

FAREWELL TO DAVE

We finally arrived in Arkansas. I sold my horse so I had some extra money in my pocket. At the rodeo, Dave entered the bull riding contest, Jack entered the bareback riding contest and I entered the saddle bronc riding contest.

Dave got bucked off his bull.

I got bucked off my horse! I was told he usually headed for the fences but when I thought he would go one way he decided to go another way and I was soon sitting on the ground. Jack rode his horse but when the ride was over the horse fell and Jack had his leg under the horse when it hit the ground. The horse got up but Jack did not because he had a broken leg and had to go to the hospital for a cast and a good night's rest. If anyone tells you that rodeo events are 'safe,' think again!

At the end of the rodeo, Dave said he was going to Arizona. A man had offered him a good job. It was a smart move for Dave because, as it turned out, this job would later lead to a high paying job with the railroad system out west.

I would see Dave one more time but it would be many years later. By then he had gotten married, had a family and settled down in northern California close to the railroad's main office. I knew he was always very athletic and light on his feet so it surprised me to see him using a crutch to get around.

When I asked what happened he told me the story. It seems he was moving a pool table that had been put in the back of a pickup truck. He was guiding the truck as it backed up to the house. He had one leg in the doorway and one leg outside the doorway when the man driving the pickup got too close to the door. The driver's foot slipped off the clutch and the truck raced backwards. It crushed Dave's leg against the house! They thought the leg might have to be amputated but Dave would not let them. It was obvious this accident had changed Dave's mood and his life.

His eyes sure did light up when we talked about the early days and that made us both very happy!

FAREWELL TO JACK

Jack's broken leg was going to take a lot of time to heal. He decided to head back home where he would have friends and family to help him rest and heal. I hated to see him go.

From the very beginning, the two of us grew up together and we had become best of friends. We shared any and everything. If I had $10 then we each had $5. If we only had money for one hamburger, we would share it. We were brothers then and we are brothers now.

Jack went back home and his leg was soon completely healed. He might have wanted to come back to the rodeo circuit but he was called into the military and ended up doing a tour in Korea.

I was also called into the military but when they called me, I had just broken my back and was in a cast from my neck to my waist. Obviously, I could not pass the physical. When they called me a second time, I had just broken my arm and there was a cast on it. Again, I could not pass the physical and they let me go. That was the last time the military called me!

Jack and I stayed best buddies but that was the last time we ever worked together in a rodeo, horse show or Wild West Show.

CHAPTER 10

SALINAS

After the Arkansas rodeo, Jan had a big event booked. She and her horses were becoming very popular and in demand. She would be working the Salinas Rodeo in California. This rodeo was located close to the place where her mother and father had worked during WWII. The sheriff of Salinas was a good friend of Jan's parents as they had worked together in the shipyard years before.

She remembered some of this town but not much. She had lived there as a youngster but only for a short time before they put her on a train and sent her back to live with her grandparents in Linton, Indiana.

Jan asked me if I would help drive when she left for Salinas. I said I would. I had learned to drive trucks and trailers when I was 15 years old, so, driving a truck of this size and pulling a large horse van was no problem for me.

It suddenly dawned on me that I would never be traveling with Jack and Dave anymore. I had a new traveling 'buddy' and the two of us were about to discover that our futures were going to be entwined forever!

Her little truck had a semi hook-up with a fifth wheel and pin. It pulled her horse van that was big enough to accommodate Jan's five horses and still provide a small living area in the back of the rig. Our route took us across Texas, through New Mexico and over the Raton Pass in the Rockies. As it turned out, I never got to use that fifth gear because there just was not enough power to reach the speed necessary to shift into overdrive. That fully loaded trailer was heavy!

I had driven the mountains of the east coast but never the Rocky Mountains of the Western United States. Boy, was I in for a surprise!

The different structure of the mountains was also something new to me. Most 4-6,000 foot mountains in the eastern U.S. do not take much time or miles to reach the top. The roads go right up and right down.

In the western United States, however, you find a 4-6,000 foot mountain and you can take hours or a day to get to the top of it! The road slopes gently to the top and it is hard to tell if you are going uphill unless you are pulling a big load or have an underpowered vehicle like ours.

When we started up the Raton Pass I was in a low gear. The motor started getting hot so we had to make several stops and allow the motor to cool so we could continue. When we were about a mile from the top of the mountain, I told Jan we would be lucky if we did not damage the motor during this climb.

Remember, there were no Interstates at this time. All we had were well traveled, curvy roads with lots of places to pull over in case you had a problem.

We pulled onto one of these emergency spots and thought about our predicament.

Jan said, "We have too much of a load. If we unload three horses maybe you can get to the top."

It made sense to me so we unloaded the white horse, Frosty, and put a saddle on him. Then we unloaded the two black mares. Jan got on Frosty, took the lead ropes of the black mares and started up the mountain. I let the truck engine cool down and then began my trek towards the peak. My top speed was between 8 and 10 miles an hour. I was trying not to let the engine overheat. I could see Jan up ahead with the three horses and as I passed her she gave me a 'thumbs up.'

When I got to the top, I rounded a curve, found an emergency area, pulled over and waited. Because of the steep incline and curve, I could not see Jan. I sat there for what seemed like a long time, wondering if she had problems. A cell phone would have been handy but they had not been invented yet! A good Interstate would also have been handy. A straight road would really have been nice. But we had none of those so I just had to sit and wait.

After a while I could see a white horse and two black mares walking beside the road. It took another 15 or 20 minutes before Jan and her horses caught up to the truck. When she arrived, we loaded the horses back into the van and continued on our trip, this time (hopefully) downhill!

We had won that battle and I was feeling good! Having never been west of these Colorado Rockies, I thought we now had it made for the rest of the trip to California. We had 'beaten' the best the Rockies had to offer and the rest would be easy pickings!

In the years to come I would travel and work rodeos all over the western states. Sometimes we would work in the Rocky Mountains all summer and I would learn the danger of the mountains compared to the flat lands where I grew up. Knowing what I know now, I would not challenge myself to pull a big van and drive that 'little' truck in those 10-11,000 foot elevations. This, like anything else, was a learning process.

We found a rodeo arena and pens where we could spend the night. The next morning, a man at the rodeo grounds heard our story and said the truck probably needed a tune-up because the timing might be off. He told us how carburetors had to be adjusted so they would not 'vaporize' fuel at this altitude. He went on to say the fuel mixture had to be 'just right' or we would continue to have trouble, especially in the mountains where we were headed next. The truck was sent to the shop to have this problem fixed. After the carburetor got an adjustment, we thought we had our problem solved.

GRAPEFRUIT! WHO KNEW?

The next day we were once more on our way. We started to climb more elevation but, after a while, we were sitting in another emergency pull off! While we were sitting there wondering what to do, a pickup pulled over next to us and a rancher got out. He asked us if we were having trouble. We talked to him and he told us the fuel pump was 'vapor locking' and if we sat there it would correct itself and then we could go on with our trip.

Sure enough, 20 minutes later the engine turned over and we were off once more. The hills continued to stare at us and 75 miles down the road we started to climb once more. I could tell we were losing power and I knew we would have to stop and rest the engine. There was a farm stand selling fruits and vegetables ahead on the left with a place to pull over across from it so we did just that. We crossed the road and began looking for some fruit.

"Where are you headed?" the lady asked.

"California, if we ever get there" Jan replied.

"Our truck keeps vapor locking," I explained.

"That happens a lot up here," the lady told us, "But I can fix the problem if you want."

She did not look like a mechanic but by now we were willing to try just about anything! Jan headed back to the truck with some fruit we had purchased and the lady gave me the solution she had in mind. "The fuel pump vapor locks because the air is thinner and all you have to do is buy a grapefruit, cut it in half and put one half of the grapefruit over the fuel pump with a string tied to it so the grapefruit half will stay in place."

I had to think about that one but we had to do something! So, I bought three grapefruits and headed back to the truck. Now, I had to explain to Jan that we were going to make it to California with the help of three grapefruits. (Put yourself in my position and figure out what you would say!) Needless to say, Jan stared at me. I was now the crazy guy holding three grapefruit in my hands and hoping they were our salvation for the rest of the trip!

"Do you really believe that?" she asked.

"Well," I tried to explain, "The lady said we put half a grapefruit over our fuel pump and that will keep the fuel pump cool and not starving for moisture."

She shrugged. I shrugged.

We cut the first grapefruit in half. Then we lifted the engine hood and saw the fuel pump. It was in a difficult place and would be hard to attach the grapefruit to it but we finally got the job done. We got in the truck and were getting settled when she sighed.

"That lady at the fruit stand can see a sucker a mile away and she knows how to sell fruit," Jan told me, "Especially grapefruit!"

"Yea, I agree but we are in a desperate situation and we have to try something to solve the problem."

I turned the key and the engine started right off. Believe it or not, we traveled all day without any problems! We were soon talking and joking about this unusual cure.

"I wonder how many bushels of grapefruit we will have to feed this truck before we reach California," she said with a laugh.

The gas gauge was now getting low. We stopped at the next gas station for a fill up. We also thought it was time to change the grapefruit as well. I opened the hood and saw the grapefruit had disappeared. There was nothing left but the string. I looked closer and it was easy to see the grapefruit had been gone for a long, long time. We had been driving for many miles and it could have dropped off at any time. I closed the hood and paid for the gas.

"Do we have more hills or lots of elevations that we have to travel?" I asked the attendant. (Just in case we needed more grapefruit!)

"No," he replied. "You have come over the worst part. The elevation here is around 3,000 feet and you have just come off a 6,000 foot peak. That is where most people have the most problems."

I looked back at the road we had just traveled.

"How far back was the 6,000 foot point?" I asked.

"Well," he answered, "You can't miss it. At the top of the peak is a fruit stand."

I shook my head.

"Yea," I told him, "I am familiar with that place."

Jan and I were soon on the road once more. She picked up on something right away.

"Aren't you forgetting about the grapefruit?" Jan asked.

I knew I had to tell her something.

"We have been going down to a lower elevation all day," I began, "And that was why the truck ran so good. We were going downhill. The grapefruit most likely fell off during the first five miles after we put it on.

"The attendant said the highest elevation was where the fruit stand was located. Apparently, that lady had a great way of getting rid of her grapefruits!"

She stared at me and then we laughed at the situation and how 'good' the truck ran with the grapefruit.

For years afterward, if a truck or car was not running good, we said we needed a grapefruit. No one understood what Jan and I were talking about, but we did! All we could think about were two young kids feeding the truck grapefruit so they could make it over the mountains to California!

ON TO CALIFORNIA

We were very relieved when we left the Rockies and the roads became straighter and much better to drive. You could see for miles in front of you and that was a relief, too.

In school, I remembered studying the Continental Divide. At the time, however, I was only interested in three things: Sports, horses and 'girlology.' But suddenly I remembered the Continental Divide and now it was staring me in the face! It seemed amazing to be at the point in the United States where there was a 'point.' The Continental Divide is unique because if you had a bucket of water and pour it on one side, it will flow toward the Pacific Ocean. If you pour the water on the other side, it will flow toward the Atlantic Ocean. (Okay, maybe not to that extreme but you get the idea!)

Our next stop was the desert and a much lower elevation. The roads were long and the terrain was flat with no hills, mountains or rise of any kind. I was driving 50 mph and it seemed like the truck was having no power trouble at all.

Unfortunately, this truck did not have any special brakes. The brakes on the trailer were electric and, in 1956, these were the best they had. The brakes on the truck were good hydraulic brakes, the kind in general use throughout the industry but we were moving fast with a lot of weight behind us. Imagine a semi pulling a fully loaded trailer, traveling at 50 miles an hour, and it has to stop quickly. You better have good brakes on both the truck and the trailer!

Since the van brakes were not connected to the truck brakes (1956 technology), you had to manually operate a hand lever to apply the brakes to the van. You could apply a little of the brake or all of it but you had to be careful because the wheels would not stop and slide, like electric brakes would later do. We were still going down in elevation (Death Valley?) but I did not realize it. The speed of the truck went to 55 mph. Suddenly, I realized what was taking place! The truck was going too fast for me to slow the truck by shifting to a lower gear! I started to 'over use' the truck and the trailer brakes as I tried to keep control of both vehicles and lower our speed.

When the brakes were applied, we dropped to 50 mph. However, when you use the brakes that much they get hot and don't work as well! In a flash, we went back to 55 mph and I had to repeat the process.

Jan was looking out the window and counting jackrabbits.

"Look, there are four of them over there," she would tell me. "Oh, there is another one and five more over there!"

She's counting jackrabbits and I had a runaway truck on my hands. All I could say was, "Yep," or, "Nope," every time she told me about her rabbits.

"You are not paying any attention to me," she commented.

Since her window was open, she soon noticed something other than rabbits.

"I smell hot brakes," she said as she pulled her head back and looked at me. I guess I was very pale and my knuckles were very white as one hand gripped the steering wheel while the other hand gripped the van's brake lever.

"Is there a problem?" she asked.

I did not have the heart to tell her we were in a runaway truck. I just kept on going!

"Nah, I got it!"

Luckily, we got to a place where the elevation leveled off. I found a place to stop and immediately pulled over. We needed to let the brakes cool off after all the work they had done. We relaxed and when the brakes were ready, we continued on our way. We reached California with only minor problems. It was a relief!

This was the first time I had traveled across the country going west. We did not know there was a northern route and a southern route that completely bypassed the Rocky Mountains. We made the mistake of taking the scenic and most dangerous middle route 'through' the mountains thinking it would be the shortest route to Salinas.

The route we took is not a place for a 'toy' truck. I would not take that truck and van over those mountains again! That is what I could call 'dumb and dumber'!

We counted jackrabbits, bought grapefruit and learned some valuable lessons but, in the end, we finally made it to California!

CHAPTER 11

SALINAS, CALIFORNIA

The Salinas rodeo was, at that time, the biggest and best one I had ever seen. I had been to many rodeos where world champion cowboys were in one or two events. At this one, however, there was a world champion in every event! These champions were current world champions while the ones at other rodeos were past champions.

I wanted to compete in this rodeo. Unfortunately, Salinas did not accept permits and I did not have a Rodeo Cowboys Association card so I could not do anything but watch. It was a good thing, too! I soon realized the cowboys here were amazing. No matter what contest I watched, I realized this was another 'dumb and dumber' moment! I needed another year of amateur riding, at least! I would have to improve tremendously and even that might not be enough to compete with these cowboys.

The specialty acts soon grabbed my attention. The best trick riders and roman riders in the United States were here. If you competed or performed at the Salinas Rodeo, you had to be the best because that was all that was here! Having this as a reference on your resume was also a plus when you were trying to get a new job.

To tell you how big this rodeo was, you have to understand that the grandstand, where people sat to watch the events, was a quarter of a mile long! It was in a huge open coliseum designed so Salinas could run Olympic events on the running track inside. The infield of the track was now hosting the biggest rodeo in the country! The track was outside of the fences. The infield belonged to cowboys, horses and some big, rough stock!

Because there were so many acts, the rodeo was in the middle of the infield and the specialty acts were performing on the track itself. The spectators could now watch the rodeo and the specialty acts at the same time. There were three of these acts performing at once. There was one at the right end, one at the left end and one in the middle of the track.

SPECIALTY ACTS

The Roman Riders would be introduced and they would ride in front of the audience stopping at a predetermined point to do their act. One man would ride four horses in tandem. He would ride the back two and two more would be in front of him. He did things I had never seen before! His stunts were daring and crowd pleasing! This man did not work very many rodeos as he was one of the best stunt performers in the Hollywood movies and they kept him pretty busy. In addition, because of the movies, he could not go very far out of California.

One Roman Rider had two very special tricks. There were several poles with kerosene soaked cloth rags on the top. A man on the ground would torch them until they were on fire. The rider would stand with his right foot on one horse and his left foot on another horse. He would take his horses and ride over the flames. (Fireproof pants?) At the end, there was a large ring that was set on fire. The rider would then jump his horses through this fire ring. It was very dramatic and dangerous!

At the end of the grandstand, Jan went through her routine with her beautiful black mares. She liked to use a lot of speed while jumping over high hurdles and riding while standing on one leg. Her act was very professional and was definitely a crowd pleaser. Jan's dream was working Madison Square Garden, but I could see a problem that she could not see. She was performing on a track with two other specialty acts. One of these acts had the best stuntman in Hollywood and another was doing fabulous things with fire.

If you are sitting in the grandstand, who is going to catch your eye? Will it be a man with horses riding over and through fire? Or will it be the best stuntman in Hollywood? Or would you watch the girl who has talent but not that kind of danger in her act?

People watching her were saying, "I wish I could to that." Their neighbor would answer, "You can if you practice!" Ah, practice! If you put out a foam pad and ask someone in the crowd to jump on it from a height of seven feet, you will get several takers. Ask the same crowd if someone will jump into an air bag off a seven-story building and you probably will not get any takers except from stuntmen who have been doing it for a long time. This is what a specialty act is. People want to do it but when they see the danger they would rather pay and watch someone else do it. Lots of people ride motorcycles but only a few will ride a motorcycle up a ramp and jump over 10 buses or 15 cars. That is a specialty act!

If you are working your horses around fire, odds are you are using your best trained horses. This act requires a lot of practice and a lot of trust between the rider and horses. When you are the best stuntman in Hollywood who did the majority of the stunts in the majority of the western movies, you have all of that and you will draw the attention of the fans and of the promoters.

Jan was very good and very professional but she did not have a 'specialty' act that would set her apart. She needed something to make the fans look at her instead of someone else. She needed something to get the promoter's attention, especially if you wanted to perform in the prestigious Madison Square Garden. (Jan did not have that specialty act in Salinas but she worked hard and years later she would have her name on the marquee at Madison Square Garden!)

Nevertheless, Jan was living a dream. She wanted to work this rodeo and now she was doing just that!

When her mother and father went to California, they lived near Salinas. Jan's dad took her to the rodeo when she was 6 or 7 years old and she never forgot the experience. Now she was a part of it but this was not her only rodeo! Jan was booked to work in three other rodeos in the western area. She had future dates in Idaho, Utah and South Dakota.

CHAPTER 12

IDAHO

Salinas ended on a good note and we were soon on our way to Idaho. This was one of the biggest rodeos in the west and, once again, there were R.C.A. world champions everywhere. The star of the show, however, was Audie Murphy. He was a very famous WWII hero who also had starred in a popular war movie called "To Hell and Back." Audie was from the Greenville, Texas, area. He was born in ranch country so it was no problem for him to ride a horse. The rodeo made him the Grand Marshall of the parade. During the night portion of the rodeo, Audie rode out, took the microphone and talked to the crowd. We all really appreciated that, hearing from a national hero and all.

The rodeo had hired one of the best clowns in the business. His specialty was fighting the bulls and he had the people on their feet with his antics! He wore a pair of wranglers with the pant legs cut off at knee level and underneath that he had red long john underwear. All you could see was that red underwear coming out of his shorts. He was terrific! I tell you about this clown for a reason. He would continue getting better and better and before long he became one of the best 'bull fighters' (rodeo clowns) in the United States. Now, over 50 years later, rodeo clowns still try to be just like him. His name was Wick Peth. He must have been good for me to remember all that!

THE GREATEST RIDE

The rodeo in Pocatello, Idaho, also had the greatest saddle bronc rider with the most recognition. His name was Casey Tibbs. He was a flamboyant person who was known for his colorful wardrobe such as purple chaps and purple shirts. He drove a Cadillac with diamonds and that impressed us. Casey was so good he could ride a wild bronc, look at any cameraman in the arena, smile and never lose any time or points in his ride. He was that good!

One particular night, Casey drew the bronc named 'War Paint.' The horse was rated as 'The Bucking Horse of the Year' and would be a headline act anywhere. There were a lot of people who came just to see the matchup between the best rider and the best bucking horse! Needless to say, I was right by the arena. There was no way I was going to miss this one! We all knew War Paint usually started out by bucking high when he came out of the chute. This night was no different! The horse came out bucking high, very high, with Casey sitting right in the middle of the saddle. The horse was amazing! He knew every bucking trick in the book to unseat his rider but he met his match on this night.

When it was all over, Casey Tibbs came out on top.

He had ridden War Paint for the full eight seconds and it was one of the best saddle bronc rides I had ever seen! Cowboys and spectators talked about that ride for years and I was there to see it. It still sticks out in my mind after all these years!

One of the photographers took a picture of War Paint and Casey that would be used for years to come in publicity and advertising material!

JAN ARRIVES

We had been there for three or four weeks but because I could not 'ride' in the rodeo, I became more of a 'camp follower.' I drove trucks and helped with the livestock. All of this while making no money and having to spend what money I had just to survive. All I knew was this was way out of my league. Without a doubt, I would have to go back on the amateur circuit and bring my skills up to a much higher level so I could compete with what I was watching.

One evening, two men in charge of the rodeo saw Jan's van and went to investigate. They were soon inviting her to a dance party in town.

Well, if there was a party out there, Jan was ready to go! We were good friends at the time so I did not think anything about it when she decided to take them up on their offer. That night, I went to my living area which was in the van near the horses. I laid there but for some reason I could not get to sleep. I kept thinking and worrying about Jan. Was she okay? Around 1 AM, I heard voices outside. It was Jan and the two men who were in charge of the rodeo. They laughed and talked for about five minutes until Jan said goodnight and retired to her living quarters at the back of the van.

As I lay there, it hit me. I was jealous! I had never been that way before. I did not know what to do but then decided to leave by train or bus in the next few days. I would stay at least a couple of days and help Jan with her act and take care of the horses. When she was settled, I would leave.

The next morning was a difficult one for me. I told Jan of my plans. She did not understand why I was leaving. I told her I thought I was getting too deep in this situation and I did not want to get involved down a 'one-way road.' To my surprise, she told me that she always had a strong attachment for me and she thought it was just her as I did not show much emotion.

"If you leave, don't you go anywhere without inviting me," she told me.

I guess this meant we were going steady. Actually, it was not love at first sight but it did grow into a 55-year marriage. In reality, we were best buddies and partners, something a lot of husbands and wives don't have.

ONE LITTLE PONY

Before we left Pocatello, Idaho, a man drove up with a trailer full of wild ponies. These were not regular size ponies. These were little 36″ ponies.

At the time, there was a big market with good prices for ponies of this size. I looked them over and saw one pony with a white mane and white tail. His body was dark, like smoke. This was the type of coloration that people would pay good money to have but this pony was dirty! His mane and tail had knots from running in the tumbleweeds and it was easy to see no one had taken good care of him.

I talked to the owner and bought him for $80 knowing that ponies like this could go for as much as $600 to $1,000 especially if they were clean and in 'show ring' condition.

When I told Jan about this ugly little pony, she wanted to know why I did it.

"I buy and sell horses," I told her. "That is how I make a living, buying low and selling higher. That is how I put food on my table."

She shrugged. Jan was not a horse trader. When she purchased a horse, it became part of her family and part of her show. It was a lifelong commitment to her. She understood what I was doing and why I was doing it but it was just not her style.

"We need to clean him up," I said. "He needs a bath and a trim on both his mane and his tail. I also need to make him gentle (tame him) and then I have to train him to stand in a 'show-ring pose'" ie, the horse is standing with his two front legs stretched out further than his hind legs, just like dogs do in a dog show.

After inspecting him, there was just one problem with this horse. He was a parrot mouth. It was hard to notice if you did not look for things like that. When I bought him, the owner did not mention this, especially when he priced the horse. I had told him I could not give much for a parrot mouth pony and when I quoted him the price I was willing to pay, he knew "the jig was up and the monkey was dead!"

Needless to say, I got the horse for my price!

When the pony was groomed, he looked really good! His snow-white mane and tail were gorgeous and the dark coat of hair covering his body really made him stand out. There was not much time for admiration, however. The next stop Jan had booked was a rodeo in North Dakota. This particular rodeo was occurring the same time as one of the North Dakota county fairs, a common thing in many states.

We finished our business in Idaho and headed for the state of North Dakota.

When we arrived, we noticed the fair had lots of 4H events and a horse show for the people who were not members of the 4H club. The horse show was for anyone who wanted to enter so I guess that included us. I helped Jan get ready for her performance at the rodeo and then went to visit the horse show committee to get a listing of the events. I noticed there was a 'halter' class for ponies.

"Will there be a lot of ponies in the halter class?" I asked one of the female committee members.

"Oh, maybe 15 or less," she answered.

"Is this a difficult class?" I asked as my curious nature got the best of me.

"Well, the owner of the bowling alley has some ponies and he has won the halter class for the last two years," she told me. "He paid over $1,000 for his championship pony."

Now my curiosity was running rampant!

"What color is his winning pony?"

"He has a beautiful black pony," she replied.

I nodded and quickly took one of their entry forms. My little vagabond pony was soon entered into the halter class. When I gave them my entry form, they asked me what the name was of my pony. I had no answer for them! With all the cleaning, traveling, setting up and other work we had to do, Jan and I had never given this little pony a name! I had been calling him 'Pony' but that was not going to work here. I had to come up with something and I blurted out the first thing that came to mind.

"Mighty. His name is Mighty."

Later that afternoon, I told Jan about entering the pony in the halter class of the horse show. I also told her what I had named him. Jan had shown horses all her life and she was elected (by unanimous vote I might add!) to handle my little pony in the ring. Luckily, the rodeo part of the fair would be over and Jan would have plenty of time, at least an hour or so, to get ready for the horse show.

We worked to get Mighty into shape for the show and when we were done, our vagabond pony looked good, really good! Jan was soon leading him into the ring for the showing. Just like the committee lady had told me, there was a beautiful black pony in the ring and it really stood out. The owner (Mr. Bowling Alley) had won two years ago and defended his first-place finish last year. Now he was trying to defend his title for a third time. He showed his horse with the confidence of the winner that he was.

After watching the ponies walk around the ring, the judge lined them up for further inspection. I was really worried the judge would see that Mighty had an overbite, something that could easily disqualify him. But we got lucky and that little vagabond stood there and showed a pose that any horse would be proud of! His 'show ring' pose was even more impressive because of his dark body and his white mane and tail.

The judge walked the line and stood at the end of it to make his decision. I watched him as he looked at the black pony (Mr. Bowling Alley) for a long time. Finally, the judge walked to the center of the line and faced the contestants.

"The winner," he announced, "Is number 6."

That was Jan's number and she was more than happy to accept the trophy and the blue ribbon. As she stood there, Mr. Bowling Alley came up to her. "Excuse me," he said, "But is that horse for sale?"

"I don't know," she told him, "Because he is not mine. You will have to ask the owner." She pointed to me.

He turned to me and we started talking. I remembered the lady told me this guy owned the bowling alley and he had given $1,000 for his black champion pony.

"Well," I said slowly as if I really did not want to sell the horse, "I guess I might sell him for the right price."

"How much?" he shot back quickly.

The price he had paid for that black pony kept popping into my head.

"We would have to have $1,000 for him," I said, as if I was hoping he would not go for the price.

He thought about it for a little bit and then said, "I can't really afford that much right now but how about a trade? Would that be okay?"

"What have you got to trade?" I asked.

"I don't have any horses to trade but I've got a really good raccoon hunting dog," he told me hopefully. "How would that be?"

I thought about it but I already knew the answer.

"I sure do like to go coon hunting," I answered, "But I can't do any hunting right now what with the rodeos and all. You got any guns you want to trade?"

"Yes, I do," he quickly answered, "But all my dogs and guns are back at my house."

"Well, we are getting ready to leave but I can probably wait for another hour or so if you want to go and get your guns and dog. I'll take a look at them and maybe we can make a deal," I suggested.

He nodded and quickly left.

By now, Jan had taken the pony back to the trailer and he could see we were packing and getting ready to go. When I got to the trailer she wanted to know what happened.

"Did you make a sale?" she asked.

"No, not yet," I told her.

That was all we said about the 'sale.' Personally, I did not think the man would return but then again, maybe…

We were almost loaded and about to leave when I see a pickup truck heading our way. There was a big coon dog in the back of the truck and I knew right away it was Mr. Bowling Alley and his dog (and guns?)

"He's back," I told Jan, "But I won't be long on this deal."

He stopped his truck and we began talking trade.

"Are you satisfied with the way our pony looked?" I asked.

"Yes," he told me.

When we were done, I hollered to Jan and asked her to bring the pony over to his truck. When she got there, I took the pony from her and gave her the dog's leash.

"We're ready to go now," I said quietly.

She took the dog and went back to our truck.

When I got in the driver's seat, she stared at me for a second.

"What did you do?" she asked, wanting to know how the trade went.

"Well," I told her, "It went like this. He got our vagabond blue-ribbon pony and we got $500 in cash, a coon dog, one shotgun and one rifle."

Jan sat there in disbelief.

To leave the rodeo grounds, there was a dirt and gravel road that led to the main road. When I looked back I could see a trail of dust and it was getting closer and closer to us. That truck was moving! It did not take long before I realized it was Mr. Bowling Alley, the man who had just traded me a dog, cash and two guns for an overbite, parrot mouth pony! Now, you could not tell he was a parrot mouth unless you looked close (something the judge did not do) and I figured this guy had finally got a good look at the pony and was ready to 'renegotiate'!

I was pulling a trailer and he was not. Before long he pulled up alongside of us and yelled out his window to me. I prepared for the worst!

"Hey," he hollered over the engines, "You did not tell me the name of the pony."

Relieved, I knew I had to tell him something so we could get out of there. "It's Mighty Mouse," I yelled back.

"Thanks," he said with a wave.

"You know," I told Jan as we watched his truck drive off, "I am pretty sure it is time to get out of this county and probably not come back!"

We moved away at a good clip and Jan just sat there. She was being awful quiet. Finally, she had something to say.

"You know," she told me, "I just worked that rodeo. I got paid truck expenses for hauling five horses and you just made more money with that unwanted pony than I did performing all afternoon."

I just looked at her and smiled.

"But I have to know," she continued, "What are you going to do with that coon dog?"

"That dog is called a Walker," I explained, "And his white and brown spots are good markings. His ears have tear marks in them and usually they get them from fighting with the raccoons they get.

"The next place we stop I'm gonna ask around and see who the hunters are and then I am going to sell that dog to one of them. I don't know if he is a good hunter or not but I'll just tell them I got him in a trade. If the man is interested and wants a hunting dog then I'll take $300 for the dog or even $10. Either way, it is all profit. The man who buys him for $50 or $75 will think he got a steal and thinks he will make money when he sells him and that means we have two happy people."

She just shook her head.

I sold the dog at our next stop!

CHAPTER 13

TYING THE KNOT

We got to a point in our travels that Jan did not have any more rodeos booked. We talked it over and decided to go back to Indiana and visit the folks. Her parents still lived in Indiana and my parents had left Ohio and moved to Indiana.

My mom and dad had opened a little appliance store and kept the people in the area furnished with stoves, deep fryers, refrigerators and some furniture. They had a plot of land about an acre in size and we used it to park the horse van and keep the horses. We did this for a short time, eventually making a campsite out of it.

By now, Jan and I had been together for some time and after talking it over, we decided to get married. We told our parents and our friends, all of whom came to the wedding if they could make it.

Before the wedding, Jan and I went to a nearby jewelry store. I did not have enough money to buy her a real diamond ring but there was this gold band I liked.

"That is a high carat ring," the man at the store told me.

I stared at it and asked, "Will her finger turn green from wearing it?"

"Definitely not," he answered quickly!

Jan saw it and was excited but I felt bad because I could not afford to buy her the ring she truly deserved.

"Tell you what," I told her, "In five years I will buy you that diamond."

We were married in a little church and my favorite uncle gave the preacher $20 and that was all it cost us to get married.

Well, five years later we talked it over. I wanted to get her that diamond ring she deserved but she said she would not trade that simple gold band for any diamond. Truth is, she never took it off and 55 years later, when she passed, she still had it on.

We had a great life and that was definitely the best $9 I ever spent!

'MAY POPS' AND A LITTLE BLACK PONY

So, here we were in Indiana and we had just gotten married after traveling all summer. I had spent all my money except maybe $300 because I was always buying, selling and trading horses. Jan had spent all the money she made on gas, horse feed, repairs, etc. She was a great horsewoman and an excellent performer but she was a poor businesswoman.

She had taken the job in Salinas, California, for a mere $400. The other Roman Riders were getting something like $2,000 and they lived in the area whereas we had to drive all the way out there and then all the way back.

Jan did not care too much about profit or expenses. She just wanted to work the California rodeo circuit because it had been a childhood dream of hers.

I called G. C. Troup, the man who owned the Circle T Ranch in Florida. I wanted to know if he needed any help at this time of the year. I knew it was time for them to gather the cows, separate them and send a lot of them to the livestock market. He said they needed help and knowing Jan and I were now married, he said we could live upstairs in the 'big house' or in his ranch house where he had a small apartment. He also said he needed us as soon as possible.

Not wanting to waste any time, we took the van over to the ranch where Jan's dad was the foreman. We parked it there and then let the horses out to pasture. He would watch over them as we planned on being back in 3 or 4 weeks.

In Florida, feed for horses was $10 a sack. Up here that same feed cost about $2.80 a sack. Seeing a chance to make some money, I drove my pickup, which was empty, to buy some feed at Indiana prices and then resell it in Florida for a big profit. I went to the grain elevator and bought 1,000 pounds of oats.

While I was there, a man walked up to me and started talking.

"Say, would you be interested in buying a pony?" I looked at him.

"Here we go again," I thought to myself.

"It is right over there, close to the elevator," he explained. "This pony is a stud and is so small it is hard to believe."

I was soon staring at an all black pony with a mane and tail that were abnormally long. I knew we were headed to Florida but we could stop at Valdosta, Georgia, where they had a horse sale that featured small ponies like this one. The wheels in my head starting spinning once more!

When I got back to the ranch, Jan came out to meet me. She wanted to know if I found the grain elevator her father had told me about.

"Yes," I told her, "I sure did. I got 1,000 pounds of sacked oats and…" I paused, knowing what she would probably be thinking, "…I also bought a small pony."

She didn't know what to say at first but she soon had plenty to say!

"Do you think that pony can eat all of that feed?"

It was a joke, but I brushed it off. There were bigger fish to fry.

"I am going to sell the oats in Florida for a profit," I began to explain, "And when we go through Valdosta in Georgia I am going to sell the pony. They have a sale every Friday that features small ponies and I think I can sell this one for a profit!" She just looked at me.

The next morning, we packed up and headed south. I had the feed in the back of the truck with the horse at the far end. There was a fence between the horse and the feed to keep both of them from getting in trouble. I had, unfortunately, misjudged the weight we would be hauling. Between the horse, the feed, our saddles, our riding gear, our clothes and the camper shell on the truck, my poor pickup was in trouble!

Today I would not even think about starting a trip under those conditions but, at the time, it did not worry me. I had forgotten one little detail, however, and it would come back to haunt me as we drove south. For years I had traveled on good, brand name tires. But now, however, I was traveling on a different brand of tires. They were called 'May Pops.'

For those of us in the country (or those of us with little or no money) these 'May Pops' were a popular brand, indeed! Back then you could travel around a 1,000 miles on $30 worth of gasoline. This was due to the low cost of gas, about 21-23 cents a gallon. This was working in our favor but the 'May Pops' were not.

I had spent most of my money on oats and a pony so we had to be careful on this trip, at least until we sold the pony. Jan and I took turns driving so we could make it to Georgia in about 24 hours. That is, if we did not stop for anything but gas and if nothing went wrong. Things went well the first 300 miles but it soon felt like we had low air pressure in one of the tires. We stopped and I got out to take a look at it. The tire was almost flat!

Luckily, we were close to a gas station (there were a lot of them back in those days) and we drove on until we got there. At that time, in 1957, the gas stations on the main roads would stay open all night and they always had a man who could fix your tires. He was good on patches, flats, anything to do with tires.

We had a spare tire but that tire was for emergencies! This tire was just losing air so we had the tire man fix it with a patch, or two or three, I don't remember. This cost was usually around $1.50 or $2. He fixed it, we paid him and we were soon back on the road.

After another 100 miles, one of our 'May Pop' tires lived up to its name and 'popped'! Of course, that is why they are called 'May Pop' tires because they may pop at any time! These tires usually had very little tread and many were just about bald.

On that trip, as it turned out, we had eight flat tires! Lots of times the gas station attendant would give us another tire and would just charge us $2.50 to put it on the truck. This was because the tire he gave us came from the 'throw away' pile and it was all profit to the repair man on duty. We 'popped' our way to Georgia and finally arrived in Valdosta.

By this time, we were low on money. Okay, we were broke! However, with luck and perseverance, we finally made it to the auction. There were a lot of 'lookers' when it came to our pony. That was a good sign.

When the auction began I ran the black pony into the ring and showed him to the buyers. Being around sales all my life, I knew how to run the sale price up on whatever I was selling and I pulled out every trick I knew. There was an opening bid of $300. Thinking I could get more, I personally bid $325. I wanted them to go to $350.

Unfortunately, they did not want to go to $350 so I was the high bidder on my own pony!

It turned into a 'no sale.' (Before the auction, when I had been asked what I would take for the pony, I had originally said $400 but there were no takers at that price.)

I took the pony out of the ring and back to the truck.

"Why didn't you sell the pony at $325?" Jan asked me.

She had been watching and was now curious why I had no money in my pocket.

"I bid that because I thought somebody would go to $350 but they didn't so I messed up," I explained.

Now, we had no money, a pony and a bunch of oats. I could have sold the oats but they were cheap in Georgia and I could get double the price if I could just get them to Florida.

Jan began to laugh.

"Well," she told me pointing to the back of the pickup, "the pony has a lot to eat and all we can afford to eat are grits!"

I was getting the pony into the back of the truck when a man came up to me and inquired about my stud pony. Jan sensed a deal might be in the offing so she went to the cab of the truck and got inside. After ten minutes, I got in the truck and gave Jan $400. She looked stunned!

"Where did this come from?" she asked.

I did not answer her but instead I quickly put the keys in the ignition and drove out of the auction yard.

As we turned a corner, I looked back and there stood this big man holding the black pony. Jan also saw him and when she saw the black pony with him she just had to know.

"Does he have a pony farm?" she asked.

"No," I said, trying to stifle a laugh, "He just mustered out of the Air Force and he wanted to breed a palomino mare he had. He asked me if the palomino was too big for the black pony and if not, could the black pony do the job."

She just stared at me. I think she thought it was a joke or something.

"I told him the pony could get the job done but I did not think he could reach her to get the job done."

That made sense and her stare became friendlier.

"Then he said he could build a ramp to help the pony get up there. I didn't know what to say so I just made the suggestion that he could dig a hole and put the palomino in it or use a pile a dirt to help the pony 'get up there' and then, if the pony 'fell off' he would not get hurt like he would if he fell off a ramp."

Her friendly stare turned into a, "What the..." stare.

"He said that was a good idea," I continued, "And asked me how much the pony cost. I told him $400. He put his hand in his pocket and brought out a wad of bills big enough to choke a horse! I took his money, gave him the pony and here we are, headed to Florida."

She stared ahead as we drove the road. I am not sure what she was thinking, but it had to be something along the lines of, "What have I gotten myself into?"

I told her I would get $400 for that pony, and I did!

CHAPTER 14

REAR END ISSUES

After selling the pony, Jan and I were in pretty good shape financially. We had gone from next to nothing (thanks to a bunch of 'May Pops') to having $400 in our hands. We stopped, had a big meal and were soon on our way. Forty miles from the Florida state line, I started to feel a vibration and it seemed like it was coming from the rear of the truck. I stopped and did a quick check. The tires actually looked good (for a change!) and I quit worrying about having another flat tire. I got back in the truck and we were off once again. We did not get very far before the problem got worse. I knew we had trouble somewhere but I just did not know where. There was a garage ahead and so I pulled into it, found a mechanic and told him what was happening. He did a thorough check of the truck and after his inspection he told me what the problem was.

"The rear end of the pickup is damaged," he said, "And you definitely need a new one. I don't have one on hand but I can order one and it will be here in 2-3 days."

"How much," I asked him?

"The cost will be in the $500 to $600 range because the rear end is new and I have to take the old one off and put the new one on."

That was not good news.

"I can't wait two days," I explained to him, "And most importantly, we don't have $500 to get it fixed."

He nodded.

"Look," he told me, "my buddies have a junk yard and I think they have a wrecked pickup truck similar to yours over there. That rear end should fit your pickup. Why don't I see if they match and then see what I can do for you?"

"Thanks," I said as he left to make a deal with his buddy.

When he returned, he had good and not so good news.

"Well," he began, "The rear end of that pickup will fit on your pickup."

"And how much is this one going to cost," I wanted to know, hoping he had lowered the price as much as he could.

"It will cost you around $300 if there are no problems," he answered, "But if I run into problems it might cost you a little more." What could I say? We needed that truck and we needed to get to Florida. "Okay," I told him.

That night we stayed with the truck. There was no motel in sight and we did not have any 'camping' equipment so we used the cab of the truck for our beds.

"Well," Jan said, "You want the top berth or the bottom berth?"

I had to laugh! The top berth was the seat of the pickup and the bottom berth was the floor of the pickup. Being the gentleman I was, ahem, there was only one answer to give my lovely wife.

"I'll take the lower berth," I said 'happily.'

She smiled and I knew it was the right answer!

We lay down in our 'berths' and tried to sleep as best we could. In the middle of the night Jan reached down and woke me.

"Hey, you want to switch berths?" she asked. We switched berths and that is how the rest of the night went.

That example is just one of the many things I loved about being married to Jan. We could stay in a fancy hotel in New York City one night and sleep in a horse trailer the next night, it did not matter! She never complained and she was always happy, all the time. She was amazing and to think I almost let her slip through my fingers!

FINALLY

The rear end was fixed the next day and we were soon on the road once more. All our profit from the little black pony had evaporated and with it some of our plans. We were now in the same situation as when we started but this time, thankfully, we were a lot closer to Indiantown, Florida.

We made it to Orlando, Florida, and knew that it would take only one more tank of gas to get us to the ranch. That was fine but while the truck needed to be 'fed' gasoline, the driver and passenger needed to be fed, too!

"Oh, look! Chicken Dinners for a $1," Jan said as she pointed to the sign. We quickly pulled over and bought two of them. We now had enough food to make it the rest of the way (about 120 miles) and we were happy.

Darkness overtook us as we entered Okeechobee, Florida. Indiantown was only 27 miles away and we thought we had it made!

POP!

Okay, we were wrong. We had been surprised by another 'May pop' that lived up to its name! Thankfully, there was a service station in sight and we hobbled into it. I had used our spare tire on the flat before this one so we were completely out of tires. The attendant looked at the tire and assessed the damage.

"I can fix this for $3," he told me.

"I don't have $3," I told him. He looked at the tire and then at me.

"Look, we have jobs at the Circle T Ranch," I explained, trying to get him to understand our situation, "And the best I can do is pay you when we get paid at the end of the week. I will bring the money here if you will please fix this flat for us."

He stared at me, sizing me up.

"Ok," he told me, "I'll fix your flat and you bring me the money when you get paid."

We made it to the Circle T and as soon as we got our first paycheck, I headed back to that gas station.

"Here," I told him as I handed him three one dollar bills. "I bet you thought I would never be back to pay you!"

He looked at me and smiled.

"No," he told me, "I knew you would be back."

BACK ON THE CIRCLE T

We arrived at Indiantown around 10 PM, just as everyone was about to hit the hay! We were good friends with Bill, the ranch hand, and his wife. Jan wanted to stop and see them first because they had an extra room and we might be able to stay with them for the night. They were happy to see us and very hospitable. It was easy to see Jan and I were worn out from our trip and they offered to let us sleep in their spare room which we readily accepted!

In the morning, Bill's wife had a big breakfast ready for us and we gladly ate until we could eat no more! When we were done with that wonderful meal, we decided to go to the ranch itself. Bill and his wife lived a half mile from the main ranch so it was a short trip to get there.

Mr. Bill (the ranch foreman) and Wiley greeted us and were glad we finally made it. As soon as the 'Hi, how are you' speeches were over, they gave each of us a horse to ride for the day. When lunchtime arrived, Jan and I had a problem. We were still extremely low on funds (tires, rear ends, etc., had taken their toll!) so we had to improvise. We drove the quarter mile to the grocery store where we each paid 5 cents for a candy bar. That was lunch! For dessert, we grabbed an orange or a grapefruit off a tree whenever we rode by one. (Remember, we were in Florida and fruit trees were everywhere!)

When the work day was over, we took the horses back, unsaddled them and fed them. It was always important to take care of the horses before we took care of ourselves. There was a block building on the grounds with two showers and toilets in them. Behind this structure was a bunk house kitchen. On certain occasions, especially if it was a party or big celebration, somebody would use this room to cook for the guests. It was filled with the usual appliances, pots, pans, dishes and anything else needed for a good old cowboy party!

Mr. Bill, the foreman, said we could cook in there for the next couple of weeks until the 'cow work' was finished. When that work was done, we would be moving up north. That night we were lucky to have a place to stay and a kitchen to cook in. Unfortunately, we had no money and, therefore, we had no food to cook! We did not tell anybody we were broke. I guess we were both too proud to say anything.

COCK-A-DOODLE-DO

I did notice there were a lot of game chickens on the ranch running free, not caged, and at night they would go to the horse stalls to roost (sleep). Naturally, being hungry adults, we decided we would have chicken for dinner that night.

My mind flashed back to when I was a child. I watched my mom kill chickens every week. Sometimes she would dress them out three at a time but I never helped. The story was that when I was three years old a rooster jumped on my head and began flapping his wings. They also said (but this has never been verified or proven!) that I was screaming and crying and acting like a three-year old. Hmm. I do know (verified) that ever since then I have been slightly afraid of chickens, roosters and pretty much anything else with feathers.

We got a flashlight and began looking for our target. I convinced Jan that she should be the one to catch the rooster and hold him. She agreed (thank goodness) and we went a hunting. Our target was soon in sight! Jan said she remembered how her uncle used to catch a chicken for dinner. He usually used a hatchet and we just happened to have one! She also said she would do the chopping. (Man, I love this woman!)

We caught our rooster and Jan tied his feet together and as she put him on the wood chopping block he got loose but his legs were still strapped together! Boy, that rooster hit the ground and went a flapping all over the place. I had the flashlight and he came directly towards the light which meant he was also coming directly at me (probably an ancestor of the first rooster I told you about…).

"Jan, get that son-of-a-bitch," I yelled as I moved backwards as fast as the rooster was moving forward!

It was at that point I learned about the other side of my wife! She started to laugh at me. Not just 'ha ha' but a big old laugh like she had just heard the best joke ever! Then she had to make a joke of her own!

"I have seen you around big bulls, wild horses, snakes, alligators and they don't scare you one bit but you are afraid of a chicken!"

What could I say? My secret was out!

Jan finished her end of the task and then we fried that bird up. It looked so good but when we tried to eat it, well, let's just say shoe leather would be just as easy to eat! This bird was so old, it was impossible to eat! We obviously did not know how to tell the age of a chicken or rooster and it cost us! Still hungry, we hunted around and found some eggs. We saved them for breakfast so we had something to eat before we had to saddle up and start the day.

BACK TO WORK

Our task for the day was to round up some yearling calves and put them into a pen. One of them tried to jump out and went head first into a pipe gate. He hit the gate so hard that it killed him instantly! If you have ever been around cattle, then you know how hard their heads are and how hard that calf had to hit that gate!

Homer, the Seminole Indian, looked at the dead calf and asked Mr. Bill, the foreman, if he could butcher him for the meat. When he was finished, Homer asked all of us if anyone wanted any of the meat. You think! Jan and I breathed a sigh of relief! We had it made! There would be steak tonight and with payday only four days away, we knew we were going to make it! (Minus $3 for the tire!)

How could things be any better!

For the next three weeks, the cows were gathered, put into pens and sprayed for ticks, fleas, mosquitoes or anything else that would feed on the blood of the cattle. The calves were then sent to stockyards to be sold. The ranch had trailers built for moving livestock along with some special cow trucks so we used them to move the beef. Homer drove the trucks but there were too many cattle for one man to take to market so Bill, the ranch hand, was assigned to the second truck and I was assigned to the third truck. For the next couple of days, we hauled calves from the ranch to the stockyards. It was 65 miles one way so each one of us drove 150 miles a day. Thankfully, there were no 'May Pops' on these trucks!

UNTIL IT'S DONE

One night, Mr. Troup and his wife, the owners of the ranch, asked Jan and I to go out with them. They wanted to go to a fancy steak house in Stuart, Florida. We had been working hard getting the cattle organized for the past three weeks and it would be nice to take a break and get away for an evening. We did not have the fanciest of clothes but Jan and I did what we could. I got my best Wranglers and ironed them so they had a nice crease down the front. I had a white shirt that was new and I worked on my boots until they had a pretty good shine on them. At least I managed to get most of the cow pen dust, dirt and manure off of them! Jan had a lot less trouble getting ready than I did. She could throw on an old sack and still look stylish! With her upbeat, bubbly personality she would fit in anywhere!

Remember, we were going to a fancy restaurant but that was not really our style. Both Jan and I grew up in an area where some of the best German and Irish descendants were the cooks. Our food choices consisted of homemade noodles, mashed potatoes, beans, corn bread, and other solid, stomach filling delicacies. Everything was cooked until it was tender, juicy and delicious! We never ate T-bone steaks but we did have pork chops, meat loaf, goulash and canned meat, all of which was cooked to perfection. As an added bonus, there was homemade butter and homemade bread to put it on.

It was not until I got out of school and hit the circuit that I discovered T-bone steaks. Usually, if someone asked me how I liked my steak, I would always say "Until it is done!" It was the same answer I always gave to that question because I wanted my food to be just like my childhood roast beef and meat loaf: tender and delicious!

When my steak came (no matter where we were), I smothered it in 'Worcestershire' sauce. I thought it was good but when I looked at other people's plates, their steaks looked red with a lot of juice on their plates. I sometimes thought, in my cowboy opinion, that their steaks were undercooked!

The next time I went into a steak house I looked at the menu closely and saw a chart showing how to order a steak. They had rare, medium rare, medium, medium well and then a note that said, “We are not responsible for steaks ordered well done.”

Learning from that I wanted someone to be responsible for what I was eating! I started ordering all of my steaks medium well. Sometimes they would come with a little pink in the middle and if they came with more pink than I wanted, I knew they had not been cooked long enough for me. To these steaks, I would simply add more Worcestershire sauce and have at it!

As I started to get a taste for steak and knew more about my taste buds, the time would come where I was ordering my steaks medium rare. If the waiter asked me if I wanted steak sauce, my thought would be, “Is the steak so bad that you have to add Worcestershire sauce to it?”

Live and learn.

OUT WITH THE BOSS

When we were ready, the boss man came by in his new Cadillac and picked us up. At the restaurant, he parked the car and we went inside. When we were seated, he ordered a round of drinks for all of us (his tab). The waiter brought us red wine and our menus.

I was kind of nervous because this was the first time I had ever been in an uptown steak house with a millionaire and his wife! As I looked at the menu, I did not know what to order. There were entrees like filet mignon and chateaubriand. I did not know what these things were but when I saw T-bone, well, I knew what that was! In fact, it was the only thing I could recognize on the menu.

“May I have your order?” the waiter asked.

“Yes,” I said trying to give him my best impression of someone who had been here before, “I would like the T-bone steak.”

“And how would you like that cooked?”

"Well done," I said.

The waiter looked at Mr. Troup.

Mr. Troup looked at the waiter.

"Uh, sir," the waiter told me, "I will have to ask the cook if he can fix it well done. He is very opinionated." I knew then I had made a big blunder and I quickly tried to overcome it.

"I like a little pink on the inside but not dark pink so I said well done."

The waiter was very polite and said, "I will tell the cook and I am sure he will cook it just right for you."

He left to get our food. I was trying to be knowledgeable and I had made a big blunder by ordering a $40 steak as "well done"! (That is $40 in today's prices.)

Well, what did you expect? Four weeks ago, I was dealing with "May Pops" and rear-end issues. Jan just laughed and said it was no big deal. But it was to me!

I have remembered that moment all my life.

CHAPTER 15

IT'S NICE TO HAVE INSURANCE

It took three weeks before we finished our work at the 'Circle T' Ranch. The calves had been sent to market and before long the cycle would start all over again.

Mr. G. C. Troup, the owner of the Circle 'T' Ranch came over to us one day and asked Jan to work his three big winter rodeos.

Florida was a 'winter' state. When everywhere else was covered in snow and had bad weather keeping their arenas closed, Florida was having winter rodeos. Mr. Troup ran three of these shows and they were good rodeos, too. Now, he wanted Jan and her horses to perform in them and entertain the fans. With a handshake, we now had three contracted rodeos to work starting in January!

Since we had some time to kill, Jan and I decided to take a trip home to see the family. We made it back in my pickup truck and without all the extra weight we had going to Florida, the trip back was uneventful. We did not even have any problems with the truck!

I know that everything happens for a reason but I also knew we were in the same position as when we went to Florida just a few weeks before. Jan never worried about money or how she would survive for the next month or the next six months. Her biggest thing was riding horses and performing in the arena for all the fans who attended the rodeos. She was a 'Leo' and that sign is very evident in a lot of performers and people who like the spotlight.

She never worried if we had $5 or $50,000 in the checking account because she knew I had that on my mind all the time and why should both of us worry about the same thing? It did not matter if we stayed in the best hotel or ate in the best restaurant this week and had to use the horse trailer next week and eat a "ring of red and a loaf of bread" the next week. Either way, we were both happy to be doing what we were doing.

Personally, my sign is that of a 'Taurus' and it seems we are always involved with financial, especially immediate money problems. These astronomical signs do not mean a lot to some people but they certainly fit Jan and I to a "T"! Apparently, we were matched by stars!

Once we got back to Indiana, we had to take stock of our situation. We had the one ton truck used to pull the horse van. When the truck was unhooked from the van it could be used as a regular truck. It was a rough ride but it was still usable for that purpose in daily situations. We knew we could get by with one truck and we chose that one (it was the only one capable of pulling the horse trailer) and I decided to sell my pickup so we would have some extra money.

Back then, you could buy a new pickup for somewhere in the range of $1,500 or so. I tried to sell my truck for $1,100 but the best offer I got was for $750. I did not want to sell the truck for so low a price but with that being the best offer and us only being home for two weeks, I decided to take it.

I called the man who offered me the money and told him it was a deal. He asked if I could drive the truck to his place and he would pay for it when I got there and then drive me back home. The trip was about 25 miles and no big deal for me so I agreed. I told Jan what was happening and that she should be ready in case I had to call for a ride.

The road to the man's house was very curvy and hilly. I was careful but when I went around one curve on a steep hill on my right, a car came from the other direction around the curve. That would have been okay but he was on my side of the road! I had no place to go and the other driver hit the left side of my truck. When I looked at the damage to my old truck, it was obvious my vehicle was totaled! There went our spending money!

The highway patrol arrived and wrote up the accident report. The patrolman was nice enough to drive me to the nearest gas station. I called for a wrecker and they towed the truck to the gas station. Then I called Jan to tell her what happened.

"You sure sold the truck quick," she said excitedly before I could tell her what happened!

"Well," I stammered, "Not exactly."

I told her about the accident and asked if she could come and give me a ride home.

The next day I contacted the insurance agency since, luckily, I had insurance. (A lot of people could not afford insurance in those days.) When the agent came to the ranch, we discussed the accident and then drove out to where the truck was parked. He looked at the truck and was quickly impressed with it.

"This truck is really clean and in good shape," he commented.

"Thank you," I replied.

After looking at the damage and doing a lot of writing, he finally tallied up the bill.

"I won't be able to have an adjustment for you today," he told me, "But give me a day or two and I will have a check for you."

That was okay with me and after driving back to the ranch it dawned on me I never asked what the adjustment (settlement) amount was going to be.

A few days later a check arrived in the mail. I opened the envelope and could not believe my eyes! The check was for $1,100!! Here I was, on my way to sell the truck for $750 and now I had a check for $1,100 in my hands! I hate to say it, but that was one of the best accidents I ever had!

Like I said before, everything happens for a reason!

BACK IN THE SADDLE AGAIN

We had money for our trip but I had no pickup and that meant there was nothing to pull my little travel trailer, so I sold it too. This extra money meant we did not have to try and eat one of those fighting chicken 'roosters' like we did on the ranch in Florida. That was a relief!

Jan's horse van held 6 horses but we were only taking 5 horses with us. That left one empty stall and got me to thinking. As we got ready to leave Indiana, I told Jan we should stop in Valdosta, Georgia, and we should get there by Friday. To do this, we would have to leave Indiana on Wednesday so we could get there on time.

"It will be a good place to stop and let the horses rest," I told her, still trying to convince her this was a good thing to do. "They have a livestock yard and it usually has some empty pens we can use and we can park the van with no charge."

She finally agreed and she probably knew there was an ulterior motive but she never said anything about it.

We left Indiana and made it all the way to Valdosta, Georgia, before she mentioned anything about our unscheduled stop.

"Isn't the place we are going the same one that has a horse sale on Fridays?" she asked "I mean, isn't that where you sold that little black stallion?"

I took a deep breath.

"Yes, it is," I replied with a smile. "When we stopped there the last time I saw a few horses for sale and I knew I could make money with them. Since we have one empty stall in the trailer, why not try it again and see what we can do?"

I learned early in life, horses had a short life expectancy (compared to humans) and I wanted to get them into the care of a person who had Jan's outlook. I was happy to get a horse and then find just the right owner for it but I also wanted to be paid for my time.

When I was young, I learned a lot about horse trading and, as I said before, I am a Taurus and my mind always reverts back to business and money. We stopped in Valdosta, unloaded the horses and put them in some unused pens. We watered them, fed them grain and got them hay for the night. The van was parked and we looked around for a place to eat. There was an old-time restaurant in the town and I had been thinking about it all day! They served some of the best grits, black-eyed peas, corn bread and iced tea and we took advantage of every one of them!

The horse sale was across the road from where we were staying. People from all over would bring in the livestock they wanted to sell at the auction. Before they entered the ring, they would be in line outside the arena. Buyers were allowed to look at them before bidding on them.

As I looked through the auction yard, I spotted a chestnut filly being ridden by a man. They were in the parking lot and I watched how the horse moved as it went around the parked cars and several other objects in the lot. This was the horse that caught my eye the most and because of that I needed to find out more about this horse. I talked to the owner and he was willing to sell the filly. We settled on a price and that was it! The auction had not even started and I already had a horse!

This type of transaction was perfectly legal. Buyers were allowed to buy outside the arena or before the auction started. All you had to do was make the deal and then the buyer and seller would have to go to the auction house office and pay. The auction house would take their commission and the buyer would get clear ownership. Once that was done, both buyer and seller were free to go their own ways.

This was a good deal since the owner of the livestock had no idea how much his animal would bring at auction (sometimes more, sometimes less) and this way he could negotiate his own kind of deal. Buying before the sale was always something I liked to do because there was the possibility of getting a much better deal. When something hits that auction ring and the bidding starts, it takes only two people bidding against each other to ruin the price and run the amount much higher than it should be.

I took the filly back to the trailer and showed it to Jan. She was pleased with the horse. We hoped to turn a good profit when we got to Florida. To keep peace in the family, I told her she could name the filly, even though I knew we were not going to have it for very long.

On Saturday, we loaded up and headed south. We arrived at the 'Circle T' Ranch and were greeted by the owner, Mr. Troup, Mr. Bill the ranch foreman, Wiley and his wife, Betty.

The corral we had used the year before was empty so we made good use of it. Things were more comfortable this time. I knew everybody and they knew me. It put me at ease and made this trip much more bearable. In addition, Jan and I had some extra money in case we wanted to have a 'social' life!

We had not been there very long when a man from Stuart, a town 18 miles away, came to visit me at the ranch. There were a lot of local people who needed extra help and I was hoping to keep cash coming in by taking advantage of their offers. I knew the man because last year I had ridden a young horse for him and got it usable for ranch work. We became good friends and now he had another offer for me.

"Heard you were here," he said as we greeted each other.

"Yep, got in a couple of days ago," I said.

"Listen, I may have something you might be interested in doing."

"I'm listening," I replied at the hope of a little extra work.

"I have a neighbor who has an unruly horse. She cannot ride it much less handle it! I told her there was someone who might be able to help her. I was wondering if you could come and look at the horse and see if there is anything you can do to help."

"Sure," I told him, "The least I can do is look at the horse and see what the problem is."

"Thanks, I appreciate that."

He told me the owners of the horse also had a charter boat deep sea fishing business in one of the nearby waterfront towns. She ran the office and he was the captain of the boat. After a day of scheduling, paperwork and financial work, she liked to relax by riding her horse around the ranch. Unfortunately, the horse usually had other ideas of what a fun afternoon was!

The next day Jan and I went out to the ranch where the horse was located. We were soon looking at a really big, stout gelding that seemed quite nice. We met the owner who I will call Helen. She told us the horse would rear up and refuse to leave the barn area. She was afraid if she forced the horse to leave the barn area either she or the horse might get hurt.

This was a problem most horsemen are familiar with. It is called 'Barn Sour' and means a horse likes to stay in the barn area and does not want to leave because it is his home. The problem can make the horse very dangerous, both to itself and anyone who tries to ride it and take it out of the barn.

"I heard you do great things with horses," Helen told me, "And I was hoping you could take him for a month or two and correct the problem."

"Well, I'll tell you something about this issue," I began, "If you take a horse like this to another location and cure him of the problem and then you bring him back to his original barn, there is a good possibility he will return to being barn sour."

There was silence as both of us understood there was a possibility this horse might never be cured. I felt sorry for her as it was obvious she liked to ride horses. My mind began to work overtime once more and I hit upon a solution.

"You know, I have a real nice filly back at the ranch that you might like," I said. "Tell you what we should do, you bring this horse to the ranch and you can take my filly back with you to ride and see if you like her. At least you will be able to ride around the ranch."

Helen nodded and I continued.

"If you really like the filly, we can sit down and maybe make some kind of deal."

She readily agreed. Jan and I thanked her for her time and went back to the ranch. The next day Helen showed up with the gelding. When we had the horse settled, I introduced her to the filly I had purchased. It was love at first sight!

Helen rode the filly and was very happy. She soon loaded her up and headed back to her home in Stuart. I told her to ride the horse and keep it for a week to see how things worked out for both of them.

A week later, Jan and I went back to her place. I had plans to either bring the filly back or make a deal, I did not know which! As we got out of the truck I knew right away we were going to make a deal! Helen was so happy with the filly I had bought in Valdosta, Georgia, that she wanted to buy it right then and there.

I told her she could have the filly and in return I would take the gelding she could not ride but I would also need $350 to finish the deal. She said nothing. She looked at me, smiled and then reached in her pocket and pulled out her checkbook. She wrote me a check right there on the spot!

On the way home, Jan looked at me and shook her head.

"How much did you pay for that filly?" she asked me.

"I paid $135," I told her.

"And you just sold her for $350 and got a nice gelding, too," she said bluntly.

"Yes, I did. Now, Helen has a nice horse to ride and I have a gelding that I will cure and in a couple of weeks I should get $250 or so for him. The lady is happy and I am happy."

She just sat there and said nothing for a few minutes.

"Well, okay," she said and that was the end of that!

I smiled. There is a rule I live by and that is to never cheat my clients, the horse buyers. If they were happy with our deal they would probably come back or, at the very least, send one of their friends to me and give me a chance to make another deal.

Helen showed up a few days after buying the filly.

"Hi," I said when she got out of her truck. "Is there a problem?"

When I saw her, I thought there must be a problem with the filly.

"Oh, no," she said quickly, "I just wanted to thank Jan and you for my new pet. I ride that horse every day and I love it!"

She and Jan were soon involved in a conversation so I quietly left them. One of the nearby ranchers had given me more horses to train and I was now a busy man! I returned three hours later and the two of them were still talking! Needless to say, they became very good friends and ended up visiting each other at least two or three times a week!

I'LL STICK TO DRY LAND, THANK YOU

Being in Florida, it was only natural that Jan and I would head for the beach every now and then. We usually made the trip on Sundays and usually went to the beach at Stuart. Personally, I liked the water. When I was a kid, my brother Jack and I would spend as much time as possible in the gravel pit 'lakes' that were near our home. Summertime was great as both of us knew how to swim like a fish!

Jan had grown up on a ranch called "The Goose Pond" where there was a big, beautiful lake next to their house. Jan's mother would go to the lake whenever the weather permitted. According to Jan, her mother could float on her back and read a newspaper at the same time! Her dad was a very poor swimmer. Jan would fight the water when it came to swimming. She told me her mother tried to help but she (Jan) could not relax in the water.

When we would go to the beach, I would swim but Jan would only go out until the water was up to her knees. This was her 'swimming pool' area. She would stand there for a few minutes before returning to the beach, sit down on a towel and watch me.

I liked to swim way out and Jan would often say I looked like a little speck in the ocean. I would catch a wave and ride it back to shore, easily swimming with the current and the push from the wave. It was great fun and a good way to relax from the work schedule of a busy week.

As I said, Jan and Helen were very good friends by now. One day, Helen asked if we might like to go out in the ocean and do a little fishing. Her husband's charter business would take care of everything and all we had to do was get on the boat. It sounded like a good way to spend a Sunday afternoon so we decided to take her up on the offer. Fishing was always an adventure for us and we both liked it but we had not done any fishing in a long, long time.

Plans were made and the following Sunday we arrived at Stuart where Helen and her husband (I'll call him Bert) had their boats docked. I was surprised when we saw the boat and how much it cost to charter the boat for just one day of fishing! It did not take long to see why they had such a good business! The boat and the gear were all first class. He had a 'top of the line' charter business.

We knew nothing about deep sea fishing but Bert had everything we needed. He got us settled on the boat and we were soon heading out to the ocean. We kept going and the beach kept disappearing and it was disappearing fast, too!

The water was like being in a canyon. If you were on the front of the boat and you were going 'down' the wave, it was like being in the lower part of the canyon. Then, in an instant, you were going 'up' another wave and it was like being on the rim of the canyon. As the waves hit the boat, it was also like being in a roller coaster! Up, down, up down.

We had not done any fishing but we kept on going and going. I was beginning to wonder if we were on a fishing charter boat or a cruise ship!

"How far have we gone?" I asked Bert as I looked around and saw nothing but ocean.

"Oh, not that far," he told me. "Sometimes I go out as far as 20 miles but we are not going out that far today."

Regardless, that is a long way for a land lover like me! A short time after I asked him, we came to a complete stop. It was finally time for us to throw in some lines and fish. Bert put Jan in one of the 'fishing' chairs. He strapped her in with a safety belt and put her fishing pole in the holder. Then he helped me and I was soon sitting across from Jan. We looked at each other and gave a half-hearted smile, not knowing what to expect next.

Bert baited the hooks. The bait seemed to be bigger than some of the fish I had caught! He put the hooks into the water, let out some line and told us to just sit tight and wait. He was soon in the cabin where he slowly got the boat moving. We were trolling the ocean!

Jan got the first strike. It bent the pole and she was getting advice on what to do so she could land the fish. She was so excited about the catch that she was trying to stand up in the chair. They made her sit down and soon she reeled the fish into the boat.

Bert wanted to put fresh bait on the hooks so we reeled in our lines. New fish were attached and our lines were soon back in the water. He left and we began waiting once more. To our surprise, Bert gunned the engines and we were speeding through the ocean. Helen was standing near us and I asked her why we were going so fast.

She pointed to our bait and as we looked out, I could not believe what I was seeing. There was a shark swimming after our fresh bait. His head was on the surface of the water. It looked like it was five feet wide and he was swimming so fast as he tried to keep up with us that there was water spraying off his body like the spray a motorboat makes!

Bert eventually slowed down. He came to the rear of the boat and told us the sharks were something he had to look out for.

"If a shark gets to the bait," he explained, "Then he could tear up the fishing equipment and this stuff is not cheap."

I understood completely. That shark was going fast and I could imagine anyone being in the water with those predators would not stand a chance!

In the time we were out in the ocean on this fishing trip, it seemed there were all kinds of animals enjoying us while we enjoyed them. We saw a turtle floating near us. It was easily 5 or 6 feet across. The birds were sitting on his shell, using him as a rest stop. There were bird droppings all over the turtle. We also saw dolphins, all kinds of fish and other sea creatures.

After a great trip, Bert told us it was time to return to the pier. I looked out and could not see the shoreline. I was not sure how he knew which direction to go but Bert was in the cabin area and he knew the way so that was good enough for me! As we got closer (and I saw the shoreline!) the waves got a little bit rougher. I could soon see the buildings and then the people on the beach.

Bert slowed down to an idle. I was in the cabin with him and when the waves smoothed out he gunned the engine and we were off to the races. I looked out the window and could see sharks swimming alongside the boat and off in the distance. They were getting nearer to the shore as we, too, got closer and closer.

I was amazed at how close these sharks were getting to the shore and to the people who were swimming in the water.

"Hey, Bert," I asked, "How dangerous is it to swim out in the water?"

He stunned me with his answer.

"I grew up in this area because my family has been in this business since I was a kid," he explained. "Me and my buddies never went swimming in the ocean. We always went to Saint Lucia River if we wanted to go swimming. There have been shark attacks all along this beach front for as long as I can remember. Most of them were never reported because all the towns up and down the beach rely on the tourist trade and if they advertised their shark attacks then the tourists might stay away and that would kill their livelihood.

"Sometimes, there might be a big attack and word would get out. Whenever that happened, the tourist trade would get weak and it might take two or three years to get back to normal."

As he told this story, my knees got weak! I kept thinking about how far I would swim out from the shore line. Guess what! I never went swimming in that ocean again! We became dry land people!

Whenever we went to the beach, I played in Jan's pool. That is to say, I only went into the water until it was up to my knees. I was a lot happier doing cowboy work! It was a lot easier than trying to dodge sharks! Still, all in all, it was a fun day and Jan and I really enjoyed ourselves!

CHAPTER 16

A NEW ERA BEGINS

Jan was soon working the rodeos for Mr. Troup. She used her black horses and was billed as "The Flying Black Clouds" on the advertisements. There was not much work for me at these events. Mr. Bill, the ranch foreman, usually hired his friends from 'up north' and 'out west' to come 'down south' and enjoy the sunshine. That left little work, if any, for me.

At this time in my life I could hold my own in the amateur rodeos. I hoped to do better at the rodeos in Florida but the weather and the good purse (prize) money drew most of the good professional rodeo riders and I knew my skills were not good enough at the time to compete with them. I could ride but they could ride better.

Thankfully, April rolled around and that meant it was about time to go north for the summer rodeo events. Wiley was going back to work for the McKinley Wild West Show. Betty had some rodeos booked for her trick riding act and then she would be off to Arizona to visit her parents.

We did not know it at the time, but when Jan and I left Florida it would be the last time we would see Wiley or Betty. We later found out these two got a divorce and had gone their separate ways.

Jan only had a couple of job offers and they were in a different direction from where I was headed, similar to the year before. I knew if we were in different areas it would be a bad business decision since we would have twice the expenses.

No! We needed to find a way to stay together so we could pool what resources we had.

I knew there was a Wild West show that stayed in the eastern part of the United States, especially around New York and the big city areas. It just made sense to look into working with them so we could both be in the same area.

The one thing I liked at all the rodeo events was the amateur contests. You paid to enter these events but they had judges, timers and all the other things you normally saw on the professional side. The events were either judged or timed but anybody could enter except for the Rodeo Cowboys Association (R.C.A.) card holders. This meant the rest of us had a chance to win!

If an R.C.A. card holder did enter one of these events (a professional trying to win a ride against amateurs) he was immediately put on a 'black list' and was not allowed to enter a professional rodeo event. This kept the balance of 'power' where it was supposed to be when it came to the rodeos.

Since Jan and I wanted to stay together, I contacted the boss man of the Wild West show. I was hoping to sell him on the idea of using Jan and 'The Flying Black Clouds' in his show. These were the shows that usually had roman riders, trick riders, trick ropers, etc. If we could sell them on the idea, then both of us could make some good money.

The boss man was very happy to hear from us and was very interested in talking about us being a part of his show.

"My wife, Jan, has a great roman riding act called 'The Flying Black Clouds,'" I told him, "Would you be interested in them?"

"I really don't need another riding act," he replied, "but there is another option."

"I'm listening," I said.

What he said next would change Jan's life and my life forever.

"You see, I work for a man that promotes different shows for county and state fairs and for several rodeos. This promoter just purchased a show from a man called Jinx Hoaglan. That purchase includes a troupe of white horses and they need a girl to ride these horses with a six-horse tandem hitch." (This type of hitch puts the horses in three sets of two, one behind the other like the old stagecoach arrangement. The rider stands on the two back horses and drives all six horses around the arena.)

"I know Jan's name came up when it came to riders," he continued, "But none of us knew where she was located! He does not have anybody to drive this arrangement or one of his three roman riding teams. He has two girls but he needs one more. Think you might be interested?"

This sounded really good to me but there were two of us and she was the one who would have to do all the work. I could ride in the rodeo events and Jan would have a paying job riding the white horses. This would be no problem since she had trained these very same horses just a couple of years earlier! She knew every horse!

I also knew Jan would agree to it and I made the deal right there on the telephone. I would do a few things in the show and they would give me plenty of time to compete in the events. Jan would ride for the show and we would carry a flag in the grand entry (opening) of the show. The show would pay for our horse feed and gas for the truck. When all was said and done, we had a deal for $375 a week.

We loaded up and headed north. Jan brought two of her black horses (as backups) and I brought a calf roping horse. The other two black mares we took to a farm and turned them out to pasture since they were not needed. We thought we would be able to use them the following year but, as it turned out, Jan never used them again.

NO PAY… NO WAY!
YOU PAY… WE STAY!

Our new job had its up and downs but Jan and I survived.

We arrived at the show and met with the rodeo producer and then the promoter. They told us there was a dress rehearsal the next day and it would include Jan riding the six-team roman (tandem) setup. There would be no money for this rehearsal, they told us. Jan and I both knew roman riding was a dangerous thing to do. The two of us agreed that if they wanted Jan to 'train and exhibit' her talent they would have to pay for it.

I approached the rodeo boss man and said we would not do the rehearsal without it being part of our contract, meaning they had to pay for the performance.

He said that was not his department and I should take the issue up with the promoter, a man named Ward Beam.

Mr. Beam was a very knowledgeable and professional man with a lot of experience in these types of shows. He knew what audiences wanted and he made sure they got it! He worked county and state fairs and was one of the first people to put on 'Hell Driving' shows known as "Ward Beam's Hell Drivers"! (It suddenly dawned on me that I had seen them at one of The Great Darke County Fairs in my early years!) These Hell Drivers would jump cars over trucks and buses. They would also drive up a ramp and make the car roll over a couple of times.

A man by the name of Joie Chitwood started his career with Ward Beam. He became an international star in shows and in Hollywood with his stunt driving skills. Jan and I worked in the same shows with Joie and Ward.

I walked into his office and introduced myself. He showed little personality and was very serious. I told him I was informed they wanted a performance from Jan for their own entertainment and to be sure she could do the job.

"You know," I told him, "She has ridden these very same horses before in the very same configuration you want. This was before you even bought the White Horse Troupe from Jinx Hoaglan. She's very capable of doing what you want."

Before long we were in a discussion about getting on a bull, jumping trucks and buses and other show related life-threatening events. I quickly tried to get us back on track.

"She gets paid by the performance," I told him, "And there was no mention about a dress rehearsal. If you had mentioned that before at the time of our agreement, it would have been different as far as I am concerned but now you are telling us and not asking us."

"We are not paying you for a dress rehearsal," he politely informed me.

I nodded.

"Okay," I replied nicely, "Jan and I will be off the grounds within the hour."

I left his office and went back to the van where Jan was waiting.

"They are not going to pay so we are leaving," I told her.

"But we spent all of our money just to get here," she replied sadly.

"Well, we will just drive until we can't go any further," I said gently. "Something will work out, it always does."

We were getting ready to leave when a man stopped me from loading our equipment.

"Mr. Beam wants to talk to you before you leave the grounds," he said stiffly.

I went to Mr. Beam's office and stood in front of his desk.

"You wanted to see me?" I asked.

"Yes, I do," he said politely.

I stood and waited for the axe to fall!

"Perhaps you and I got off on the wrong foot," he said with a new understanding of our situation. "I mean, maybe you are right and we should pay you for the performance, even if it is just a dress rehearsal. Would that be okay with you?"

"No problem," I told him, "I'll tell Jan and we'll start unpacking our gear."

That may have been the moment he fully realized that Jan and I were ready to leave. If we had left, he would have no roman rider and no act.

"You ride today," he said as he reconfirmed his status as the boss, "And tomorrow we will knock out any other problems we have."

And that was the end of that! I went back and told Jan what had happened.

She was happy because now she was doing what she loved with the animals she loved. It helped that the audiences loved her, too. We unpacked, Jan rode in the rehearsal and we were off and running in our careers! Jan told me later that she was proud of the way I stood up to that promoter!

GABBY HAYES

In the days to come, I would enter saddle bronc riding, calf roping and steer wrestling events. When I did the bronc riding, I had to use a new saddle. It did not have a 'broken tree' like the one I learned on and this new saddle beat me to death! I could not get 'in time' with the saddle and the horse and that cost me dearly, especially physically!

My calf roping and steer wrestling were doing much better. I was in the money most of the time and was often the winner of these events. Because things were going so well, Jan and I were making from $500 to $700 a week and that was plenty for us to live on throughout the summer.

Before long I decided to enter just two of the events. Since my calf roping and steer wrestling were making the most money, I settled on those two.

I helped to hook up the six-horse hitch for Jan. She rode those horses with authority and skill, so much that Ward Beam liked what he saw. He became friendlier to us. Once he even came around to thank us for helping him with the entertainment. At the time, he was just another promoter (and there were a lot of them!). Later, I would realize that Ward Beam was like another Wiley to me.

From Ward, I would learn the art of getting jobs at fair conventions, how to price the jobs, how to hire big name stars to bring in the big crowds, to fill a grandstand and so much more! What Wiley did to teach me about cowboy ways, Ward did to teach me about the ways of show business. I remember what happened on one of the first days we started with this show.

The horses needed to be fed so I walked into the barn. The horse stalls were on either side and as I walked down the aisle there was a man in a nice western suit sitting down and watching me. As I walked past him he spoke to me.

"Hi, Sonny," he said casually.

"Hi," I replied, too busy to really start a conversation.

I was walking to the horses when suddenly a strange urge hit me. It seemed I had seen that man somewhere before but for the life of me I could not remember where it was! The horses got fed but my mind was still wondering about that man in the suit. The townspeople came to look and visit the show and I figured he was one of them.

"Maybe he is just one of locals," I thought to myself as I finished feeding the horses.

On my way out of the barn I decided to stop and talk to the stranger. Sometimes you get an itchy feeling and you just have to scratch it! We started a simple conversation but the more we talked the more I kept thinking I had seen or knew this man from somewhere.

Finally, it hit me!

The man I was talking to was none other than Gabby Hayes! He was the sidekick of Roy Rogers and appeared with Roy in movies and on the "Roy Rogers Show" which was on Saturday mornings! Gabby was very popular and here I was talking to him, a movie and TV star! All I knew about him was his stage name, Gabby Hayes, but that was enough for me!

I went back to the van and told Jan I had just met Gabby Hayes. It turned out Gabby was one of the big stars the show had booked and he would be the featured entertainer. We could not wait for the show to start and when it did, everything went off without a hitch! Jan rode her horses and I came in 3rd in the steer wrestling contest.

And I had met Gabby Hayes!

STEER WRESTLING

After our work at this rodeo, Jan and I made about $500. That was good money for those days but we had expenses to pay and we had to make as much as we could while the rodeo season was in full swing!

We were soon off to another rodeo about 150 miles down the road. This rodeo furnished us with gas money for the truck and it looked like we had found something that fit both of us. She performed her act and I competed in the events!

This new rodeo had some really good talent in it. In the next few years one of the barrel racers would go on to become the world champion of the United States and of Canada!

There was also a rodeo cowboy who became a good friend of mine. His name was Jackson and he worked all the eastern rodeos. He was also one of the best steer wrestlers in the east. This was not easy and to achieve this feat Jackson had a pair of horses he took with him wherever he went. The horses were specifically trained for steer wrestling and any good rodeo man will tell you that the horse is as important as you are when it comes to steer wrestling!

This sport requires two horses. The horse ridden by the contestant is called the 'bull dogging' horse. The other horse is called the 'hazing horse' and is ridden by the 'hazer.' The steer is released from a bull doggin' chute and the two horses must run along opposite sides of the steer and keep him going in a straight line. When the time is right, the contestant slides off his horse, grabs the steer by the horns and wrestles him to the ground, hence the name! The fastest time wins. It is not for the faint of heart!

As you can tell, the hazer and the horses are very, very important to the contestant who is trying to win. Oftentimes, cowboys cannot afford their own steer wrestling horses so they will rent their horses from someone who has trained a pair of horses for this event. The owner of the horses usually gets one fourth (1/4) of whatever the contestant wins.

This is where Jackson made his money! He had a good team of steer wrestling (often called 'bull dogging') horses. He had no problem keeping these horses busy at the rodeos where he decided to go! Even I used them because they were good!

The horse ridden by the contestant was named 'Shorty' but this horse did have a fault during the event. The horse would chase after the steer but would then 'fade' out away from the steer when the contestant was ready to ease off the horse and grab the horns of the steer. He was fine for the first 50 feet (about what it takes to get in position), but after that it was anybody's guess if he would hang in there or just fade away!

There was also another problem. The bigger rodeos had a barrier and this allowed the steer to have at least a 10-foot head start.

In the beginning days of amateur rodeos, this start was called 'lap and tap.' This meant the steer and the riders got out at the same time. However, there was a flagman at the 5-foot marker and when the steer left the chute and passed the marker the flagman dropped his flag and the official scorekeeper's time would start. Additionally, the bulldogger's feet could not touch the ground before the flag was dropped.

There was no head start for the steer. This might cause problems, especially if the contestant and his horse left early. If the rider left early, the steer would come out, see the rider and he would stop dead! The rider would just keep on going, chasing after nothing and the steer would watch him, knowing he had outsmarted another cowboy!

Jim Warvell steer wrestling (c. 1960s)

I got to know Shorty really well and I think he got to know me, too. We had good timing together and would leave the same time as the steer. We could catch the steer fast before the steer would get up to full speed. We would catch up to the steer and I would soon be in a position to 'slide' myself off the horse and grab the steer's horns and wrestle him down to the ground as fast as I could.

My official times with Shorty would always be several seconds faster than if I used another horse. This was not because I was that good but because Shorty and I worked together well and it showed. Most steer wrestlers might not catch up to the steer for 50 or 60 feet. I could catch them in the first 10 feet or so. With that kind of 'extra' time, I could make a lot of mistakes and still have a faster time!

So, for that summer, I made money in about every amateur rodeo we attended. In the years that followed, this would all jump up and bite me in the butt!

The bigger rodeos decided to give the steers a longer start out of the chute. Since the steer had a fair start and could build up to full speed, it changed the event of steer wrestling, making it more appealing to the audience. Now, the public could see the steer leaving the chute with a good head start. It would be running full speed as the bulldogger and the hazer caught up to him. The bulldogger would then slide off the saddle and grab the horns to wrestle the steer down.

To ensure the steers had a fair start, the bigger rodeos incorporated a 'barrier' which was usually set at 10 or 15 feet even though some bigger rodeos gave more. The bulldogger would be penalized if he 'broke the barrier,' meaning he did not give the steer a 'fair' start.

That was the end of 'lap and tap.'

This new development required a whole new technique! You had to 'shape' that steer into the right position. Before, (when he did not have a lot of running room), I could catch him and pull him around enough to put my hold on him and down he would go!

Now, to do the same thing on a much faster steer, you had to slide off, grab the horns and put both feet on the ground into a sliding position and, the most important thing of all, *hang onto those horns!*

This required some real delicate movements! When you slid off the horse you grabbed the left horn. Your feet were soon on the ground trying to slow the steer down. At the same time, you are pulling the left horn toward you and down. As the head of the steer is turned it will be higher in the air and you get a proper hold on him. Do it right and the steer will go down in one quick motion. Do it wrong and you will not get the steer down or, in cowboy terms, 'throwed.'

Personally, I never really had to put much pressure on the inside (left) horn but with this new change it became a whole new ball game for all of us! Now I was throwing steers in 10 to 12 seconds instead of the 4 to 6 seconds using the old method. That time would never be good enough at the bigger rodeos where the R.C.A. cardholders were the contestants and I knew it!

You have to remember that back then there were no schools that taught you the finer things to do and the know-how when it came to rodeo events. We all had to learn on our own because even though they might help you a little, the really good cowboys and riders would not give you their trade secrets because that would just take money out of their pockets.

To make the grade with the 'big' boys, you had to wrestle a steer in 7 or 8 seconds and you had to learn how to do it on your own! There were no instant replays, no video and no slow-motion replays to study. This was a watch them and learn and then watch them and learn some more process. It can be frustrating but that is the nature of the beast.

We knew that in the wintertime the steer wrestlers would all get together and 'winter' in the same location. They would get some steers and continue to practice their craft. They had made enough money during the rodeo season and they could do this. The rest of the 'amateurs' had to find work to keep on living!

At one time, many of the steer wrestlers would go to Bakersfield, California, for their winter 'vacation.' Still others went to Burkburnett, Texas. These were two of the 'hot spots' for anyone who was a steer wrestler, as long as they were good at it!

Things have really changed since then. Now there are schools that help youngsters who want to get into the rodeo profession. It is a good way to let rodeo 'wannabees' see if they can really do it or not. It also helps pass on the history and honor of the profession.

KEEP AN EYE ON JACKSON

Jackson, the owner of Shorty and the other steer wrestling horses, was by far one of the most interesting characters I ever met! I never did ask where he was from, but I do know he spoke with what sounded like a deep Georgia accent. If you shut your eyes and only heard him talk, you would know right away it was him!

When I first met him, he was in his fifties and had been a horse trader. He worked many of the big rodeos in the east as a steer wrestler. Between renting out his steer wrestling horses, judging the rough stock events and having the show furnish his gas money, Jackson and his wife had it made.

His wife was a trick rider and she was very beautiful. She was now in her fifties and thought she had lost her beauty and because of that she was very shy and stayed in her trailer most of the time.

But Jackson had a problem! Those of us who knew him usually kept a close eye on him. If he 'found' something or 'picked up' something, he never thought about who owned it and he certainly never looked for the owner. Today we might say he was a kleptomaniac.

For instance, I have seen people feed their horses and then leave the barn area. Jackson would then come in and take their feed and give it to his two horses, Shorty and Gump Stump. Later, if someone inquired about the problem, Jackson would say he ran out of feed and had to 'borrow' some from them because his horses did not have enough to eat. Like I said, we had to keep an eye on him!

That is not to say he was not a nice guy and a character because he was. He would sit around most of the time playing cards and drinking beer and having a good time. When he was around we would all laugh and have a great time but, we always had an eye on him!

Still, you had to like him!

One morning, I heard him arguing with another cowboy.

"Jackson," the cowboy yelled, "You took the blanket off my horse and put it on Shorty."

Jackson just looked at him and shrugged.

"Well," Jackson explained, "It was a cold night and my horse, Shorty, is small and he was cold and your horse is bigger and has a lot more hair and likes the cold weather."

By the time Jackson was done talking and the cowboy was through arguing with him, the cowboy felt sorry for Shorty! He turned and walked away leaving Jackson standing next to Shorty.

He turned to his horse, petted him and said, "You had a good night, didn't you?"

Like I said before, he was very likeable but you had to keep an eye on him…all the time!

There were a lot of card games in the barns and everywhere else. One night, Jackson was playing cards in one of the barns. It got late and the game broke up so the players cashed out and headed for their respective campers or trailers. As Mr. Jackson headed home he noticed the lights were on inside his trailer. Being the fun-loving guy that he was, he had to throw out a comment.

"Hey," he yelled out pointing to his trailer and the lights, "Look at that! The little lady loves me! She left the lights on just for me!"

He walked over to the trailer and opened the door. He expected to find his wife in something sexy. Instead he found her standing there with a gun in her hands! She began to fire and he began to run! That man was running for his life and she was playing 'shoot the rabbit' as he ran all over the grounds!

Actually, she was firing up in the air so she would not hit anybody but Mr. 'Jack Rabbit' Jackson did not know that because he did not look back! That man was moving fast! The next day he took a lot of ribbing from everybody.

Jackson had a lot of other issues, too. About a week later he came out of his trailer with a big bump on his head.

"What happened?"

"Well," Jackson began, "The other night we were all playing cards and I told my wife I would be back in about an hour. I was only a half hour late and I thought she would be mad but she wasn't. We talked for a while and then we went to bed. I fell asleep and thought that was it."

"Was it?"

"Well," he began again in that Georgia twang, "I slept good but when I got up in the morning my wife was standing there with a broom in her hand and she started beating me with it! I jumped out of bed and that is when my head hit the floor and I got this bump."

"You got the bump on your head from hitting the floor?"

"Yea, I did," Jackson continued. "You see, she had tied a rope around both of my ankles and then tied the rope to the bottom of the bed post. When I jumped out of bed, I went nowhere fast except down to the floor.

"My head hit the floor and she kept beating me with the broom stick!"

(Jackson weighed about 200 pounds and his wife weighed about 115 pounds.)

"Know what she said?" Jackson asked.

"No, what did she say?"

"She told me, 'I can't whip your ass when you're awake but I can beat the hell out of you when you are asleep!' That's what she said!"

From that moment on, Jackson said he had a hard time sleeping! He would feel something and jump up thinking she was going on the attack again. He would look over and she would be fast asleep.

Go figure!

GOTTA KEEP AN EYE ON HIM... ALL THE TIME

A cowboy has to rely on several things to make a living. While his ability to learn and adapt is critical, so are the items he needs to perform his job. For me, I was always concerned about my ropes and my knife. My ropes were kept clean and my knife was kept sharp, very sharp.

If you don't know why a knife would be so important then you have never been tangled in a rope and needed to get free! My knife was very important and I did not like to loan it out to other people because they would not be as careful as me. I was always afraid they would let the blade touch a hard surface, turn the edge and possibly ruin the knife forever.

One day, Jackson wanted to borrow my knife. He said it was going to be used to cut a piece of rope. I was reluctant to do it but I lent him my knife. He went to cut his rope and I did not see him for over three hours.

"Are you through with my knife?"

"Yes, I am," he told me.

"Where is it?" I asked.

"Well," there was that Georgia twang again, "I finished cutting my rope and then I laid your knife down somewhere and now I can't find it."

Knowing Jackson, I could see the handwriting on the wall. Now, I had no knife and the next day I had to go steer wrestling. I would have sure felt better with my knife but it was nowhere to be found!

I was using Jackson's horse for my steer wrestling and because of that I had to pay him one-fourth of whatever I won. Since I was in the money more often than not, he stood to make a few bucks. When it came time for me to get the horse, I had a talk with Jackson. I knew if I wanted my knife back, Jackson would have to have some pressure put on him.

"Look here," I told him, "I'm not going to use your horse today."

"But why not?" he asked me.

"That was my good knife and you lost it," I said bluntly.

"You mean you are not going to ride my horse because I lost your knife?"

"Yep."

I could tell it made him mad. He turned and walked away.

About an hour later here comes Jackson and he was laughing and joking like usual.

"You won't believe this," he told me, "But your knife must have dropped out of my pocket while I was in the trailer because my wife found it!"

"Good," I said, happy to have my trusted friend back in my pocket, "Now go get Shorty ready because I want to ride him in the steer wrestling event."

That was the way it was with him. We were still good friends and it stayed that way until he died a few years later.

There will be more about Jackson later because we did a lot of horse trading down in Florida and my life would not be complete without some of the outrageous things that happened down there!

A ROSE IS A ROSE BY ANY OTHER NAME, BUT A WARVEL CAN BE A MAGGOT

Growing up in Darke County near New Madison and Greenville, Ohio, I never thought much about my name. Back then my family name was Warvel (one L, pronounced like Marble but with a 'V'). Like others, my family was proud of our name.

Then things started to change. As my name got out into the public (newspapers and the like) and it was used more and more, I started to see a problem. People were misspelling my name in ways I never thought possible! I was Mr. Warbel or Weavel or Waddle.

Now, if you look in the dictionary you will see there is a warble fly, also called a maggot. Being from farm country and proud of my name, I did not like being teased or called a maggot. Since I was entering a new arena of my life, I knew this was going to be a potential problem. I remember when my brother Jack and I were doing horse shows. The announcer always had trouble with our last name, Warvel.

When Jan and I went back east we did not know anybody. Jackson was the first person we met as we arrived on the rodeo grounds in New York. As mentioned, he had a long, drawn out southern way of talking. Again, you sometimes had to listen closely to what he said in order to understand him.

One day Jan and I were talking to him and his wife walked up to us. We had never met her before so he introduced us to her.

"Honey," he said as she got closer, "I want you to meet Jan and Jim Warvell."

My last name was always pronounced Warvel. Mr. Jackson pronounced it War-vell (two distinct syllables like Bar-bell). At first, I was a little miffed! Here we go again, I thought to myself. My name is being mispronounced.

As the days went by, everyone started calling me Jim War-vell. Even the announcer over the public-address system found it easier to say War-vell than Warvel!

So, we ended up changing our name to Warvell (2 "Ls"), sort of like what big name movie stars have done. (Some guy named 'Marion' changed his name to John Wayne and he did pretty good with it!)

Jan and I took that new name and made it our own. We traveled all over the world to places like Canada, England, Brazil, Kuwait, Singapore, Puerto Rico, Mexico, Japan and many more places. Wherever we went our shows played in the biggest stadiums and arenas they had. In New York, Jan got to fulfill her dream when we played in Madison Square Garden (the original one). In Salt Lake City, Utah, we played in the Salt Dome. In San Francisco it was the Cow Palace and in England we were honored to play in Wembley Stadium!

We were billed as 'The Warvell Family from Weatherford, Texas' whenever we performed. We had two daughters and both of them were a part of our act. What I am getting at is this: we took an unknown name and made it recognizable in the world of horse and specialty acts in the entertainment field and not just the rodeo circuits.

If someone calls me Jim Warvel (one "L") then I know automatically that the person knows me from my days in the New Madison or Greenville, Ohio, area. It means they knew the teenager part of me that grew up there. Some of them do not know the difference in the name and when I tell them they often think we are uppity or arrogant and that is just not the case at all.

I am proud of my early family name but there was a pronunciation and printing problem with it and when you are a performer and your name is in print and announced wherever you go, something has to be done to make it easier for people to recognize you because that is how you make a living. If it is a problem it needs to be solved and that is what I did.

My Grandma (who delivered me and brought me into this world) once asked me why I had changed my name. I had to explain it to her and she accepted it with no problem. From that time on, I was Jim Warvell (2 "L's"). When she wrote a birthday card or letter it was always Warvell and I thank her for that.

It was an achievement and acknowledgement for me. I was proud of the name that was pronounced correctly and glad I was not confused with Warble or Warbel which, did I mention, is also a maggot?

In our society, it is sometimes important to stay positive as much as possible. I know that everybody is proud of their name and I am no exception. Some names are funny to say and in their meaning, too, but they, like me, have the right to change it if they feel it would make their life easier and less conflicting. Heck, women change their name every time they get married and if they get married three or four times they change their name three or four times so why can't we all do it?

CHAPTER 17

PARTNERSHIP

Jan and I continued our eastern Wild West venture as Mr. Beam began to book all the places we worked. At each place, there would be a headliner who was the feature act of the show. We were one of the 'add-on' acts.

The money we made was good and we were getting along nicely. As time went on, Mr. Beam began to realize that Jan was the one who made 'The White Horse Troupe' work like a well-oiled machine. Because of this he made sure we were taken care of wherever we went.

He became friendlier toward us and even asked us out to dinner one night.

As we ate he began to talk business.

"What are you going to do after the Wild West Show ends?"

We shrugged because we had never thought about it. There were no plans for us except our usual winter routine.

"Well, there is something you should know. When I bought The White Horse Troupe from Hoaglan, he had a big show booked. To seal the deal, I had let him in on half of the contract for that show. The show is at the Harrisburg National Horse Show in Pennsylvania."

We stopped eating. This was getting interesting.

"This show has Olympic teams from all over the world," he continued. "Places like Germany, Japan, England and Canada will all be there. The people in charge would like to have you and the white horses there for next year.

"I am going to break away from this Wild West Show. I think it would be great if we just booked the horses into as many fairs, rodeos and even circuses that we can. I am already booking other acts in these events so the contacts will not be a problem."

We were both glued to his words because we knew there was something else going on.

"What I am trying to say," he continued, "Is that I think you and I should go into a partnership."

Interesting!

As the evening progressed, we worked out a deal. We would split everything 50/50 after paying for expenses. We would furnish a horse truck and a house van for the girls to stay in at the different shows. Jan and I would have no salary. We would just have what was left after we made the split. In addition, Mr. Beam would give us $1,000 to appear at the Harrisburg show.

Later in life I realized that I probably should not have taken the deal but at the time it was the best thing we had.

We still had one more week to go in the Wild West Show. Mr. Beam told the owner of the show he was not going to promote or book them the next year and they would not have the white horses, either.

That did not sit well with the owner and there was a big disagreement between the two of them. This caused bad blood between the owner and Mr. Beam and that bad blood spilled over to Jan and I. We were accused of stealing The White Horse Troupe.

I told Mr. Beam we were not going to stay under these conditions. Mr. Beam understood and said he would stay and I should send a truck the following week (after we had fulfilled our contract obligations) to pick up the white horses, our wardrobe and our equipment. We never expected to get into the white horse business but you never know where the road will lead you.

THE SPARE WHITE HORSE

Jan and I went back to Indiana. We went to a little county fair grounds that had a horse show arena used by the 4H club and the local horse riding clubs. We rented it for a month so we had a place to work the white horses and refine the act. We also hired some new female riders and this would also give us time to incorporate them into the show. We had to do all this before the big show in Harrisburg.

We did, however, have a few problems. One of the horses was getting old and we wanted to find and train a new one. This was a pretty important thing because it is always good to have an extra horse available in case one of yours gets sick or, in this case, gets old! We also had to find two or three riders. Our contract called for eight girls to be in the act. At the moment, there were only six girls in the show.

Jan reached out to a couple of girls she knew when she worked with Jinx Hoaglan. She found out where they were and contacted them. They could work the Harrisburg show but they could not work for us the following year. That was okay with us! We had to deal with one thing at a time and the first thing up was that Pennsylvania show.

As for the white horse we needed, well, who else would you call but Jinx Hoaglan who had the original white horses? Unfortunately, he had no idea where we could find another one. I thanked him and said, "There are other white horses around here. In fact, there is an auction over in Rushville, Indiana, so I'll go there and try my luck."

The auction had more than a hundred horses every Thursday or Friday. I can't remember for sure what the day was. When I got there, I saw only three white horses. Two were old and not the kind we needed. The other one looked very athletic but he was also very young, maybe 20 months old or so. He was small, around 14 ½ hands tall. Most jumping horses are at least 16 hands tall or bigger. He was narrow between the front legs but very smooth otherwise.

This horse was not the kind we really needed but with no other choices available, I bought him. I hate to say it but most of those other horses were on their way to the dog food processing plant.

The bidding began for the white horse and I threw out the first bid. Some man bid against me and I saw that he was the man who bought horses for the dog food plant. I had seen him buy the other, old, worn out horses and now he wanted to get this one?

Not on my watch he ain't! I outbid him and bought the white colt for $135. I knew we would have to use him until we could get a more mature white horse for the act. Jan was anxiously waiting to see what I had purchased. When she saw him, she just stared and then spoke the same prophetic words I had thought about when I saw him.

"What are you going to do with this baby?" she asked.

"Tomorrow we will start riding him and try to have him ready for the big show," I commented, trying to justify my purchase.

"We can't get him ready in time," she commented.

"Well, we gotta try," was all I could say.

The next morning, I took that colt and started training him. He was nervous and he did not want to get hurt and he wanted to move ahead all the time. Thankfully, he did not fight when I pulled the bit and moved his head to the right and then to the left. No matter which way I pulled he would go in that direction. That was the end of day one.

The next day we were trotting in a circle and as I tightened the circle (made it smaller and smaller) he did not fight me. Before the day was over, we were galloping around in that circle! Sometimes it takes a horse a week or two to do what this young colt was doing in just a couple of days!

I had a halter on him and a 30-foot rope as he was running around in a circle. I got him to move out and trot and then take off at a gallop. He was working unbelievably good! There was a barn with a long side on it so I fixed up a jump stand. This consisted of two poles in the ground several feet apart and then another pole is put between them at varying heights, similar to what you see at equestrian events.

I ran him through the two poles a few times before I put the jumping pole between them. I then laid the pole on the ground to see what he would do. He ran to it, ignored it and just galloped right over it. Even with the pole on the ground, he jumped three feet high and broad jumped at least eight feet from where he started to where he finished! And the pole was on the ground!

In the next few days we took one of our trained white horses and worked them together. Jan rode in front and I rode in back on the colt.

Jan would go over the jump and the colt would follow. We had to do this because in our performance, all the horses had to jump over obstacles. They would jump two at a time, then four at a time and then eight at a time. Right now, we were jumping one at a time. We always had two horses in the arena so they had to get used to working together, regardless which horses were there. To our surprise, Jinx Hoglan came to see how things were going and when he saw the colt he about had a fit!

"That horse will not work in the show," he told us bluntly! "It will mess up the show, I tell you!"

As for me, I did not worry about what he was saying. I had an ace up my sleeve and her name was Jan!

PRACTICE PAYS OFF

Jan and I worked the colt every day. He was a little on the nervous side or 'flighty' side but as the days progressed he got better and better. When we rode him, it seemed as if he did not want to stop. He did not care and he was willing to go wherever you pointed his nose!

We blended him in with the other horses and after three weeks of jumping and riding with the rest of the 'herd,' he was doing remarkable! He looked like he had been ridden for four or five months, he was that good!

Having the horses for your troupe is one thing but you also have the riders and support personnel, too. Jan reached out and found just what we needed. The girls she found had worked with "The White Horse Troupe" so she knew them and knew what they could do.

Jan met all of them at the fairgrounds. We had been at these fairgrounds for over a month and we rented the arena almost every day to practice and perfect the act. She told them what she expected of them and they were ready and willing!

We had three Roman Riding teams of horses. Jan would ride one and the other teams were ridden by the girls Jan had hired. Both girls were experienced and were quite good. The six-horse hitch was the toughest to ride so Jan rode them. She had been training and riding them all summer at the Wild West Show. They were used to her and she was used to them.

Before long, we had seven girls working for us, eight including Jan. Our contract for the National Horse Show at Harrisburg, Pennsylvania called for eight riders so we were ready when the time came. Jan made sure the act was polished and ready to go.

There was a white horse drill the girls liked to do. They would ride bareback and wear circus type wardrobe. The girls would do a dangerous 'crisscross' pattern at a fast rate of speed. At the end, they would go over a jump in the show ring. First, they would jump in pairs. That would be followed by jumping in sets of four and then all eight of them would jump together. As they jumped, they would throw both of their arms up in the air. It was not easy to do because they were obviously not holding on to anything!

This part of the act was always done using a spotlight and it looked very impressive! Imagine eight beautiful white horses with eight beautiful young women! That was beautiful in itself but when they rode together and jumped together, it was more than impressive and the fans loved every minute of it!

Jinx was watching as Jan mounted our young colt. You could tell he was nervous about the horse and it showed. As Jan and the horse entered the show ring, the colt looked like a snake going through the grass! Just in case the colt did not perform, he had good horses waiting in the wings and he was ready to use them at a moment's notice.

I was not worried but I knew that horse was a handful to ride! Jan, however, knew how to ride and she kept him in the correct place at all times. If the horse was going to give her a rough moment, it would be at the jump sight. If he refused to jump (as many horses will) it would create a serious situation for all of us.

It was not long before Jan and the horse were headed for the first jump. He was going towards the jump pole and I could see that horse just staring at the pole.

(The jump pole is simply a pole laid on two stands, one on the right and one on the left. To keep from injuring the horse or the rider, the pole will fall off the stands if it is hit during the jump. This is a safety measure and is used by all jumping contests. Even those 'brick' walls you see at equestrian events are really small blocks that will tumble easily when hit.)

Jan was ready for the jump, but was the horse? He had his ears back and looked a little scared when he got to the jump pole. I wasn't sure but when the time came, he must have been scared because that colt jumped much higher than was needed!

People in the grandstand were expecting a jumping show and they got one! Many of them could easily see the difference because they were experienced and knowledgeable individuals who were here to see jumpers, including some of the Olympic horses.

Jinx watched in awe. He shook his head when he saw me.

"I can't believe it," he said with a look of amazement. "That horse did in one month what it usually takes me a year to accomplish."

I just smiled. Jan was all smiles, too. She came out of the arena rubbing and talking to the colt. We both knew we had something special with this horse but did not realize at the time that this horse would fulfill one of Jan's childhood dreams.

Jan and her crew performed every night. She rode the six horse Roman riding team and then she would switch to the young colt. When it came time for the 'big jump,' all the show people and horse lovers would crowd around the arena and watch. This little horse would jump very high but as good as the height was, the length of the jump was also amazing!

Every night this horse did it, over and over again! Not only was it fun to watch, but Jan said it felt as if he had wings!

It was wonderful to know our patience and training had paid huge dividends!

COWBOY STRIPTEASE

The National was over and winter was about to set in. I made a deal with Mr. Beam. He would furnish the money to feed the horses over the winter if I found a place to keep them. When he got the bookings for the next summer and we worked the first show, the cost would be split and after feed, gas, and paying the salary of our seven girls, we would split everything right down the middle. I was hoping this would make enough profit to keep the White Horse Troupe up and running.

Before we went to the show in Harrisburg, I had found a man that owned a small dairy farm. He had sold his cows and gotten a job in a local factory. His farm was now empty but he still had a barn full of hay. I talked to him about housing the horses and he said he would feed them. We settled on a price and the horses soon were boarded and settled into their new surroundings.

Jan and I were now ready for Florida and our winter home. As we got ready to go, I found out there was a contest rodeo in Cincinnati, Ohio, and another one in Richmond, Indiana, the following week. I also discovered that Jackson was going to be at both rodeos with Shorty, the horse I liked to ride.

As always, Jan and I were broke. This would give us a chance to win some money in the steer wrestling competition. We decided to head for Cincinnati.

I was surprised to find that they were using the 'lap and tap' method in the steer wrestling event. This was right down my alley and I got excited! There were two rounds at this rodeo. This meant you had to make two 'runs' and you would get two different steers, one for each round. They were paying the first four finishers and another sum for the best average time. If you had the two best times in each round, it was possible that you would even get another check!

I entered and got lucky! I won both rounds and also had the best average time. It was a nice payday.

We loaded up and headed for Richmond, Indiana. This was only a three or four-hour drive from Cincinnati so we easily did it in one day.

They ran their rodeos a little differently in Indiana. There would only be one shot at winning. You got one steer and that was it. The fastest time would win it all.

Thankfully, I got lucky again and won this contest, too. Jan and I now had enough money to make it to Florida. Jackson talked to me before we left the rodeo arena.

"I will see you in Florida and we will work the Kissimmee rodeo."

As long as he brought Shorty, his trained horse, I knew I would be there. We did not go to Florida alone. Jan and I took the colt, Frosty and two other white mares with us to Florida. We also had a horse I was training as a calf roping horse in case I wanted to enter that event, too. We were traveling with five horses but not for long.

Jan's two black mares were taken to a farm and turned loose so they could retire in comfort and peace. They had some age on them and we wanted to work the white horses over the winter. The black horses had served us well and we were happy they had a nice place to rest and retire.

When we hit the sunshine state, we did not go to the Circle T Ranch. Instead, we went to a friend's ranch near Kissimmee. He had a nice roping arena that we could use to work the white horses and get them ready for another year with Mr. Beam.

The rodeo in Kissimmee was soon upon us. I talked to Jackson and he was anxious for the steer wrestling to start since I was making money in just about every event I entered, especially with Shorty as my partner. When the time came, I entered and then waited.

The rodeo was set up in such a way that you could see the livestock and I was soon staring at a pen full of steers. After watching and evaluating them, there were a few I wanted to draw but that was a pot luck thing so only time would fulfill my destiny. These steers had just come off a ranch in Kissimmee and most of them were a Brahma cross-breed.

The Brahma breed of cattle are known for a hump on their shoulders. They flourished in the Florida swamps and extreme heat. They were often crossbred with the Angus and/or Hereford breed of cattle. These particular steers had a slight hump showing traits of the Brahma breed. They were big and wild-looking.

When evaluating a steer for the contest, you, as a rider, want one with a thin neck. Unfortunately, there were not many in this lot. There was one steer with very large horns that really got big around the base of the horn where it attached to the steer's head. His neck was very thick and you could see a little hump on the top of his shoulders. His number was '2' (all steers had a number so when a rider picked his number at the draw, he could see which steer he had drawn). A quick look at the other steers told me that I would take any of them but I did not want to draw that one!

When the draw arrived, I reached in and son of a gun, I got number '2'! I took a deep breath, let it out and probably said a few things I should not have said!

There were four or five riders ahead of me and all of them managed to "bulldog" their steer in good time.

Now, it was my turn. Jackson knew who I had drawn so he was laughing and having a good time with it. All I could see was this monster steer as they put him in the chute and waited for me to get ready.

I signaled I was ready and they let the steer loose. Shorty did his job and took me to him. I caught the steer quickly (thanks Shorty!) and tried to stop this massive steer, but sensing danger, number '2' decided to fight back.

A steer or cow can take their hind foot, strike it forward and knock a fly off their ear if they want to. That's what this steer did. He thought I was a fly and he was going to knock me off! His foot went between my shoulder blades and ripped my shirt down to my belt. Unfortunately, his foot did not stop there! He missed my belt and caught my pants, ripping them down to my knees! I did not know if I was 'bare' or not, but those onlookers got a really good look at my 'tighty whities'!

I let him go and the arena was laughing hysterically at my predicament. Here I was, in front of all these people with my rear end hanging out to dry! I was so embarrassed, my face looked like a fire truck! I raced out of there to the sounds of cheers, laughter and applause. My truck seemed to be miles away but I made it there and changed my clothes.

When I returned and saw Jan, she wanted to laugh but she was trying desperately not to do it. I thought she would bust out laughing as she stood there and tried to look sympathetic. It was something wives are supposed to do but looking back on it now, had that happened to someone else, I would have laughed as well!

For the next two days, we watched number '2.' He was caught once but got away. The last time they used him the steer outran the steer wrestler and got away scot-free. That was one tough steer!

That was it for the next two years. Jan and I had a talk and we knew our future was in a different direction. We were going to concentrate on our white horses, the circus dates, the fairs and the other events we could book.

We were now performers and entertainers on a full-time basis.

DEALING WITH ADVERSITY

We trained and worked the horses all winter long. When spring came and it was time to leave Florida, we gathered our gear and headed back to the farm we had rented in Indiana. There was also a place in Ohio where we could put the horses out to pasture since the grass had now returned. The horses were soon happy and ready to go but we had other people we had to train and make sure they were ready, too. Jan quickly gathered the girls together and got them in shape for the coming events.

Mr. Beam had also been working. He had booked several events for us and the first one was 'Tom Packs 10 Ring Circus' in St. Louis, Missouri. It was the biggest circus during the 4th of July week in the entire United States.

Most circuses have three rings under a tent with a grandstand around the walls of the tent so the spectators could see all three rings at once. If you were lucky, you could put 200-400 people inside to see the show.

Tom Packs held his show on a football field with a cinder running track around the outside of the field. There were 10 rings on the field and all of them would go at the same time. The people in the stands (remember, this was a football stadium) had a very busy time trying to watch everything that was happening in front of them.

This concept was a great idea as far as Tom was concerned. He had a stadium sized seating arrangement (seats went all the way around the field) and he could sell tickets to 10-12,000 people. He made a lot more money in one show than some of the other promoters did in three or four shows!

And now, here we were. The White Horse Troupe was performing in the biggest circus arena in the country. But we had a severe problem.

The girls we used the previous year at the National all had prior commitments. We were supposed to have eight horses and eight very talented women riding them. Instead, we had seven horses and a young horse (who did not even have a name yet! We just called him 'The Colt'). Other than Jan, that was it. We were a little shy on the people side of things.

To say I was getting nervous would be an understatement. It was not the fault of Mr. Beam. Promoters know what you have for an act and that is what they book. It is their job to get you work and your job to show up and do it. We did not know at the time about the girls. We were now getting a little desperate. We did not know where to find seven girls who could ride in the act, especially in the local area.

With no other choice, we decided to do what the White Horse Troupe did in Nebraska. We sent out advertisements for young girls that wanted to ride horses and be in show business. One of our ads was in the "Western Horseman Magazine," a well-liked and well-circulated magazine that is very popular throughout the United States. It is read by lots of horse people, trainers, breeders, riders and many more.

Our advertisement stated that we wanted the girls to send photographs and to include their height, weight, experience, etc. We hoped for the best and feared for the worst. Boy, were we surprised!

We received replies from New York to California and all locations in between. We knew we had to make the decisions as to which girls to choose. We needed girls who knew how to ride and were willing to ride bareback, jump over obstacles and do Roman riding. All of these had to be done while running and going through different routines. They had to be hard working girls who wanted to do the work and would be proud of their accomplishments once they learned the routines.

It took several phone calls and a lot of conversation to try and get just the right girl with just the right attitude and work ethic. We got lucky because when our choices arrived, that is exactly what we got. The girls we picked would turn out to be great assets to their family, their community and the business world. We had seven girls from seven different states which made it interesting for us.

We were soon listening to southern drawls, Wisconsin twangs, New 'Yawk' accents, California expressions and Midwest slangs. Still, they were great and that is what we needed. Jan, who had to train them, was totally pleased. The girls were hard workers and wanted the show to be spectacular and it was!

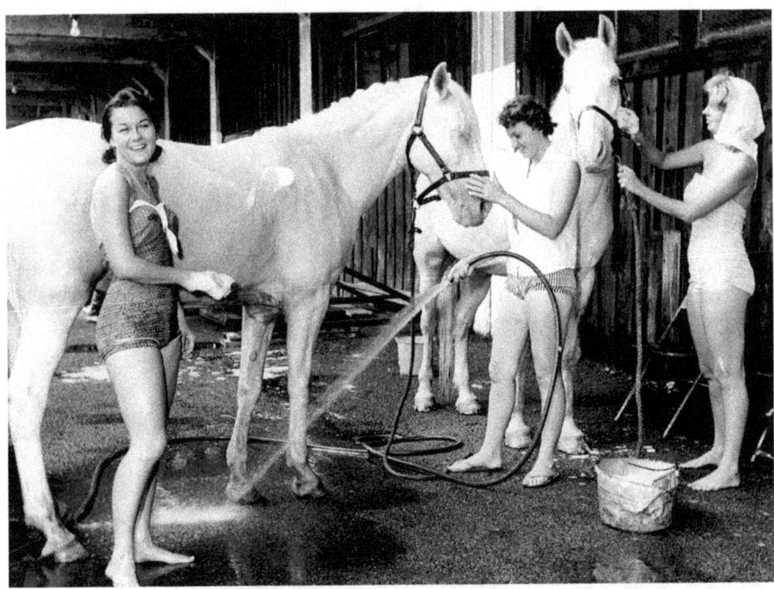

White Horse Troupe bathing the horses before the performance (late 50s). Left to right: Della Townsend, Barbara Ames and Helene (Cookie) Voelkel

White Horse Troupe

Jim holding award trophy, Jan at far right (late 50s)

Jan Warvell (early 60s)

Jan Warvell and Sharon Egan (early '60s)

Our horse van was turned into a bunk house with eight beds. These great gals were more than special to us. They were All-American girls. We never saw them have a beer or cuss. If they were doing those things, they gave Jan and I the respect of not letting us see them do it and not telling us about it. They were very professional around us. (After the White Horse Troupe was finished, we would stay in contact with several of the girls and that would be 30 to 40 years later.)

When the girls arrived, it took every minute of every day for them to learn the routines. They had to know the act, do the drills, jump the horses (with both arms in the air) and ride bareback (no saddle). They even had to bathe the white horses before every performance.

By the time the circus arrived, we knew the girls were as ready as they were ever going to be. It was still a nervous time for them and for Jan and me. The girls had to perform their very first show in front of over 10,000 people. They had to do the act with precision and perfection while 'styling and smiling' the whole time and showing no fear at all. Whew!

Jan was the leader and she had a lot of experience. The girls had developed confidence in themselves and in Jan. They knew she would take them through their first performance. They had been trained and were ready. We hoped.

Because of the size of the arena, I was worried about the six-horse hitch. Jan was supposed to ride all six of the horses completely around the cinder block track. We knew she could do it but one of the older lead horses had to be replaced.

The new horse was only two years old and it was the one we named, 'the colt' and yes, it was the same one we had used at the National! We had been training 'the colt' for six weeks as a leader in the six-horse hitch and he was doing a fairly good job. His training, however, was done in a show ring with no spectators and no other animals.

As we put the colt into the lead position, we were not sure how the horse would react. It was well-trained and would go where you wanted to go but we did not know how it would be in front of elephants, bears, circus performers in all ten rings and above all, 10,000 screaming fans. We were about to find out.[4]

Jan kept her wits and got through the first performance with no problems. There were no stumbles and no mistakes. The crowd got to see her and from our viewpoint, it was a success.

Our new ladies also performed at a high level. They were now performers and they loved it! They wanted more of the spotlight and their smiles and eagerness proved to be a major asset.

As we continued to perform, 'the colt' lived up to all our hopes and desires. It was a perfect spot and the horse gave us solid performances in the six-horse hitch and in the jumping arena.

---

4 The two lead horses are very important. They set the pace for the other four horses to follow. If one of the lead horses should stumble, get spooked or just plain stop, there will be a major wreck as the other horses behind have no place to go.

There was also an added bonus. The girls were becoming a big family. All of us knew each girl, their strengths and weaknesses, and we also knew the horse that fit their skills and personality. We were now ready for the world and the 'fun' of being entertainers.

THE SHOW MUST GO ON

Jan always rode the replacement or unruly horses. She did this because she was the best at training and making a horse understand what she wanted it to do. Once she had the horse performing well, she would turn it over to one of the other girls who could ride and wanted a 'challenge.' Then Jan would go out and find the next most unruly horse.

One of the girls who liked a 'challenge' was from the state of New York. Her name was Sharon and she had seen the ad in the magazine and was quick to answer it. When we talked on the phone, we told her we would give her a try. Two days later, we got a phone call from her saying she was at the local bus stop and needed a ride to our training facility!

She was about 5′7″ tall, nice looking and, of course, had a Yankee accent. On the ride back, it became obvious she had a terrific personality, liked horses a lot and was going to fit in well with our crew.

Two days after getting her from the bus stop, I received a phone call. The woman introduced herself and said she was Sharon's mother. She informed me that Sharon (her daughter) had run away from home. She had received a letter from Sharon with our telephone number in case there was an emergency.

Her mother told us Sharon had no money but if we would watch over her for a few days, she would send her daughter some money for a bus ticket back home to New York.

I assured her we would take good care of her daughter. I also told her that Sharon would stay with us for four or five days and, at the end of that time, if she wanted to go home, we would make that happen for her.

To make a long story short, Sharon stayed with us for four years and became like a daughter to Jan and I. During that time, Sharon became a professional Roman rider and trick rider. Like I said before, we got lucky! Real lucky!

Mr. Beam had scheduled a lot for us. That first summer was made of mostly circus shows and a few big fairs. The last one would be at Danbury, Connecticut, about 65 miles north of New York City. It was ten days long and ran over two weekends. This was one of the most outstanding events you could attend with 75 to 80 thousand people in attendance every single day! They would come from near and far to see the shows. For guests, it would cost them a one-time fee to enter the grounds. After that, everything was free.

There was a high fence around the outside of the entertainment area. Just beyond the fence were fiberglass figures of deer in a jumping pose. Each of these deer was 10 feet long and painted snow white with a red ribbon harness. They were mounted 8-10 feet off the ground in a single line as though they were flying. Red ribbon 'reins' stretched from each deer back to, who else, Santa Claus who was sitting in a nice sleigh.

This area was once owned by a man who let it be used for the county fairgrounds. Over the course of time, he and the fairgrounds had gone bankrupt. The property was bought by a man named Leahy who had a plan for this large plot of land. He wanted to turn it into a mini Disneyland. Once he took over, the land soon looked like a real farm, including animals.

The centerpiece was the barn area. Inside he had milk cows where, at certain times, families could watch a real farmer milk the cows, something seldom, if ever, seen in the city. But the man did not stop there! He installed all the equipment necessary so the visitors would see the different stages used to make milk. He also had areas where they could see how cottage cheese, regular cheese, ice cream and other dairy products were made.

At the end of the tour, there was a store selling all the products made by the farm. After seeing how things were made, the families were more than willing to buy them and take them home. For someone who lived in the city, this was way more than a petting zoo! It was a learning experience, worthy of a school field trip or a family's weekend trip.

In the summer, there would also be lumberjack contests. Two 40-foot high poles would be firmly placed in the ground. Lumberjacks would then climb to the top of the pole, saw off a 12-inch section of the pole and then race back to the bottom. The fastest time would win.

There was also a large area designed to show how a tree was transformed from a big round piece of 'tree' to lumber that could be used for building homes.

Mr. Leahy had a barn for our white horses. There was a walkway down the center of the barn where people could go and see them. The horses were protected by large screens so the people could see the horses but not touch or feed them.

To our surprise, thousands of people were going through the barn on a daily basis. Most of them were 'city' people and had never seen a live horse, much less a beautiful all white horse. There was more than just a farm atmosphere on the property.

The fairgrounds had a huge grandstand. Inside were wild animal shows, stunt car driving shows, cars jumping over busses, trucks (and whatever else they could find) and, of course, the circus and entertainment acts of which we were an integral part. These were called 'Grandstand Shows' and we performed with all of types of these different shows, day in and day out.

We always started these Grandstand Shows with a parade. We joined all the other performers and marched along a special route. Usually, the crowds were huge, sometimes as much as 60-70 thousand people who just wanted to see what was on the agenda for the day. Mr. Leahy had taken precautions by having guards and security posted along the parade route.

Our White Horse Troupe was one of the highlights. The girls now had one season of performing under their belts as this was the last summer show for us. As they rode in the parade, the girls would 'work' the crowd by waving and talking to them. It was easy to see they loved their job and had developed into seasoned performers!

These girls had spent the summer with some of the best circus performers in the United States. They had been with the Wallendas, the high wire performers who were world renowned and the best of the best. We also performed with The Hannefords, a family act that dated back to the 1700s in England. There was also The Budweiser Hitch, a man named Gene Holder, who traveled all over the United States with his wild animal acts.[5]

The girls worked with all these big names and many more. This would be our last outdoor performance. Mr. Beam had booked us to do the Winter Shrine Circus which would be indoors. These were the best winter circuses in the United States and it was an honor to be booked into their arenas.

These indoor shows would not start until January and it was now the end of October. Most of the girls would go home for a couple of months, except for Sharon. She had left her home in New York and decided not to go back. She had found a new home with Jan and I and our beloved white horses. This would be her home for the next three years.

Our first year came to a close and after we settled up financially with Mr. Beam we found there was very little money to show for all the hard work we had done. But, we had made it! We were very familiar with the old expression of 'chicken one day and feathers the next day.'

Even with the lack of funds we knew we were on the plus side of the ledger. Our gain was the experience we were getting in learning show business and how to promote ourselves and how to book our own shows. This is difficult to learn as promoting and booking are completely different than being on the performance end. I was watching, listening and learning.

Ward Beam had already booked us for some very nice shows during the coming year. We knew we had the horses to perform the shows

5 He had other acts and I once saw him at the Darke County Fair with his racing ostriches and the best Hell Driving show at the time, "The Stunt Drivers."

but many of our young women were heading in a new direction. Some were off to college while some returned home to start a new career. We now had to get replacements but because of our ads and contacts, there was not as much urgency as there was before the previous season had started.

There was a better feeling between our troupe and the circus people with whom we worked. You have to understand that circus people stick to themselves. They tend to stay together and do not like outsiders. We had worked with them for almost a year and they had accepted us as members of their family.

Our first show was in Detroit, Michigan, and it was cold outside! But, thankfully, we were inside and we were now with some of the very best acts in the entire circus world. The Detroit circus had hired the Wallendas (the high wire act), The Hannefords, John Boady (the large cat trainer who worked the center ring) and, of course, The White Horse Troupe (not to say we were in the same category as the headliners but we were proud to be there!).

It was unfortunate but the next year would be when the Wallendas fell while performing their famous 'pyramid' routine. Seven of their family fell from the high wire and some were injured, crippled and even killed. This was world news at the time.

Mr. Beam had booked this circus through a man named Al Dobritch. Mr. Dobritch was a man that was known to be very crafty, a reputation I would learn firsthand as the year went by.

Detroit was soon over and we went on to work many more circus and horse shows. We worked many of the winter circus events and then, as the seasons changed, we started working the outdoor arenas. We worked one rodeo, The Annual Salt Lake City Rodeo in Salt Lake City, Utah. It was starting out to be a very busy year.

When it came to booking our act, Ward Beam and I had an arrangement. He would book the event, send me the contract and I would sign it and then return it to him. It was a deal we had worked out a long time ago and had served both of us. Al Dobritch saw us and liked the act. He then hired Mr. Beam to hire us. Mr. Dobritch had access to a variety of venues, including some in Canada so Mr. Beam thought it would be advantageous to work with him.

This arrangement sent us to the circus in Toronto, Ontario, in Canada. This circus was one of the biggest in Canada. The headline act was Struppi Hanneford. She was a beautiful woman from Germany who had married Tommy Hanneford. They became known as The Hannefords. He was well-known as a 'rosin back rider.'[6]

Struppi made her appearance riding bareback on one of our white horses. Her husband, Tommy, would lead the horse into the arena. The troupe's appearance was show stopping because Struppi wore a white ostrich, Indian style headdress and our girls wore purple ostrich, Indian style headdress. Her entry alone probably cost in the neighborhood of $5,000. We felt it was worth it because when the spotlights hit them, they were a sight to behold! It was something the customers were willing to come back and see again and again!

The White Horse Troupe was a beautiful act but you need a lot of acts to fill the arenas where the circuses are held. We were blessed to work with and learn from some of the biggest, best and most revered acts in America!

LIFE IS FULL OF UPS AND DOWNS

The next year would be our last year with The White Horse Troupe. Some of the things that occurred during that next year are entertaining in my mind. I still think and laugh about them. We went through a lot, but these events only made us stronger.

We still had Jan's old van truck and we used it to pull the horse trailer. Well, it used to be a horse trailer but now it had been 'remodeled' and was now our bunkhouse for the girls of the show. To pull the real horse

6 A rosin back rider is someone who rides horses standing on a free galloping horse while doing all kinds of difficult stunts. A good rider can perform a back flip and land on a galloping horse that is behind the horse he started from! It is not for the fainthearted! This is all done with nothing but balance and talent!

trailer, we used another old truck. Money was tight and although we could have used new trucks, we had to make do with what we had.

Back in those days there were no Interstates. All we had were the state roads that everybody had to use. These were very curvy and hilly roads with a 50 mph speed limit on the straight and well paved stretches.

I kept up with the mileage (cost accounting) and we were lucky if we averaged around 35 mph, slow moving by today's standards. We would be in one town for maybe ten days and sometimes for as little as three days. It just depended on what kind of show we were doing.

That summer sticks out in my mind because we seemed to have trouble with every move we made. One of the trucks would have tire problems or motor problems or the lights would go out one at a time (naturally!). To let the other driver know there was a problem, our signal was to blink the lights. We would then pull over and see if we could correct the problem.

On one occasion, Jan was following me during a rainstorm. Suddenly, her windshield wipers quit working and she could not see anything! We quickly pulled over at the first safe spot we could find and I went to work trying to figure out what the problem was. It turned out the wiper motor had died and there was no place to get a new one. We knew we had to keep going because we had a show commitment for the next day.

We were stuck but ingenuity still survived in our world! I rigged up a string and tied it to the wiper motor. This motor was located under the dash of the car and had arms on each side of the motor which made the wipers go back and forth. You pulled on the right string and the wipers went to the right. You pulled on the left string and the wipers went to the left. Hey, it worked!

Jan knew we had to keep going. Luckily, she had a girl named Della that liked to ride shotgun[7] (in the front passenger's seat) with her when she drove.

---

7 The term *shotgun* came from the Old West during the stagecoach era. The man sitting nearest the stagecoach driver carried a shotgun because he had to be on the alert for bandits, Indians and any other trouble that came their way. He was the driver's lookout and protector.

Once we were ready, all Della had to do was pull the strings to keep the windshield clear. That is how we managed to get to our next location. They laughed about it later because sometimes Jan would say, "Faster, faster," and Della would be frantically pulling the strings as she tried to keep the windshield clean!

On another occasion, Jan was blinking her lights at me. That meant trouble so at the first safe location we pulled over. It was 2 AM and we could only hope that it was something simple. I walked back to her truck to see what was wrong.

Her truck had a five-speed gear box with the shifter coming out of the floor next to the driver's right leg. The driver had to shift with their right hand while pushing in on the clutch with their left leg and steering with their left hand. It was complicated until you got used to it.

As I walked back with a, "what now?" look on my face, Jan rolled down her window.

"I am having a hard time reaching the gear shift lever," she told me.

I didn't say anything but I thought she was either getting sleepy or her arm had somehow gotten shorter!

"I'll have a look," I told her.

She got out of the truck and I looked at the gear shift. I could not believe my eyes!

The gear shift was now at least six inches further to the right than where it should have been. I may be a 'jack of all trades and master of none' but this situation had me perplexed!

With no other choice, I crawled under the truck trying to find the problem. The first thing I saw ran a shiver down my spine. We had lost the motor mount bolts. These are the bolts that hold the motor in position. I crawled out and got the jack and put it under the motor. Using the jack and a tire wrench, I got the motor back to its correct position. Luckily, one of the bolts had wedged itself in the frame. I took it and bolted it back into one of the holes through the motor and into the frame.

We were soon back on the road but we drove carefully and kept a wary eye on the gearshift lever until we got it fixed.

Jan later told me that if we had gone much farther the gearshift lever would have been out the passenger side door!

We continued our journey from one town to the other. Another occasion found us on the Pennsylvania Turnpike. We were making good time until a Pennsylvania State Patrol Officer pulled us over. I guess we looked like a pack of vagabonds with two trucks and two big trailers.

The patrolman walked past the trailers and came up to me. He asked me a few questions and I told him we had a trailer of horses and a trailer of eight pretty young women. By now, the girls were sticking their heads out of the trailer to see what was happening.

With something new to occupy his mind, the patrolman began to walk around the trailer with these beautiful young women still looking at him. He talked to them and asked them a few questions. I am sure his mind was racing with all these women in front of him.

Finally, he came back to me.

"Sir," he began, "Can you please tell me what is going on here?"

"We are a traveling troupe," I told him.

I reached over and grabbed an album. As he looked at the pictures I told him about our act, The White Horse Troupe. He went back and looked at the trailer with the horses. He stared inside and saw the white horses. I think it was at that time the patrolman was finally convinced we were legitimate!

"Go on," he yelled to me. "Have a safe trip!"

When the patrolman left, one of the girls yelled at me.

"Hey, Jim! If he had found a red light in the bunkhouse trailer we would have been in big, big trouble!"

Everybody laughed. Believe it or not, at this time I was 22 or 23 years old and my wife and I are pulling horses and a bunkhouse full of beautiful women.

Ah, the American dream!

INGENUITY AT WORK

When you are young, your experience level is low. You do things 'on the fly' and the best you can. Jan and I had eight girls (young women) who were our bread and butter. We took care of them the best we could and when it came time to replace one of them, we selected girls who were more interested in horses and performing than they were in boys and partying.

It was my responsibility to be sure they had respect for Jan and me even though we were just a few years older than they were. If I was overbearing or being a little strict, they knew Jan was there and could confide in her with their concerns. She was more of a mother figure who gave them good advice.

Throughout those years we never had a serious problem with any of our girls.

Jan and I had our hands full. We were dealing with eight horses, eight girls, worn out trucks and Ward Beam. Our job also included giving a good performance at every show so we would get a good recommendation and be set for the next year's booking. We were soon used to the challenge but nothing was ever a sure thing, especially in the entertainment business.

When my brother Jack and I were running around at the horse shows, we had a friend named Dick. He married one of our good friends. Both of them had great jobs but they lived in a small farming town where things moved slowly and everybody knew everybody. Things were always in order and that was okay for them but not for Dick.

Dick went on vacation, he tracked me down and met me in one of the little towns we were traveling through. He wanted to know if he could travel with us for a couple of weeks. I said, "Sure," and that was all it took! He jumped in the passenger seat and off we went.

Our destination was Toronto, Canada. This was the same big circus we had attended the previous year. We were about 25 miles south of the Michigan state line when a weigh station came into view.

Now, I don't like weigh stations! There are too many forms, laws and different paperwork that differ from state to state and we were always traveling from state to state. I was not too worried about this weigh-in because we had already been through one weigh station in this state and they had waved me through. This time, however, the patrolman told me to pull over and bring my papers into the office. It was 10:30 at night.

"Where is your gas stamp?" he asked after looking at the documents.

I was stumped.

"Sorry, but I do not know what you are talking about," I told him.

"Well," he explained, "When you go through this state you need to have a gas stamp so you can keep track of the gas you use as you travel and go through the state."

I soon learned that at one time there was a form a driver had to send to the transportation department with a penny for every mile you had driven in the state. I did not have the stamp so I said I would buy one from the officer.

"I don't have them," he told me. "You will have to go to the nearby town. There is an office there and you can get the stamp when they open at 8 o'clock tomorrow morning."

"Oh," I told him. "Well, we'll drive there and wait."

"Sorry," he informed me, "You can't drive those vehicles anywhere unless you have the stamp and the only place to get it is in town."

"We have horses in our trailer," I told him bluntly, "And we need to unload them because they cannot stay in there for that length of time."

He thought about that for a minute and then said, "There is a county fairgrounds located about five miles down the road. I'll let you go there to unload the horses and wait until the office opens."

"How do I get to the town where the stamp office is located if I am at the fairgrounds and can't drive my truck?" I asked.

"Your truck is legal," he told me, "But the trailer is not. Just unhook the trailer, drive your pickup into town and get your stamps."

Dick, my friend, was standing near me and listening to all of this. We went outside and headed for the truck.

"What if we don't go to the fairgrounds and just keep on going?" I asked him.

Dick said, "You can, but that guy said if you get stopped again you will be arrested."

We both knew that Toronto was a long drive away and if we were going to make it we did not have time for being arrested, seeing a judge and paying a fine.

I decided to head for the fairgrounds. As we pulled in, I looked in my mirror and could see a pair of headlights following us way back down the road. We parked and sure enough, a state patrol car rolled past our location.

We were now 15 miles from the Michigan state line. Once across that boundary we would be legal and not have to worry about anything. But should we take the chance?

"Look, Dick," I told him, "We cannot stay here all night and still make it to Toronto on time. We have to do something."

Dick listened like a true friend but I knew he was nervous. He had only smoked 6 or 7 cigarettes all day but he was going at them now! There was another trailer at the fairgrounds. It had an elephant painted on the side and we saw the owner had the elephants out of the trailer and tied to a walking post.

I decided to talk to the owner of the elephants. That ingenuity thing was at work again.

"I have a problem," I told him, "And I was wondering if you would be willing to hook up your truck to my trailer and drive it 15 or 20 miles to Michigan. The law says my truck is legal but not if I have the trailer attached. I'll pay you $50 to get my trailer to Michigan."

He stared at me for a few seconds and said, "Sure, why not? I got nothing else to do and it will be a quick $50."

I thanked him and went back to my truck and told Dick what I wanted to do.

Dick began smoking a little faster. The man with the elephants came and hooked up my horse trailer to his truck. Dick rode with him in the truck and I followed them in my truck. Things went good for the first ten miles. We were now at a small town with one stop light and, of course, it was red. I had to stop and as I was waiting for the light to change, Dick came running up to the driver's door.

"Hey," he said as he took the cigarette out of his mouth, "You know that pink slip the cop gave you at the weigh station?"

"Yea, I got it," I replied.

"Well, this guy says he has one, too, and they sent him to the fairgrounds as well!"

I nodded and noticed that Dick was extremely nervous. He had a cigarette burning but he went ahead and lit up another cigarette. Now he had two of them going at the same time!

A policeman was driving by and saw the gathering. He stopped, came over to the truck and asked if anything was wrong. I told him we were fine, just talking. He smiled, went back to his patrol car and drove off. The cop made Dick even more nervous. He managed to go back to the elephant man and we managed to cross the state line. We unhooked the trailer from his truck, I paid him and he returned to his elephants.

It should be clear sailing to Toronto but we had one more obstacle to clear: The Canadian border.

OH, CANADA

To cross the border, you need a work contract, sort of like a modern-day work visa. Mr. Dobritch had sent Ward Beam a contract for the Toronto Circus. Ward had signed it and then sent it to me. I signed it and sent a copy to Dobritch, keeping a copy for myself to use when we got to the Canadian border. With the contract, I would need to be bonded and a few other items that I was sure had been completed by Ward. This was the usual way things were done.

We arrived at the border parking lot (called a 'holding lot') and I went inside to take care of the paperwork. I had the work contract, the health papers for the horses and my bond papers. They looked things over and told me the bond papers were not in their files.

"You will have to go to the bond office and pay $25," the man told me.

I shook my head. Somebody (Ward Beam) had not done their job. I paid the money and we were soon in Canada. After all the worrying I did, it was amazing that it only cost me $75 to get there! We were here and things were okay.

Or were they?

THE TORTOISE WINS THE RACE

We pulled into the Toronto Exhibition Grounds and headed for the circus area. This area was closed to the public so only the performers were allowed to be here.

"Hi," I told the gate guard, "Can you please tell me where we are supposed to park?"

He pulled out his pad, looked at it.

"Sorry," he said politely, "But I do not have you on my list."

Well, things like this happen.

"Do you know if Mr. Dobritch is on the grounds somewhere?" I asked.

"Yes," the guard replied, "He is in the office."

I walked over to the office. We had been working together for over a year and a half so we were familiar with each other.

"Hi," I said, trying to be cordial, "Can you tell us where we are supposed to park?"

Dobritch gave me a strange look.

"What are you doing here?" he finally wanted to know.

"I have a contract to work here," I said bluntly, hoping to remind him.

He looked at me with no guilt at all and said, "No you don't."

"Ward Beam signed a contract and I signed it and I sent it to your office!"

"Yea, I know," he told me, "But we can buy more and better acts than The White Horse Troupe and we can do it cheaper. I never signed that contract so you don't have a job here."

I was getting upset but I tried to stay calm.

"Then why was I not notified?" I asked.

He shrugged and said, "Don't know. My office took care of those details."

Reluctantly, I left his office and returned to the truck.

"I think we made a big mistake," I told Jan. "I don't have a signed contract from Dobritch and Ward Beam did not notify me of any problems so I assumed the job was here."

Apparently, the mail had a hard time catching up with us and Beam had never told us there was a change in the itinerary. We now had a problem. The girls had to be paid, the horses had to be fed and we had gas and other expenses as well. There was another job for us in the states but that was nine days away and we would be living off of what we had which was not much.

There was no choice. We had to drive and that is what we did. The troupe made it and we managed to survive. There were lessons to be learned here and we would use them to our advantage during the rest of our entertainment career.

(They say what goes around comes around. I don't know if that is true but a few years later a casino opened in Las Vegas called "Circus Circus." They hired Mr. Dobritch to get the acts they would use. We may never know what happened but Mr. Dobritch somehow managed to get on the roof of the casino where he proceeded to fall to his death. Maybe his office forgot to notify somebody?)

Dick decided to go with us to Texas. He would help drive the trucks and that way we would not have to stop as much. We knew the roads and were only worried about one very steep, curvy hill we would have to climb but that hill was a good 15 hours away.

One of our trucks was old, very old. Sometimes, on a long, heavy pull, it would jump out of gear. You could slip it back into gear using the clutch but the clutch was slipping, too. There was no problem on a straight, level surface but hills were a different thing.

When we got to the hill, we stopped the vehicles. All of us got out and talked about what we should do, especially what to do with the old truck. The main topic was what to do if the truck stalled on the hill. It was decided that Dick would jump out and put some blocks we had under the tires to keep the truck from rolling.

"Do you want me to drive?" I asked Jan.

She was a very good truck driver but I still was going to leave it up to her.

"No, I'll be fine," she answered. "I can handle it."

"If you put it in compound low gear," I told her, "Then you won't have any problem but our top speed will only be 7 miles an hour."

She nodded. We loaded up and began our journey. Jan started out okay but she did not get enough speed to shift gears. She missed the gear but the hill was not real steep. She decided to put it in compound low and that is where we stayed for the next mile and a half. It may not seem like a long way when you are driving but try doing it at 7 miles an hour!

The gear slipped out once so Dick ended up holding the gear shift in gear. This was something he had to do because if the truck stalled on this hill, we might have never gotten it started again. The steepness of the hill and a slipping clutch would have really made it hard to get the engine started.

When you are only going 7 miles an hour, you tend to be at the head of a very long line of fellow travelers and we were! Boy what a mess that was! We had semi-trucks blowing their horns, cars with screaming drivers, air horns and a lot of angry travelers.

But we were moving! At the top of the hill we pulled off and let everyone pass. We got out of the trucks. Jan was relieved and Dick was trying to smoke two cigarettes at once, again. I did not want to look at the passing cars but there was no choice when it came to listening to them! They told me later a lot of people were 'waving' at us as they passed.

Apparently, that was the last straw. Dick never made any more trips with us. He returned home and went back to his factory job. He might have done it if I asked but I think he was perfectly content to stay at home and work in the factory.

We have been friends since childhood and he still talks about those two weeks he spent with us.

At the end of the summer, we once again had a contract for the Danbury, Connecticut, exposition. This place was always packed shoulder to shoulder with people and when we arrived, Mr. Leahy was more than pleased to see us. He considered us a perfect fit for what he had planned.

We had been discussing several options and when we finally decided what we wanted to do, I called Ward Beam and offered to sell him our half of The White Horse Troupe.'

Jan and I were ready to move on and try something else.

AN IDEA IS BORN

Ward was a little stunned at first and he declined, saying he was not interested in buying, especially if Jan and I were not a part of the act. We were still interested in something new so at the end of the Danbury contract we sold the horse truck and a couple of the horses. We kept 'the colt' and one of the Roman riding teams. We said goodbye to all of the girls, save two of them. We were going to mold what we had into one good specialty act.

Sharon, the runaway, was now a part of our family. She had developed into a terrific performer and was Roman riding very professionally. She was a great showman and there was no doubt she would be in the new act.

The other girl we kept was from Detroit, Michigan. She had exceptional balance, was a good rider and was definitely ready for an adventure. I knew we needed one more act. We could have done the six-horse hitch but a lot of people were doing that because it was a popular addition to any circus or show. We needed something new and completely different. I had an idea but it was so crazy I decided not to let Jan know until I had worked out the kinks. First off, I wanted to see if it was possible. (Yes, it was that crazy!)

We went back to Florida for the winter, staying at a friend's ranch as they had a roping arena we could use. I started riding 'the colt.' He never had a name except 'the colt' and we just left it at that.

I used a western saddle and a bit that was used in driving buggy horses. The reins were a one piece and when I dropped them they would settle on his neck. To get him to turn, I would pull on the reins and point him in the direction I wanted him to go. In no time at all he got the idea and when I pointed, he turned. To stop, I pulled on the reins and put my hands above his head.

In time 'the colt' was being ridden and I only had to use hand signals.

When I was happy with the way he performed, I went to the junkyard and bought an old junk convertible. I put it in the arena and dug holes where the tires were. This put the convertible low to the ground and at the right height for my experiment. Next, I put up a jump pole (two rods in the ground and a bar hanging between them). 'The colt' was used to jumping over the pole so I made sure the pole went across the side of the car.

I got on 'the colt' and rode him for a few minutes. Then I turned him and we headed for the car. He jumped and cleared the pole and the car by at least three feet in each direction. It was an amazing distance! He never even came close to the pole or the car!

With the way he jumped, I was sure he could jump over a car but this is the first time it had ever happened. Now I was ready to tell Jan about my plan.

When Jan heard my idea about jumping 'the colt' over a car she said it sounded good but she was not sure it could be done.

"Look," I told her, "I will finish training the horse and then if you don't think it can be done or you don't want to do it, we will scrap the idea. Oh, there is more. I am going to train the horse to come to you when he sees you."

"I don't understand what you are talking about," she told me.

"This is my idea," I explained. You will go into the arena wearing a white feather ostrich headdress and walk to the middle of the arena with the spotlight on you. Next, we turn 'the colt' loose at the entry gate and he will run around the arena like a wild stallion."

Her look did not give me confidence but I continued.

"He will see you and come to you. When he gets there, he will bow down in front of you on one knee. You will get on him and ride him around the arena in circles and figure eights with no bridle, no saddle, just hand commands."

She was still staring blankly at me. So far, the act was not very impressive.

"Then," I continued, "I drive a convertible into the arena and you and 'the colt' will jump over the car. Then you circle the arena one more time and leave through the entry gate."

Now she was getting excited.

"That sounds like a great act but do you think it can be done? We are going to be embarrassed if we have a horse running around the arena and no one can catch him. Plus, the horse will have no bridle and no saddle."

I told her, "I know what you mean but I am taking all the chances here."

She laughed at my comment. My idea was now out there and it was up to me to get 'the colt' ready for a showstopper of an act. There were three things to accomplish.

1. Ride him without a bridle
2. Teach him to jump a car
3. Have him run to Jan so she could ride him without a bridle and saddle

Yeah, that would be easy!

Jumping the car would be the easiest thing to do. He could already do that with room to spare. I just had to keep riding him without the reins and using nothing but hand signals.

He still had to be taught to identify Jan and run to her. This is done by a process called 'whip breaking.' It sounds harsh but the process I used was not mean and did not hurt the horse. I start the process in a small box stall. The horse is turned loose and you enter the closed stall and shut the door behind you. If the horse is a little nervous or scared, it works to your advantage. You have a 6-foot buggy whip with a 10-inch piece of leather on the end of the whip. As with most whips, when you flick it the end will break the sound barrier and create a loud 'snap' or 'pop' noise. The whip never touches the horse or any other object in case you are wondering.

'The colt' was a horse who was afraid of certain things. However, when you were riding him he felt safe and secure as long as you were on his back or alongside of him. In his mind, I was his buddy. When he was in the box stall, it was a different story.

I would enter the box stall and he would look away and go in a corner with his butt facing towards me. When I touched him on his rear, he would get scared and try to get away from me but there was no place to go. If he turned and tried to get away in the other direction, there was still no place to go.

Before long he would turn around and look at me. I would pet him and talk gently to him and rub his face.

If he turned and tried to get away, he would discover there was still no place to go. He would then turn his head and look at me. I would take the whip and rub him all over his body and show him there was nothing to be afraid of. I would touch his rear with the whip and say, "Come here."

He would come to me and once again I would pet him, talk to him and rub his face. Once he figured out that coming to me meant he would get a reward, he did it right away. When he stuck out his tongue and licked his lips, it meant he was looking for a friend and this was the time to reward him with a rub on the nose and neck.

This is how you start the process.

CHAPTER 18

BECOMING FRIENDS

I moved us to another pen. This time the pen was approximately 10 feet wide and 30 feet long. I would crack the whip. The sound would scare him but that is what I wanted. He was scared and confused. The horse would then come to me when I said, "Come here."

Not knowing what else to do, he would come over and I would rub his head and nose. By doing this the colt would feel safe and secure. The goal was for me to be inside his 'zone' and make him know we were 'buddies' and I was his refuge and best friend.

During this time, we would *never* give our horses a slice of apple, sugar, candy mints or anything else because that would turn them into beggars. You give them treats and they would like you only because you gave them some kind of treat. If you have been giving them treats and then you don't give them treats, the horse may decide to 'nibble' on you or give you a little 'bite' to let you know he is waiting for that treat. I never wanted a beggar for a horse so I never gave them treats.

There are certain things you notice when you turn a horse loose into a field. The first thing he does is look to see if there is another horse around. If there is, you will notice the horse will run over to the other horse and they will just stand there together. The reward is that they just want to be friends and be near each other. Dogs and other animals often do the same thing. Companionship and having a 'safe' zone is important to all living creatures.

Understand that I am not saying the 'treat' system does not work because it does, especially with animals like dogs. You can train animals to do wonderful things by using this method and if it works for you, so be it.

Jan and I never used this method. We did not feed sugar or candy to our horses. I have seen strangers come up and try to give our horses a treat and they would not take it. We did not tell the horses not to take the treat, they just did not take it from the strangers!

Our horses looked at us like good friends, companions and safe zones. It was a feeling of trust and cooperation we instilled in all our animals. We made them feel as if they were part of our 'family' (which they were!) and we tried to let them know we were part of their family, too! They never had to 'beg' for our respect. Respect was given and received (both ways) because it was earned.

This was how I trained "the colt" to come to me. He was taught that being by my side was safe and I would protect him and be his friend. It would not take long before "the colt" would hear the crack of the whip and then hear me calling out, *"Come here!"* That was his cue and he would immediately come to me and I would rub his head and his nose and play with him. I would repeat this process over and over until he understood what I wanted him to do.

You must remember that this has to be done in a small, narrow pen and not in a big round pen. Do it in a large pen and the horse will run around looking for an escape route. By running around, the horse loses his focus. His attention will not be on you and you want his undivided attention so you can train him.

After the whip training was over, Jan would take the colt to the end of a long wooden alley, turn him loose and slap him on the rump. Then she would ring a bell or make some other loud noise that would startle the horse.

That noise was my cue! I would be at the other end of this alley and when I heard the noise I would shout, *"Come here!"*

The colt would come running to me. He needed a friend and there I was, waiting for him! As soon as that colt reached me the obligatory scratching and rubbing would commence and the colt would feel safe.

The horse came to me because he knew I was happy to be with him. Companionship and safety were his and all he had to do was come to me.

If we had trained our horses with sugar cubes or treats, he would have come to me because of that and not because he wanted to be near me. Treats will get animals to do what you want them to do but that is the beginning of the begging process. When they are performing their trick, the animal is only thinking about the treat they will get when they are finished. Their focus and concentration is on the treat and not on the task at hand.

In my case, I needed the horses to concentrate on the performance and the commands we were giving him. They had to perform because they trusted us and not because they were getting a treat when we were through. These horses had to trust us just like they trusted their mother and they did not have to beg to get that trust, either!

Over time, the colt we were training would come to me whenever he heard me shout, "COME HERE!" It did not matter if there was any noise. All he had to hear was the sound of my voice.

During this time, I was still riding the horse without a bridle and using hand signals to tell him the direction I wanted him to go. I would put both hands down close to his neck and pull on the reins for him to stop. I would raise my hands, pull on the reins and then drop them on his neck. Sometimes I would have to raise the reins higher and pull but I never used the word "Whoa" or "Stop" and the horse eventually learned to stop using just these hand signals.

If the horse started galloping faster than I wanted, I would say, "Quit," and pull back on the reins slightly. Over time the horse learned to slow down when I said, "Quit," and stop when I pulled hard on the reins.

Through constant practice we got the horse to do amazing things just by using hand signals and a few exact and precise words. The horse learned to adjust his speed, turn right or left, stop, slow down, speed up and even to back up! We also taught him to kneel down on one leg so Jan could get on him in a way that it looked like he was being polite and Jan was welcomed as a friend.

Once we had all this accomplished, it was time to put everything together.

START OF THE ARENA KACHINAS

Jan was nervous about the idea of working a liberty horse but we both knew if it worked we would have a one of a kind and very beautiful act! We now had our horses, our act and most important of all, each other. It was time to go out there and make it or break it. We were now a rodeo specialty act!

The next thing we needed was a new and different name. We liked "Arena Dolls" and thought we could not improve on that name. Then Jan came up with the name, "Arena Kachinas." (Kachinas is the Indian word for dolls.) It sounded perfect as Jan was going to use the new colt in an Indian setting.

Next, we needed a name for the new colt. After much discussion, we came up with the perfect name: "White Feather" and Jan would be known as "Princess Kachina"!

We now had a name for our act and a name for our colt. All we had to do was get our wardrobe. You have to remember that we had just come from working in the circus community. In the circus, it is nothing for management to spend $5,000 just on the clothes and accessories for the headliner of the show. In addition, all the other members of the circus wore eye catching clothes, especially the women. I did not forget how much of an effect this had on the audience and when we put our show together we decided this was what we wanted to do.

For our rodeo specialty act, we wanted beautiful girls in beautiful outfits. We wanted them showing their accomplishments in Las Vegas style wardrobes. Our act had to have a unique and different look when we entered the arena. Your eyes will go to the flashiest and best-looking act and you will always remember that act. We wanted to be that act!

There was no western wear store that sold the style of clothes we needed for the Arena Kachinas. We wanted a cowboy look with a Las Vegas presentation.

We started with the Roman rider attire. Beginning at the top, we knew we needed unique hats. Our choice was the best white cowboy hats we could find.

Promotion for the Arena Kachinas

Next, we needed body suits that would not get in the way when riding Roman style, standing on the horses or doing any of the other special feature events that needed to be performed. The leotard was used by women gymnastic teams and since the gymnasts moved freely in them, the leotard seemed to be the way to go.

We started with a shiny, stretchy type of leotard material. The fabric was red with western style 'yokes' on them. These yokes were made with wide strands of rhinestones sewn to the uniform. In addition, the sleeves had cuffs that were also covered in rhinestones.

The legs of our performers were covered with flesh-colored fishnet stockings. This was the same material and style used by Las Vegas showgirls on stage in the big casinos.

We had to be very careful in the selection of our cowboy boots. We had to get something safe with a rubber or non-slip sole. Cowboy boots had a hard bottom on them and that presented us with a problem, because with hard bottom boots you cannot feel what is beneath you. We had to try something else.

Then I got hit with a brainstorm. I went to a boot maker and had him make just the tops of the boots. I did not want the bottom soles to be on the boots. At the bottom of these boot shells I wanted a strong, elastic band. Now, when the performers put on their boot shells, they would stretch the elastic over their footwear. This allowed them to wear sneakers, tennis shoes or whatever was appropriate. These shoes would give them good contact with the horses and allow them better control of their bodies. They looked like they were wearing cowboy boots but in actuality they had boot shells over tennis shoes!

Jan's wardrobe for the finale presented us with other problems. As the star of the show, she would be in an Indian outfit. Our first task was to get her an Indian headdress made of ostrich plumes. The head band was made of white soft leather with one heart shaped ruby stone in front surrounded by rhinestones. The entire ostrich plume headdress would be set into this head band. At the back of the band, two straps, one over each shoulder, would hang down. These 3-foot long straps had 10 ostrich plumes in each of them.

The headdress itself had 25-28 plumes in it. Although this may sound heavy it was not! It weighed about 2 pounds or so. (The ones we saw in the circus and in Las Vegas were four to five times as heavy, at least!) This light weight allowed Jan free movement. It was easy for her to turn her head as she rode around the arena.

In the years to come, we learned how to make our own costumes. It was not long before we started making them, saving ourselves a lot of money in the process!

We now had horses, performers, costumes and a very good act. That was fine and dandy but now we needed the most important thing of all: *jobs!*

Jan Warvell (c. 1961)

CHAPTER 19

GETTING JOBS FOR THE SEASON

January was getting close. We wanted to work the professional rodeo circuit which in those days was called R.C.A. (Rodeo Cowboys Association) since this was the best circuit. (Now known as P.R.C.A. Professional Rodeo Cowboys Association). Every year the R.C.A. had a rodeo convention. It was held in the lobby of the Brown Palace Hotel[8] in Denver, Colorado during the month of January, the same time the National Western Stock Show and Rodeo was being held. It was during this convention that the planning for the next year of rodeos was developed. This lobby, which could hold up to 100 people, was where all acts were signed, dates were verified and all the other details of making rodeos attractive and presentable to the public were finalized.

Each town or city's local rodeo organization would send a committee to hire the stock contractors. These stock contractors were the people who furnished the bucking bulls, wild horses and other livestock for the rodeos. The committee, usually 2-4 people, would also hire the rodeo specialty acts such as the bull fighting clowns, trick riders or any other act that would be entertaining. All with the hope of bringing in people to see one of the greatest sports on earth!

On most occasions it was the committee that hired the acts but sometimes the stock contractors would hire the specialty acts. You had to be aware of this because if you were a specialty act, you needed the attention of the committee and/or the stock contractor.

---

8 The Historic Brown Palace Hotel in Denver, Colorado is the second longest operating hotel in Denver. Built in 1892, it was the first atrium-style hotel. It has a rich history of guests ranging from Presidents to Hollywood stars.

We had worked circuses for the past couple of years and had an act that fit their requirements. Now we had to switch from the circus environment to the rodeo world. Our act was now designed for the rodeo circuit. Before, we had Ward Beam as our agent but now we were on our own!

One problem we had was our act was new and no one had seen it. Many knew of our reputation when we worked with the circus and they 'assumed' we were still a circus act which we were not!

This was going to be a hard sell! As they say, talk is cheap and all I had was a lot of talk, a few pictures taken in a practice arena (with no people in the stands) and a lot of hope. It was very frustrating. The people of the committee asked us if we could show them our act while one of their representatives watched us. That was not possible!

The first year we had problems trying to talk in private to people who we hoped would hire our specialty act for the season. All the other acts were after the same thing we were after (a contract!), so we got interrupted on several occasions.

Back then, acts would carry around a photo album with pictures of their act. They had no problem interrupting your conversation or your business deal. They then would show the promoter their album. This was a cutthroat business and you had to be ready for anything!

The R.C.A. convention ran for three days. After the convention was over, the big National Western Stock Show and Rodeo began. It seemed to be the rodeo to work especially since a lot of rodeo people were already in town. It was also one of the three biggest rodeos in the United States and only the top acts worked this rodeo. If you could work this one, then next year you could work a high volume of rodeos based on this job alone. This was our target as everyone at the convention would see your act live and in person.

I talked to the man in charge of hiring the specialty acts for the National Western Stock Show and Rodeo, Willard Simms, and he told me he had never seen one of our acts, but he would try to go to a rodeo where the Arena Kachinas were performing. After he saw the act, we could talk about the possibility of working the National Western Stock Show and Rodeo in Denver. I did not get a commitment, but at least I had gotten acquainted with the man in charge. That was the first step and we had taken it!

By the time the R.C.A. convention was over in Denver you would have your best dates lined up. If you did not get a lot of work you could kiss the rest of the rodeo year goodbye! It would be feathers and not chicken for you!

I do not blame the committees for not hiring us. They did not want to hire a new act they had never seen and then take the chance that it would turn out to be a terrible act in front of a huge rodeo audience. They would have to go home with egg on their face and a loss of reputation to boot!

Jan and I got only four weeks booked for the year. It was not what we wanted but it was a start, so we left Denver very satisfied with our accomplishments. Now it was time to hit some Fair conventions and try to negotiate with the promoters of the Shrine Circus.

We got lucky with one of the most popular stock producers. We were hired to do a few jobs and we only got them because of an agent who handled TV stars and big-name personalities!

This man had worked with Ward Beam and had seen us when we had The White Horse Troupe. Thankfully, he put in a good word with the stock producer that did the biggest indoor and outdoor rodeos in the entire United States!

The stock producer's name was Lynn Beutler and he hired almost all the people that worked his rodeos. He had an excellent record and he produced what was acclaimed as the best rodeos in the states.

Mr. Beutler was one of the few rodeo stock producers that would hire specialty acts for his own 20-week tour. He hired us for one show. It was the last rodeo of the season in Roswell, New Mexico. During the rodeo week, the rodeo would draw up to 20,000 people and we could not wait to showcase everything we had! We now had a job for the end of the year that could make or break us. The Arena Kachinas now had a good job. What more could you ask for?

I also got us a contract to work the one-day rodeo in Los Angeles, California. It was in the Los Angeles Sports Stadium and was sponsored by the Sheriff's Department of Los Angeles. This stadium was actually a football stadium with a cinder track around the outside of the field. They usually sold out because who is not going to buy a ticket from the Sheriff's department?

The idea was to get the acts as close to the people in the stands as possible. We knew the promoter who was in charge of the rodeo. He had worked the Tom Packs Circus in St. Louis, Missouri. He thought it would be a good idea to use the cinder track for our Roman Riding. This would get us close to the audience. He thought the Roman Riding would be a success but he was not sure about the untested Arena Kachinas. I guess you can't blame him but we were excited to get the job!

The rodeo was early in the year and it was the biggest one-day rodeo in the United States. Just like before with The White Horse Troupe and the Tom Packs Circus our first rodeo performance would be in front of 60,000 people or more.

The pressure was on us once more. It was another make it or break it moment.

We left Denver and went back to our campgrounds in Florida. We knew we had to generate more work. Thankfully, when we were with The White Horse Troupe we had developed a lot of contacts.

When we got settled, I called Mr. Leahy in Danbury, Connecticut. He was satisfied with our work in the past and, sight unseen, he gave us a job for that year.

We also got a call from the producers of the Society Horse Show at the State Fair in Springfield, Illinois. It turned out the agent who helped us get the rodeo in Roswell put in a good word with the Springfield planners who then called us. After some discussion and a sales-pitch they sent us a contract for their fair.

This was our first Big Society Horse Show and the engagement turned out to be very good for us. From this showcase we booked "The Kentucky," billed as the "World Championship Horse Show." From there we went to New Orleans and then to the Alabama Society Horse Show. We also got some winter dates for the Shrine Circus.

After all of this, we had a variety of performances on our resume. We also developed some great connections to most all kinds of outdoor entertainment venues in the United States.

In the middle part of the year, I got a message from Mr. Willard Simms who was in charge of the National Western Stock Show in Denver. He was offering us a job to perform in the Stock Show after the R.C.A. convention next year! Through several phone conversations we took the job and hammered out a contract!

Now we had booked the best rodeo job for the next year. Anyone who worked this rodeo would be in high demand and we were very excited! During the year we also did a few small rodeos. Among them was the winter Detroit, Michigan Circus. We had worked this event in the past when we had The White Horse Troupe.

We were now booked for 10 weeks. It was not as much as we had hoped to get but we had a variety of places to showcase our new acts. We could smell the chicken but we were still looking at feathers!

This year would determine our future so we had to be ready to outperform our competition. We could also not afford to make a mistake since we had no idea who would be in the audience. If we were good and impressed the right people we might get more bookings. If we messed up, we would lose whatever good we had accumulated. The pressure was still on and we felt it!

SHOWTIME

Early in the spring we made our way to California for our first show. Our act was simple but untested. I would turn White Feather loose at the gate to the arena with 60,000+ people watching. The horse had no bridle and was supposed to run free and wild through the stadium. Jan would stand in the middle of the arena dressed in an Indian Princess costume. The 'wild' horse would run all over the place! After a minute or two of 'running wild,' the horse would see Jan and then run to her, kneel down on one leg and allow Jan to get on its back.

Jan would then use her hand commands to get the horse to gallop in a circle, do figure eights and then, for the finale, jump over a convertible car. All of this is done with hand commands and no saddle. Jan was a master at it! Before we went into the arena, however, we were treated to a great surprise!

The act we followed was a guest star brought in from Hollywood. Her name was Lucille Ball! Yep, that's right! It was Lucy herself!

The entrance to the rodeo arena was blocked from the audience's view. They could not see anything until the gate was opened and the act rode into view. The producer told us we would be following Lucy and she would be in the arena about 5-10 minutes. We were to be ready for a quick entrance.

We stood and waited behind the back drop that led to the arena. Jan was in her beautiful Princess Kachina wardrobe and I was holding White Feather.

Lucy walked by us just before entering the arena. She stopped and commented on Jan's outfit. She really liked the ostrich plume headdress. Then Lucy walked over and asked if she could touch White Feather. I nodded.

"This is a beautiful horse," she said to me.

I stood there and all I could say was, "Thanks!"

She nodded, turned and walked into the arena. The crowd went wild with cheers and applause.

I stood there thinking, I must be crazy! We are about to follow Lucille Ball, a well-known and well-loved movie and TV actress, with an act that has never been seen before and we are going to do it in front of thousands of people!

I wanted to run but it was too late. Our Roman Riding act was at the first part of the rodeo and the Arena Kachinas were a smashing success!

We felt good about that but now it was time for the main event of our act: Princess Kachina and White Feather.

We waited and soon Princess Kachina (Jan) was introduced. She walked stately to the middle of the arena. It was now time to turn White Feather loose and hope he did what he had been trained to do. He ran into the arena and acted like a wild stallion, running all over the place. He had his tail over his back and when the crowd saw him they all started to clap their hands and cheer. This was all new to White Feather. He had been in front of thousands of people before but this was 60,000 people who were producing noise, a lot of noise!

I watched as he ran faster and faster around the arena. I could tell he was scared. Then he saw Jan and he knew she was his friend and safe zone. He made a bee line for her. When he got to her Jan asked White Feather to kneel down onto one knee. Like so many times during our practice sessions, he gracefully knelt down and Jan deftly got on his back. She gave him the proper hand commands and they rode around the arena (she is doing this without a bridle and saddle!).

The convertible was driven to the middle of the arena. Jan then rode White Feather up to the car and let him look at it. She turned him around and they rode away from the car for approximately 100 feet or so. She turned him around once more so they were facing the car. By now the audience knew what was coming and they were looking on in great anticipation.

Jan and White Feather began their race to the car. That horse knew what he had to do and he went over that car with a style that showed what he was made of! It was as if he was that 2-year old colt back at the Harrisburg National Horse Show! He was amazing!

The cheers of the crowd told us we had stumbled onto something special, very special! They rode out of the arena to thunderous cheers and a steady stream of applause. It was a good day!

We were soon back at the stalls. Jan had a huge smile on her face and tears were coming down her cheeks. I was not much better off but they were tears of happiness. The pressure was finally off of us.

The performance was over and it was a big success. People came back to the stalls to congratulate us, especially Jan who had done all the work! Many wanted to check out our liberty horse, White Feather. This was a first for us and we got a lot of comments on how quiet and gentle White Feather was. He stood still as many of our visitors reached out to touch and pet the star of our performance. He had seemed like a dangerous, wild stallion running wild but now he was the peaceful horse who was the center of attention.

MONTIE MONTANA, SR.

Finally, the big day was over for the Los Angeles Rodeo. We now had a week of no work. I had talked to several people in hopes of finding a place to camp with all our equipment and horses. No one could give me a good location. Our next show was in Texas, almost 1500 miles away. It would be nice to stay in California and rest for a couple of days in the mild weather before making that long, hot trip.

At this time, most of the television shows were westerns. There was Gunsmoke, The Rifleman, Have Gun Will Travel, Maverick, Roy Rogers and Dale Evans, The Deputy and many more. The producers of these shows often hired props such as horses, wagons, stand-ins and other cowboy items they needed for their scenes. These props were usually hired from different 'stables' that handled these items. Liberty horses were always a hot item and White Feather got some attention on this particular night.

I did not know anything about the movie rental business, especially for the Roy Rogers TV show. I always thought that Roy took his horse Trigger with him and trained him. I soon learned that is not the way things worked!

At the time, there were two men who trained and owned many of the extra items (especially horses) used in the shows. They also owned 'stables' that contained just about everything you needed to make a western movie or television show. To say they competed with each other would be a severe understatement!

Both of them came back to the stable area where we were. They wanted to see White Feather. I met them and discovered they were two of the most popular horse trainers in the entire film industry! If you were in the horse training business, they told me, then California was the place to be.

They had just seen a well-trained horse act wild, kneel down, take on a rider and then jump over a convertible car. Both of them asked us to stay at their movie stable location. Life can be really funny! It is amazing what five minutes can do. Jan and I felt it would have been very entertaining to stay at their movie stables but things were happening quickly.

While we were getting ready for our performance, we had been talking to Montie Montana Sr., a well-known trick roper and a western personality. After the show, he found me and offered us a refuge.

"Why don't you guys come to a rodeo arena and fairgrounds near my ranch?" he asked. "They shoot a lot of commercials and do film work there. At least you will have a place to stay before your trip."

Needless to say, we took him up on his offer! Like I said, it is amazing how life can change after only five minutes! First, we had no place to stay and now we had a choice of three places.

The next day we headed for Montie's fairgrounds in Van Nuys, California, just north of Beverly Hills. As we pulled in, there was a guard at the gate. We identified ourselves and he said they were expecting us.

The guard told us we could use some empty horse corrals but first we had to park in a certain location. It seems they were shooting a television commercial on the grounds and we had to stay away. He took us to the rodeo arena fence. It looked good to me especially since we had no other place to go! We took the horses out and tied them to the side of the trailer. This was not a problem since we often tied the horses to the side of the trailer before performances. Then we waited.

After the commercial work was done we were allowed to put the horses into the empty corrals so they could run and let out some energy. About an hour later three buses loaded with people arrived. They were dressed in cowboy hats, western attire and scarves. It looked like a square dance party was about to begin. Jan and I thought it might be a family reunion or maybe even a hog roast but there were no picnic tables or fire pits.

The bus people were soon directed to the empty grandstand where they took their seats. Someone went to the front of them and directed all of them to crowd down to one end of the seats. They were squeezed closer and closer until the man was satisfied.

This man had two sticks. One had a green flag and the other had a red flag. He looked like one of those guys you see at road construction sites. They wave this way and then that way and you have no choice but to follow their directions. The people in the grandstand were in the same boat as those drivers on the road!

Once he had the people where he wanted them, the man gave them instructions to show different kinds of emotions. To start, when he raised the red flag they were to, "Ooh," and, "Ahh," until he told them to stop. When he raised the green flag the crowd was to clap their hands and cheer. After 15 minutes this 'director' had the crowd making all kinds of different noises. He would tell them what to do and they would do it with no questions asked.

After watching this for a few minutes, Jan and I finally figured it out. These people were what the movie business called 'extras.' They would appear in different TV shows and movies doing whatever the script wanted them to do. Some of these people would be paid a small amount while others just did it for free because they wanted to be in the movies. All of them must have gotten a thrill each time they saw themselves or their friends walking in a crowd on T.V. or in a film.

Needless to say, the afternoon was an interesting one! Besides watching the grandstand show, Montie did some great rope tricks and there was even a man who was dragged by a horse because his foot was caught in the stirrup of the saddle! It looked like he was in trouble but there was a small rope, unseen by the camera and the audience in the dragging man's hand. After he passed the camera and the scene was over, he pulled the rope and released a device that allowed him to break free and roll away from the horse.

In real life, it seemed simple but on the screen (movie or TV) it looked like a man being dragged to his death! Of course, the stunt man knew what he was doing and survived, unhurt and ready to reshoot the scene if necessary.

Yep, we were in Hollywood!

All of this (and more) made for a few very interesting days. Watching made us realize that what you think you see is not necessarily what you are really seeing. But again, that's Hollywood!

Life was now a little easier for us. We had worked our first big show and it was a smashing success! We now felt confident about the Arena Kachinas and White Feather. We enjoyed our time at Montie's place but we soon had to fulfill our contract so we headed for Texas.

THE LAST RODEO OF THE YEAR

The weeks rolled by and we continued to work the circus and rodeo circuit as we had promised. We did have one very important rodeo to work and it was soon upon us.

The Roswell Rodeo was the last stop. Lynn Beutler usually hired people for all of his rodeos (25-30 weeks of work) but he had only hired us for the last one. Roswell was a small town of about 12,000 people. The grandstand could only seat 5,000 people but it was packed to standing room only every night of the 4-day event! The arena was in ranch country and was the biggest and most anticipated event of the year. The fans got their money's worth because Beutler did have the best rodeos so obviously he had to hire the best talent.

We knew if we did well at this last rodeo our future would be secure in booking our specialty acts. Jan and I were excited to work this New Mexico rodeo, one of New Mexico's oldest and best. There would be a lot of talent scouts at this rodeo and, once again, the pressure was on us to do good.

We arrived at 3 AM not knowing where the rodeo grounds were located. We stopped and asked for directions. Thankfully, we got good directions and did not get stuck going the wrong way down a one-way street with trucks and trailers. It was pitch black when we arrived at the fairgrounds. We spotted the grandstand in our headlights and drove by it. We then saw the pens holding the bucking stock but they were empty.

There was no way we were going to put our horses in those pens since we did not know when the bucking stock would arrive or be released into those pens. We could tell this was a ranch-type rodeo arrangement. There were no barns for the horses and many of the participants had just tied their horses to their trailers.

We discussed the situation and in the end Jan and I decided to park next to the pens and leave the horses in the trailers where they would be safe and under our full control. The horses could rest and when it was daylight we would find a safe place to park or at least ask someone where we could park.

It was in the early fall and the weather was just perfect. Jan and I laid down to get a few hours of sleep. Since the night was so nice, we opened the windows and let the cool breeze take us away to dreamland.

Before we could even try to sleep we were hit with an odor, a real strong odor! The odor soon got to us so Jan got up and closed the windows. We did not have the cool breeze anymore but we still had that odor! We tried covering our heads with a blanket but we could not get away from the odor! Still, we tried to rest as much as possible until the morning sun made sure we were wide awake.

Jan was the first one up. She went to the trailer door and looked out onto our new surroundings. All of a sudden, she started to laugh.

"Hey, what's so funny?" I asked her.

She could not answer because she was laughing so hard. I dragged myself over to the window and what I saw filled in all the missing pieces!

It seemed I had parked the vehicles as close as possible next to a pipe holding corral. These are fenced in areas designed to hold animals until you were ready for them to go where you want them to go. I parked here because I was hoping to stay out of the way when things got hectic in the morning. What I did not see was the pen next to the pen where we had parked. That pen had about 30 goats in it. Among this group were five Billy goats and if you have ever been around Billy goats then you know they have an odor as strong and as bad as any skunk you will ever find. It is a different kind of smell but it is not good, not good at all!

After Jan and I got ready to sleep, the goats came through the pen area and the Billy goats came with them! They were probably using our trailers as a windbreak because they were sleeping not six feet from us. Jan and I were, for all intents and purposes, sleeping in the middle of a goat herd!

Wow! I quickly remembered why I worked with horses and not with goats!

We later found that one of the local cowboys was using the goats to train his horse. He would put one of them in the rodeo arena and follow it around until the young horse got the idea. A goat was worth around $7-8 dollars as opposed to a calf which was worth between $40-50. This cowboy would bring them to the fairgrounds this time of year and we just happened to be their babysitters for the night.

This was just another private joke that Jan and I would have. It would often bring a laugh whenever an 'odor' appeared or we saw goats. It was kind of like the old grapefruit story. Sometimes the problems in life are some of the things you laugh and joke about later in life. You can always remember them and laugh about them later but at the time…

At 10 AM the boss man showed up and gave us directions as to where we should park our trailer. He showed us where we could keep the horses and, best of all, he gave us a copy of the program. We had two acts to perform and it was nice to know when we were supposed to do them.

During the time we worked in the circus (especially the Shrine Circus), we used flashy costumes and a good musical score was also helpful in getting the crowd involved. It was a lesson I learned and used in our new act.

I had hired a good musical conductor and had him write a musical score that fit perfectly into our act. Each member of the band had his own book. The trumpet player, the drummer, all of them had an exact script to follow. I was concerned that with over 15 books and over 15 musicians there would be problems. I can't read music and know nothing about it except that I like to listen to it.

Our acts (Arena Kachinas and Princess Kachina) required at least 30-40 minutes between them. Besides the timing we also needed to be sure our music coincided with our acts. When I told the boss man in Roswell we would like to have our own music played he did not seem overjoyed at first.

"Oh, don't worry about that," he told me, "Our band and organist play a regular set of music and all the acts like it."

"I understand that," I replied, "But we have our own music and it needs to be played during the act."

He was still not sure. I gave him a couple of the notebooks and waited.

It was not until he saw the score that he changed his mind.

"Where did you get this music?" he asked me.

"I have been working with professional musicians and writers," I told him.

He looked over the books once more and was impressed.

"Yea, we can do this with no problem. Just tell the conductor to be sure it is okay with him."

(I did not mention anything about getting the idea or the music from our time in the circus because western people, especially rodeo people, did not like circus people at this time.)

To help things go smoothly, I got the conductor's name, found him and introduced myself to him. My biggest fear was the conductor would ask me musical questions and I would not be able to answer them. The conductor who wrote the score, said there was no problem and it would work at all the places we visited. For instance, if there was no drummer or trumpet player, then the rest of the musicians, no matter how many were there, had a notebook to follow.

It worked like a charm.

"I have a musical score that we need for our act," I told him.

He looked at me and smiled.

"Don't you worry none," he said bluntly. "I already have music for your act. It is good music, too. No one has ever complained about it and I use it all the time so don't you worry."

Worry? This was exactly what I thought would happen and what I did not want to happen. I had to set him straight.

"I appreciate that," I said politely, "But I would like to have my music played during our act."

He was not overjoyed. This would take some selling.

"Would you at least look at it?" I asked as I held out the conductor's book.

He took the book and looked at it.

"I have a notebook for each instrument," I said, hoping it would help.

"You have others?" he asked looking at the pile I had with me.

I handed him a few of the other books and he scanned them.

"Where did you get this score?" he wanted to know.

I explained to him that they were done by a professional writer.

"We have used this score at all our other performances," I said, letting him know it was really no big deal.

He surveyed the books and I could see he was putting together the music in his head.

"This is good," he finally said. "This is very good! We can do this with ease. You will have your music."

"You know there is some tom-tom and flute music in there," I said, knowing these were not common musical items. "Will there be any problems getting that sound?"

"No, I'll be sure of that," he replied. "You know, this is the best musical score any cowboy has ever handed me. I am impressed!"

I gave a huge sigh of relief!

Daytime rolled into the night and it was soon time for us to perform once more. This was another tension-filled evening. The man who ran this rodeo was our ticket to future bookings provided there were no errors. We needed his approval since he could open doors in all sorts of venues!

The Arena Kachinas performed first and they were perfect! They looked great and made no mistakes.

Jan and White Feather went on 40 minutes later. I worried about the music being there when we wanted it but the band was terrific and the music was played exactly where it needed to be. As for our finale, it, too, went off without a hitch! The pressure was off once more and we were more than happy!

After the show, I found the band conductor and congratulated him on an excellent performance. He was all smiles and very happy that the music matched the act and was written to take full advantage of what was happening.

There were smiles all around in the camp that night. People were talking about all the acts and the beautiful music score for our act. We had three more performances to go and all of them went off without a hitch, much to our delight.

After the last performance, Lynn Beutler, the owner, came over to our camping area. He gave us the check for our work. He seemed pleased with what we had done but said nothing else. We were about to go back to the trailer when he stopped me.

"Say, will you be available for all my dates next year?" he asked. "There are two big rodeos that have not been fully booked and, as for the rest of them, well, trust me, I can make that happen."

"Sure," I said, not wanting to pass up a golden opportunity.

"Good," he said with a smile. "I will get you a list of the dates and times and have them delivered to you shortly."

I nodded, we shook hands and he left.

When I told Jan, she could not believe it! Heck, I could not really believe it, either. The thing we had been working for had just arrived and just like that we were booked for the whole of next year. That five-minute rule applied once more!

We soon had a list of his rodeos and the dates. He called, we accepted once more and he said he would send over the contracts.

"There is no need for contracts," I told him. "Your reputation is worth everything."

In all the years we worked for him we never signed a contract. It was all done with a shake of the hand. He had his reputation and we were creating ours!

As we imagined, once we were working for Lynn we received offers to work all sorts of rodeos in all sorts of places. America had opened up to us!

SECOND ATTEMPT AT THE R.C.A. CONVENTION IN DENVER

During the 2nd week in January we again attended the convention in Denver. Before arriving this time, I told Jan we had to do something different. We prepared early and made a brochure with pictures of all our stunts and a list of all the places we had worked. (This was the first time brochures were used to promote contract acts!) We had 500 brochures made, and before we went to the convention, we mailed out 200 of them to all of the upcoming rodeos. We also put a personal letter in each mailing letting them know we were very interested in working for them. We also told them we would see them at the Brown Palace Hotel for the convention.

While the convention was held in the Brown Palace Hotel, it was not the most affordable place to stay. The majority of the specialty acts and their agents would stay in the surrounding, much less expensive hotels. They would either walk or take a taxi back and forth each day saving their money for other things.

Jan and I made sure our acts were done with a classy appearance and lots of showmanship. We needed to carry on this type of appearance in getting our jobs lined up for the coming year. We came up with a plan and immediately put it into action. We knew it would be an expense for us, but we rented a two-room suite in the Brown Palace Hotel. One room we made into an entertainment room complete with a bar and finger food. This room had a sofa and cushy chairs for the agents.

The second room we used as a bedroom and a storage room for our personal items.

We could now make "appointments" with the rodeo committees. They would come up to our room, have a drink and we could sit and do our business without being interrupted. When our clients arrived, I would have the bar set up with snacks and all sorts of the other 'necessities' needed to close the deal. This was a good situation for us. There were no distractions or interruptions and we could get their full attention while giving them our full attention.

We would not have to deal with the lobby and all the other agents and acts looking to take away our time with the promoters. This was a completely new and innovative approach to booking contract acts such as ours and was really successful for us.

We were soon getting signed contracts for the upcoming season and by the end of the second day, we were booked for events we really wanted!

First brochure for the R.C.A. Convention

CHAPTER 20

TIME FOR A CHANGE

After that second year a rodeo producer wanted to hire us. It was so nice to tell him, "We would love to do your rodeos but we are already booked for the entire year."

You should have seen the look on his face! In the time, it takes to snap your fingers, Jan and I had the most sought-after act on the entire rodeo circuit!

Unfortunately, our expenses were still eating us up. We had hired two girls for the Arena Kachinas and had 7 or 8 horses that were also our responsibility for 12 months of the year. All of us had to eat and that was getting expensive. We also had the trucks and trailers and they needed gas, oil and an occasional repair.

We were paying the girls $250 a week each. If we made $1,000 a week, the girls got $500 and we got the other $500. It seemed the girls we had trained were making more than we were!

I had to do something. You know, when you are on the road and you sit and drive all night long, strange things go through your mind. That was how I came up with the idea of Princess Kachina and White Feather. Now I had to come up with other ideas that would keep our family afloat.

We had worked the Arena Kachinas from Salinas, California, to Cheyenne, Wyoming, to Fort Worth, Texas, and to most of the smaller rodeos in a variety of states. We disbanded the Arena Kachinas and went entirely to calling ourselves The Warvell Family. This would create more revenue for Jan and I in the face of increasing prices on just about everything.

We knew the first year after the name change would be difficult. The promoters and rodeo people knew us by one name and now we were going by another name. Thankfully, the rodeo stock producers and rodeo committees were sold on our act no matter what name we used. Our act still consisted of Princess Kachina and White Feather and they were a huge selling point.

We were offered 20 plus weeks with one stock producer. It would be enough to showcase our new acts (you need to add new things all the time) so we gladly accepted the offer.

We met Harry Vold the next year. He was a Canadian rodeo producer and he wanted to hire us for his Canadian rodeos. He later moved to Colorado and became one of the biggest rodeo producers in the United States.

You have to understand how rodeos and shows work. For instance, we worked the Society Horse Show and based on our performances we got even more work. When you are at the big rodeos or something as important as the Society Horse Show, important people attend these big events and your act will stick in their mind. Just like reruns on TV, no one wants to see the same show twice so, for the next year, the producers may want to hire new or different specialty acts. We were so well received they hired us for two years in a row before we had to change the act.

A lot of circus promoters liked to hire you for 4 or 5 years in a row with several different acts working at the same time. This made it very difficult for the audiences to see and watch all the entertainment at once. This way no one really had to change their act. What I am saying is, you had to have a good specialty act but variety and change were always well accepted.

Once I figured it out, I told Jan my idea. I would do comedy work on two little white ponies. At the end of the year we could quit The Arena Kachinas (saving money on the girls and on the horses) and keep Jan's routine. We would bill ourselves as The Warvell Family.

We had to do something because by now we had two daughters. One was three and half and the other was twelve.

It was a big gamble because The Arena Kachinas were still popular and in demand. Jan and I were now well-known in the rodeo circuit and our reputations had been established. We might lose The Arena Kachinas but we still had the equally as popular Jan and White Feather act. Then, too, there would be my new act to help us out. We fulfilled our contracts for the year and spent the winter in Weatherford, Texas. We practiced and worked on the new acts.

The second week of January we again attended the convention in Denver.

We did not have many pictures of our new act, The Warvell Family, but I made the rounds anyway. Our reputation was important and I used that, too.

I did a lot of talking to people we knew from the years gone by. Our past record was worth its weight in gold and we walked out of there with 18-20 weeks of work. Many people hired us because we had produced for them in the past.

We now had jobs with a new act and a new name. The pressure was on us once more and we were in a position to make some money because we did not have the expenses like we did with The White Horse Troupe or with The Arena Kachinas.

The Warvell Family could do what they wanted to do, get paid for it and actually make some money.

We still had the Roman Riding. This was something Jan could do and I had also mastered this skill. What concerned me was putting together a comedy act that was different from what the people had seen in the past. We had watched circus acts and witnessed the best comedy they had to offer. Unfortunately, most of these acts did not involve horses!

I once saw a high wire act that worked very well and was a crowd pleaser. A man posed as a newspaper photographer and climbed to the top of the high wire pole. He took a picture of the people in the grandstand. At first, the crowd believed he was a photographer who was actually taking pictures. He walked out onto the wire and as he did, the announcer told him to get down. The other high wire performers acted like they were trying to protect him and get him down.

It was a scary sight for the people in the grandstand. As he got further out on the wire, his camera fell! He went after it, fell but caught himself by draping one arm over the wire. He hung on and pulled himself back onto the wire. Then he ran across the wire to safety on the other side.

Of course, he was a professional high wire walker but he acted like the photographer that he wasn't. The crowd loved it and it made for a good stunt.

Jan Warvell as Princess Kachina and White Feather

After thinking about it, I decided this was the act I should do. It would be done while Jan was Roman Riding on two horses. I would pose as a newspaper reporter and photographer. I would go into the arena, with a flash camera wearing a hat with "PRESS" written on the front and take pictures of Jan and the family doing their Roman Riding act. Slowly but surely, I would become a nuisance. I would get in the way of the horses and right in the path of my family. The announcer would tell me to get out of the arena because I was putting the family in danger.

It would not be long before the audience would start to yell. Of course, I did not listen and the audience would just get more and more vocal. By that time, I would be heckling the audience and they would be heckling me. Jan would then ride by me closer than ever. I had a pair of breakaway pants on and I would slip a rope on a hook which was attached to the roman pad she was standing on.

Whoosh! She would run by and the pants would fly off my body! There I was in a suit jacket with no pants except for a pair of swimming trunks that, I hoped, looked like underwear to the crowd! The audience loved it! They laughed at me and were happy to see me leave the arena. It was not long before they all realized I was just part of the act.

Jan and Toni would continue with their Roman Riding. As they did, I would come back into the arena riding two small ponies showing the crowd that I, too, could do what they were doing, though on a smaller scale!

Actually, I was sitting on the two ponies Roman style with a leg on each side of each horse. The audience could see I was cheating again so I got a mixture of reactions. I would race around the arena one time at full speed. Then I would signal them to stop and when they did, I would somersault over their heads and land on my rear end. This sudden stop delighted the crowd! They had just had a bad experience with the 'photographer' and now they got a little revenge.

I took a lot of these 'falls' and they looked a lot worse than they were! They may have looked like accidents but they were planned, well thought out falls that did no real damage to my body.

I took five falls every performance and if we did three performances a day then I ended up taking 15 falls. I will admit that occasionally one of them would hurt but when you are young, agile and have fallen many times before it is not so bad. I did a lot of different routines and things always managed to work out for us.

For the next 5 or 6 years we worked the best rodeos in the U. S. and Canada. We worked some of the rodeo dates two years in a row and that became a hard thing to do as new acts showed up every year. People liked to see you but promoters liked to keep the acts fresh and different for their audiences. We needed a new and different 'never seen us before' venue. Once again, that five-minute rule applied and we got lucky, very lucky.

Warvell family in costume, ready to perform (c. 1960s)

The Warvell Family: Jan, Toni, Sonna, and Jim.
Practice arena, Texas (c. 1960s)

Toni and Sonna performing

CHAPTER 21

We finished doing the Los Angeles Rodeo and our contract for that year. Then we changed our name to The Warvell Family. After that we were booked solid for the next three years.

Things were going exceptionally well for us. On one occasion, we were on our way to Venita, Oklahoma, traveling through Colorado. We had just worked a rodeo and were on our way to the next one.

It was about 2:30 AM when Jan, who was driving the truck behind me, blinked her headlights at me. That was our sign to find the next rest stop. When we stopped, she came up to my truck and leaned on the windowsill.

"You won't believe what I just heard," she told me.

"What's that?"

"I was listening to the radio and they said that somewhere near Venita a case of anthrax has been reported."

This was serious! Anthrax is a killer among animals.

She continued by saying, "The announcer said that any animals entering the state of Oklahoma will be quarantined and not allowed to leave the state."

We both knew the consequences of that action! There was a lot of work for us in the west and southern states so we could not take a chance and cross the state line of Oklahoma. Jan's parents lived on a corner of the land we owned in the state of Texas. We told everyone if they wanted to get in touch with us to get in touch with them. We would then check in with her parents every few days to get our messages. Remember, there were no cell phones back then so we had to find pay phones to keep in contact with them.

This anthrax issue created quite a problem for us. We decided to go to the next truck stop and talk things over. In the morning, we called her folks and told them our situation. We also needed to see if they had any messages for us.

They did.

Montie Montana Jr. wanted us to get in touch with him. Only then did I remember he had called before we left for the summer's work. He said he was putting together a Wild West Show in North Platte, Nebraska. It was located next to Buffalo Bill's original farm where the house and barns were still standing.

(Buffalo Bill's property was now a Nebraska tourist attraction and historical site with hundreds of visitors stopping by every day.)

At the time he asked us to join him, we were under contract to other rodeos.

We knew how Montie was and 'putting together' a show was a lot harder than 'putting on' a show. Sometimes he could go overboard and we just let this go because he was in the planning stage and we were in the 'putting on' stage.

THE QUARANTINE EFFECT

With the quarantine now in effect, our rodeo and show dates were cancelled. We had no more work until the State Fair in Albuquerque, New Mexico. That would not happen until the fall season. This was the big rodeo where Lynn Beutler had booked us. They were featuring The Warvell Family with special guest star Charlie Pride, one of the hottest country singers at the time.

Other than this fair, we had no place to work or to camp. I called Montie, Jr., and he was happy to hear from us.

"How much work did you lose because of the quarantine?" he asked.

"We lost a lot of work," I told him.

"Sorry to hear that," he replied. "So, what are your plans?"

"Well," I said slowly, "We are in Colorado now with no work and no place to even camp."

"Where in Colorado are you?"

"About 200 miles from North Platte, Nebraska," I answered.

"Great," he quickly answered! "Come to North Platte. We have a place you can park your Airstream and a place to keep your horses. When you get here we will sit down and talk some business."

I thanked him and hung up the phone. I went back and found Jan leaning on the truck waiting for an answer to our problems. I smiled at her.

"Get in the truck," I said happily, "We have a free place to camp up at Buffalo Bill's Ranch in North Platte. If we get going now we can be there before dark."

"What about work?" she asked.

"Montie said we will work that out when we get there."

I wanted to sound positive and put her at ease but there was still a lot of 'what ifs' in the air.

I started out in Wild West shows with Cherokee Hammond. This was the show where my brother and my buddy worked. The announcer gave us different names every time we entered the arena, making it look like they had many cowboys instead of just his three relatives and a few extras. Then I worked for shows with the likes of Milt Hinkle and, there was my time with Ward Beam and His Daredevil Auto Show and all the fair dates we did with them.

So, with all that behind me, what could Montie Montana, Jr., throw at me that I had not already seen? We were on the road once more.

NORTH PLATTE AND MONTIE, JR.

We got to North Platte when it was just getting dark. I could see a lot of horse trailers, campers, horse-drawn wagons and buggies scattered on the property.

We found a place to park the Airstream and horse trailer. We had an awning 'roof' on each side of the horse trailer and that created shade for the horses. (Actually, it was canvas tightly tied to iron stakes driven into the ground. It was crude and simple but it worked!) This arrangement kept the horses out of the sun and rain but our biggest concern was the wind. If the wind got to over 35mph we had to take it down and put the horses in the trailer.

When we got up the next morning I was surprised to see some of the best performers I knew walking around the grounds. Montie had hired all of them to work the show he was putting together. After talking to some of them, I discovered this was the 100th Anniversary Show for Buffalo Bill and all of his accomplishments in his home state of Nebraska. His home and horse barns are a tourist attraction in the state bringing in hundreds of people who stop every day to visit. The state of Nebraska wanted to celebrate his life with a Wild West show that duplicated Buffalo Bill's original show.

Montie had gotten the contract and was putting it together. It would be the biggest Wild West show in the United States and by far the best! This was the dream of Montie Montana, Jr., and it looked like he was going to pull it off!

He had started out by putting on shows in California with talented Indians from different tribes who came from all over the United States. His other performers included stunt people, singing cowboys, horses and anyone or anything else that paid the bills. They performed in parking lots, malls and anywhere else that people would let them perform. He started small but was looking at the big time.

This event in Nebraska was a dream come true for him!

"Jan," I said as we sat in our camper, "Do you want to go with me when I discuss things with Montie?"

"No," she replied softly, "You go ahead and visit with him. We have no place to go for the next two months so maybe this will work out for us." I nodded and headed for the main office. I had not seen Montie in several years. I think the last time was at the Los Angeles Sheriff's Rodeo. It was after this show when he invited us to his house for supper.

Montie's office was now one of the rooms under the grandstand. The room was full of people working different promotions. There were several girls typing so fast they did not have time to look up at who was talking! The place was a beehive of activity and I was a little intimidated with all the people working on what was obviously a *huge* project.

As I stood there a man came up to me. "Hi, Jim," he said as we shook hands.

I looked at him and tried desperately to remember his name, much less who he was. He began to talk and even then, I could not remember anything about him. After several long and confusing moments, it dawned on me who he was!

He was a man from the Midwest who had a show with camels and a few other exotic animals. He would sometimes appear at one of Ward Beam's shows.

"Are you going to be working here?" I asked him.

"I am working the phones and promoting a few ideas to bring people into the show," he told me.

He was hustling and his words took me back to the days when I was riding bucking horses and bulls for $5 a ride and maybe making $15 in one day. Back then, my bed was the back of my pickup truck with its homemade camper that leaked whenever it rained.

For a few seconds, I thought my life was going in a circle. Then reality hit me! If I was going in a circle it was a pretty good circle. I had a beautiful wife, a talented family, a $12,000 Airstream that did not leak, horses, a horse trailer and so much more!

As I stood there among these people, the early years of my life were running through my brain. Looking around I realized there were more people in this office than there were in some of the early Wild West Shows where I had performed.

Wow!

Montie, Jr., came up to me and we greeted each other. I did not know him very well. He and I met many years ago and although Jan and I did have supper at his house one night we were not what you would call good friends. We were acquaintances and had a working relationship. He was a very positive person and if you talked to him for five minutes it was as if you had known him all your life. He was just that kind of person!

"How much time have you lost because of the quarantine?" he asked me.

"Well," I said trying to figure it out really quick, "I guess we have lost as least two months because all of our southern dates were cancelled."

"That's great," he told me in his upbeat manner! "We should sit down and do some business."

"Fine with me," I told him.

In reality, I was a little worried. I told him we were out of work for two months and he says, "That's great!" There was optimism in his voice and I waited for it to be expressed in words.

"I am going to do this show just like one of the original Buffalo Bill shows," he started out, "But we do have a problem with your act."

The axe was about to fall!

"What kind of problem?" I asked him.

I thought our act was pretty darn good!

He said, "This is a western show from way back when, and back then, they did not have any convertible cars, you know. Now, I really love White Feather jumping over that car and I definitely want that in the show. Is there any possible way we can have them jump over a wagon instead of the car? I mean, we want to keep the old west theme."

I knew this was a major change. White Feather was a great horse and would probably jump anything we wanted but with animals you just never know.

"We can have a rehearsal and see what happens," I finally told him still unsure.

"Great! How about 1 PM this afternoon?"

I mean, what could I do? I agreed and left to tell Jan and start the preparations.

Jan listened intently to the new arrangement. I was not sure what she was going to say. Finally, she answered me.

"Let's go and find a flat-bed wagon," she told me.

I asked around and one of the ranch hands told me there were a lot of wagons in the back of the barn and I could use any of them. One of them looked like an old-time buggy a doctor would use to make his house calls. We found a flat-bed wagon which seemed our best bet because there was not a lot of distance to jump.

The one big problem with this wagon were the wheels on the back. They were more forward on the body and the wheel itself looked like a major obstacle. The spokes of the wheel were dangerous and we did not want White Feather to jump and get his legs tangled up in the open area between the spokes. That would spell instant disaster.

Jan agreed this might be a problem so we decided to use heavy saddle blankets and put them over the wheels to hide both the spokes and the open area between them. When finished, the wheel would look like a solid object and White Feather would then jump over the lower area between the seat and the wheels. At least that is what we hoped would happen!

While we were surveying the buggies and wagons, a man walked up to us. He had just driven a wagon in a local commercial. He also had a 'wagon horse' that he used in the commercial. The horse had been around noise and was used to it. Things like people, equipment, flash bulbs, etc., did not bother him at all.

I asked if he would be interested in using his horse to pull the wagon into the center of the arena. Since the horse was used to distractions, we also wanted the horse to stay while we jumped our horse over the wagon.

"Are you crazy?" he shot back.

"We jump over cars almost every day," I told him with a smile.

He still did not believe us and I had to produce pictures of White Feather and Jan jumping over a white convertible.

"There's no saddle?" he asked with a surprised look.

"You are right," I answered, "There is no saddle and we do it almost every day! I only have one request."

He did not seem too happy as he asked me, "What is it?"

"I need someone to hold your horse by the lines so he does not move when our horse jumps over the wagon."

He thought about it and said, "I have a buddy who helps me all the time. He can do it."

We moved the wagon to the arena and found Montie had several Indian teepees scattered inside the arena. I assured Montie we could work around them and none of them would have to be removed. He was glad about that.

Next, we went and found the 'Buddy' who would hold the horse. I asked him and he agreed to stand there and make sure the horse did not move during the jump.

We looked around and finalized a quick plan. The wagon, driven by a man named Pete, was moved near one of the teepees. 'Buddy' would go into the teepee and wait while we started our Princess Kachina and White Feather act. When Pete drove the wagon into the arena, 'Buddy' would come out and put the heavy blankets over the rear wheels. He would then run to the front of the wagon horse and hold him to keep him calm. Our act would then go on as usual.

When we had everything ready, the next step was to find Montie, Jr. I told him we had found a horse and flat-bed wagon and would attempt the jump at 1 PM He said he would definitely be there.

CHAPTER 22

AUDITION TIME

The time finally arrived and we went to the arena. To our surprise everyone from Montie's staff to the performers were sitting in the grandstand. Jan was decked out in her beautiful ostrich plume Indian headdress. She looked amazing and to those in the stand I am sure she looked more than impressive! She smiled at me and said, "We have never had this many people for just an audition!"

Princess Kachina (Jan) walked to the middle of the arena just like we had done a hundred times before. Jan was now standing between two teepees separated by about 150 feet. When she was ready I turned White Feather loose. He ran into the arena just like a horse on the open range. As usual, he ran free with no bridle or saddle. It was an awesome sight especially to those in the grandstand.

We expected him to run free then run directly to Jan, just like he usually did. This time, however, things were different. White Feather ran into the arena and went right past the teepees. He had never seen a teepee before and his curiosity took over. He stopped and went over to one of them. He looked at it and was examining it when he saw Jan.

Now his showmanship took over! He ran over to Jan and knelt down so she could get on his back. As Jan sat on this magnificent horse our two daughters, Toni and Sonna rode into the arena dressed as two young Indian maidens. Each of our girls was riding a horse with no saddle (bareback.) They rode to one of the teepees and made their horses lay down. They sat off to one side and watched their mother perform.

Jan rode White Feather around the arena. She used nothing but hand and voice signals to ride around the teepees and our daughters. I signaled for Pete (stunt extra, part of Montie's cast) to drive the horse-drawn wagon into the arena. He parked it between the two teepees. This was usually the time when we would drive the car into the arena. Jan would then take White Feather to the car where they would both 'inspect' it. Then she would go back far enough for White Feather to get a good running speed for the jump.

Buddy (the other stunt extra, part of Montie's cast) did his part by covering the wagon wheels with blankets (for White Feather's safety), before going to the front of the wagon horse to keep him calm. So far, everything was going according to plan.

Jan walked White Feather to the wagon and they 'inspected' it. I don't know what was going through that horse's mind. There, sitting in front of him, was this funny looking object. It was certainly no car! Maybe he thought our budget had been cut but who is to say!

She turned him and they got far enough back to make their run. Then, the moment of truth arrived. Jan and White Feather began racing toward the wagon.

I could see no fear in Jan's face. All I saw was confidence in everything she did.

When I looked at White Feather's face there was also confidence. He was looking straight at the wagon. When he jumped he usually had one ear back (as if listening to Jan) and one ear was forward toward the object he was going to jump. That was the way his ears were now. It was a wonderful sight and put me at ease.

My worry was Pete. He had to hold those lines and make sure the horse and the wagon did not move.

Jan and White Feather were now at full speed and we all watched as they jumped over the wagon. The people in the stands were clapping and cheering. I was, too!

Jan, White Feather and our daughters exited the arena to congratulations and praise. When Pete drove the wagon out he, too was congratulated. There was a smile on his face. He had always wanted to be part of a stunt and now he had accomplished that goal.

Montie found us and said the act would fit in perfectly with the rest of the show. His main concern was the man sitting in the buggy as White Feather jumped over it. Montie said the man had been hanging around the place for a couple of weeks and all he talked about was getting a job as a stunt person. Montie wanted him to go away because the man had no talent and he would probably get hurt.

"I can hear him now," Montie told us. "He will be claiming the show can't go on without him and he will be demanding $300 or $400 a week for all the stunt work he is doing."

When he was done, I had to laugh.

"That's not a problem," I told him. "We can always get another driver."

"Good," he answered.

"Oh, by the way, we have another act, too."

"What is it?"

That was my cue and I proceeded to tell him about the Roman Riding act with my comedy thrown in as part of it. He listened and liked the idea.

"When can I see it?" he asked.

"We can do it in about an hour," I told him.

"I'll see you then!"

AUDITION #2

An hour later we were ready to go again. Jan and our two girls entered the arena and began their act. As they were riding around, I again posed as a local newspaper reporter and photographer. As mentioned before, the audience loved it!

But I wasn't through with them.

I would return on two of our fast ponies. I was sitting with both horses between my legs. Jan would come over and try to show me how to do Roman Riding and this would result in several falls and comedic mishaps.

Finally, Jan got me to stand up on the horses and as soon as she did the horses would take off and speed around the arena. It looked like

I could not stop them. I would then turn around and sit down on the horses. They are now racing around the arena and I am looking in the opposite direction.

Jim: Comedy Pony Act, riding as a Press Man (c. 1960s)

The finale was me stopping the horses at the end of the arena. At least that was the way it was supposed to end. This rehearsal/audition, however, did not quite end that way. So, here I am riding backwards on two fast ponies. As they are running I cannot see where we are going. The horses decided to take a different path than the one I had planned for them. They spotted an opening and headed straight for it.

The opening was not one of the arena openings, however, it was one of the teepee openings!

Someone had opened one of the large teepees by throwing the flaps to one side. The ponies saw the opening and ran right into the teepee!

This was definitely not part of the act!

Jim: Comedy Pony Act, as a Press Man, riding backwards (c. 1960s)

As I turned around for a quick peek as to where we were, I was flabbergasted! A lot of things went through my head. The first thing was I knew I had messed up. We were in the teepee before I could get control of the horses. As I looked around I noticed someone had hung an Indian headdress inside the teepee. I quickly grabbed it and put it on my head. I did not have time to tie it down so I used one hand to hold the small straps under my chin. This at least kept the headdress from falling off my head. I turned the horses around and out of the teepee we went as fast as those little ponies could go! We were barely outside the teepee before I could hear Montie yelling and laughing from the grandstand.

Good or bad, Jan, the girls and I finished the act and our second audition of the day. When we got back to our horse tent Jan was still laughing about me riding out of that teepee wearing an Indian headdress! I told her thanks and how good she was at jumping over that flat-bed wagon. She would not take any credit saying White Feather knew his job and had performed admirably. We put everything away and then decided to go and see Montie. This was necessary in the hopes we could make a contract with him to work his show for the next two months.

"No," she told me, "You go. Whatever you work out with him will be fine with me."

Jan loved riding horses and doing the acts but she did not like the contract and negotiating part of the business. To me, it was just like horse trading. You give and take until both parties are satisfied it is a good deal.

I knew I had to be careful in making this deal. The rumor was that Montie would sometimes over extend himself and he would not have enough money to pay his acts come payday.

NEGOTIATIONS

Montie's office was just like it had been the first time I walked into it. There were office staff everywhere. The first time I only knew one man in the whole room and no one even looked up when I walked in the office. This time was totally different.

This time several people were saying, "Hi, Mr. Warvell." Others were waving and smiling at me. It made me feel like I was part of the family. Montie was standing off to one side with a phone up to his ear. I discovered later this was not an unusual position for him. When he put the phone down he saw me and nodded.

"Let's go out to my pickup truck," he said motioning to the door.

I was taken aback at first but then I realized he wanted to talk in private. I followed him out to the parking lot where his truck was located.

"I really like what you and Jan do," he began. "I also like the family concept you have put into the act. I like the idea that you guys are so versatile."

"Thank you," I said.

"Most of the acts here can only do one thing," he continued, "And they won't change, saying it has worked in the past and will work now."

I nodded. He was right.

We got down to discussing our salary and he offered us half of what I had in mind.

"I think we are a little too far apart to do business," I told him.

"Well, this Wild West show has a lot of scenery changes in it," he explained. "Those scene changes require a lot of extra material, people and money. That is the best I can do."

There was only one way to get what I wanted. We either walk away and did nothing for two months (and that meant no income) or fix his problem so we could get paid more.

"Can I see a rundown of your events?" I asked.

He showed me his acts and the way he wanted to present them.

"You know," I told him as I reviewed the list, "I could work many of these events as long as it did not conflict with our family acts. That would save you some money." He liked the idea.

I also told him Jan needed time to prepare for the Princess Kachina and Roman Riding acts.

"Jan and I could ride in the opening of the show, carrying the American flag for the national anthem," I added.

"Okay," he told me, "That would be great. Can we meet back here at the pickup in about 30 minutes?"

"Sure," I told him.

We went our separate ways and half an hour later we began our second round of talks.

Jim and one of his comedy acts

Jim performing

Montie arrived with a list of different jobs he wanted to discuss. His list was pretty specific about what he wanted Jan and I to do during the show:

1. Jan and I would start the show by riding into the arena carrying the American Flag, with everyone else (the entire show!) following us. This would mean there would be about 40 horses and 40 people behind us. They would each be carrying a state flag.

2. Jan would do the Roman Riding act.
3. I would do the comedy act at a different time in the show.
4. Jan would do the Princess Kachina and White Feather act.
5. Jan and I would work on a new act. She had a fancy dressage horse doing complex movements and at the end of her routine, as they exited the arena, she would have the horse walk on its hind legs.
6. When Jan left the arena I would come into the arena looking like a local farmer. I would be pulling a big farm/work horse with a huge horse collar as if I had just removed the horse from a plow. The announcer would say this farmer wanted to show that his plow horse could do the same thing as the fancy dressage horse that had just left the arena. What they did not know was this horse was amazing! He could actually do all the dressage movements and a few other silly tricks as well. At the end of the act, Jan would come out and we would have both horses walk out of the arena on their hind legs! As it turned out, this would become a very popular part of the show.

Montie also had an act emulating a pioneer scene. He had covered wagons with pioneer people walking beside the wagons. These pioneers would be carrying their life's possessions as they searched for their final 'dream' spot. He wanted me to dress and be either Lewis or Clark, the great American explorers. I don't know which one I was, but I was one of them! I would walk out with my guns, my fur hat and the other items a famous explorer would have.

Montie did not stop there. He then had a mounted cavalry unit ride into the arena. They were fully equipped just like the cavalry of the olden days. He even had a Gatling gun mounted on a horse-drawn carriage.

I went through all of these 'wants' and knew they could work in my favor especially since the next thing we had to discuss was money and how I wanted us to be paid. We negotiated for several minutes and when both of us were satisfied, Montie had a smile on his face. His show would become a reality with some of the best acts in the business and he felt he would still make money on the deal.

Jan performing

We shook hands and I went back to the Airstream to tell Jan about the agreement. She was always okay with any deal we made as long as she could keep riding her beloved horses. This time, however, she was not sure we could do all the things Montie wanted us to do. She wanted to sit down and list all the things we were supposed to do.

The list was daunting.

We had to ride in the grand entry carrying the American flag. We would do our three acts. I would work the pioneer act. I would also drive a stagecoach. Then there was the cavalry charge (if possible) and last, but not least, our girls would do their trick riding act.

Hmm.

After we looked at the working schedule of the acts, Jan said we would be in eight different events. I understood and agreed with her. One of her main concerns was all the costume changes we would have to make.

"Remember," I told her trying to be convincing, "Montie has some of the best wardrobe people in the business and they will be working on this show.

"He has even hired Edith Head and she is one of the best when it comes to outstanding wardrobes." (Edith Head would go on to provide wardrobe designs for some of the biggest movies that came out of Hollywood. She would also win Academy Awards for those designs!)

That did not totally convince her so I continued.

"Montie also has a big tent for the costume changes. All we have to do is go in the tent and there will be people waiting with the next costume. They will help us change and then be ready for the next one. It looks like a Hollywood production.

"He has the money for the Buffalo Bill's Wild West Show and it will be used for the production of the biggest show in Nebraska."

Both of us also knew the tourists coming to this show and traveling through North Platte would bring in thousands of dollars. They estimated the grandstand would be filled or three quarters filled each and every night. This was why the budget was so huge!

We also knew Montie and how he would plan and stage these 'big budget' shows and then come up short. Still, I told her this would be a good deal because the show was supposed to last for the next three months. We would make good money and have work until our next big show which was the New Mexico State Fair featuring Charlie Pride and the Warvell Family. By staying put there would be no travel expenses and, in addition, our horse feed was free.

I think what sealed the deal was something I had in the contract. We would be working on a week to week basis for Montie and he would have to pay us IN CASH at the end of every week. That meant if we did not get paid at the end of any given week it would be our last week working for the show. We would not accept a check or an IOU. He could pay the others with a check and I would not say a word. Us, he had to pay in cash!

It was the best deal anyone in the show ever got.

SHOWTIME

Montie wanted a full, dress rehearsal to see if everything would fit. When the schedule was done even Montie said it was too 'tight' for everything to work. I did not have time to change into the military uniform for the cavalry change so that, for me, was dropped.

That was okay with me. Jan could stay with our horses and I would just do the rest of the show as outlined in our agreement. This was not something new to me. I remember being with the small family shows when I had to change hats and costumes many times to make it look like there were a lot of 'cowboys' riding and performing in the show. The only difference was in the size of the shows. This was a *huge* show and the others were small ones. The other big difference was the money. We now had a really exciting set of acts and were making good money. It was a lot better than getting paid $5 a ride!

Montie's great adventure was to have its grand opening Saturday night. He set up half price nights for Thursday and Friday nights before the grand opening. This way the show would get rehearsals and be 'polished' and ready for the full price crowds.

In addition, Saturday had to be 'polished' because Montie knew the governor of Nebraska, the press from Omaha (the state capital) and all the people from the state of Nebraska would be at Saturday's opening night. Montie wanted them to be surprised and impressed at what they saw.

We worked hard and when Saturday night rolled around, all of us were ready. The show was a hit! Everybody was happy and I must say this was the best Wild West Show I have ever seen!

Toni Warvell performing the "Hippodrome" (c. 1970s)

Toni performing the "Fender Drag" (c. 1970s)

Sonna performing the "Texas Skip" (c. 1980s)

THE BEST OF THE BEST

The crowds started out slow but, after the first month, word got out and we were having crowds of 3,000–4,000 people every performance.

Jan asked me one day why we were working so many acts when we could work just our three acts and make just as much money. She was right but there was something special about this show. I had never seen so much incredible talent as I did at this show.

We had Dick, Connie and little Tad Griffith, the best rated trick riders in the United States and maybe even in the world. In later years, Connie would be killed while doing one of her trick riding events. Tad would become a stuntman in Hollywood doing dangerous things on horseback. Tad would then turn to driving automobiles over ramps while performing dangerous wrecks. His kids would eventually become movie stars.

We also had John and Vi Brady who were the World Champion Whip-Cracking Artists. Vi was also the All-Around Australian Cowgirl and both of them had been featured on stages all over the world.

Joyce Rice was also with us. She was the baton twirling world champion from the east coast.

We had stunt people from Hollywood. One of them, Phil Spangenberger, eventually became a Hollywood consultant on western guns and old cowboy wardrobes.

The Peterson family was also in the show. They were trick riders. One of the boys, Rex, would go on to work with Glenn Randall Sr. who trained lots of horses for the western movie business. Glenn trained Roy Rogers' horse, Trigger and the horses for the original Ben Hur movie. When Glenn died, Rex took over and went on to furnish trick horses for the movie industry. He was another man that became a success after working for Montie's Buffalo Bill Wild West Show.

George and Kathy Taylor were also in the show. They were riders who were always in high demand by fairs and other shows.

FESS REYNOLDS

I cannot forget Fess Reynolds. He was a cowboy character from Electra, Texas, a little town named after one of the daughters of a man who owned the Wagner Ranch. The Wagner ranch was 40 miles wide by 60 miles long so if you were born there you had a choice to become either a cowboy/ranch hand or a worker in the oil fields. Neither one of them appealed to Fess because he wanted to get out and see the world. He had been to local rodeos and had seen the specialty acts.

Since Fess had grown up with wild animals for pets he decided to train these animals to do tricks. He had a pet coyote, a raccoon, a skunk (The skunk had been 'de-scented' of course!) and any other animal he could catch in the wild. He had a way with them and could train almost any animal! Fess would dress up as a clown and with his animals he had his own specialty act. He later became a rodeo clown.

There was one sure thing about Fess. When you saw his horse trailer you made sure not to walk up to it unless you were with him. There is a compartment on most trailers that holds saddles, bridles and other items. I have seen Fess open that door and I watched as a young bear or cheetah jumped out of the compartment! You learned to expect almost anything to come out of that trailer!

Fess had a son who was known as 'Little Brown Jug' or 'Sled.' This son would later play the role of Little Beaver in the Red Ryder movies and TV shows.

The best part about Fess and what I liked more than anything was sitting and listening to him tell his Wild West stories.

Fess had a white Brahma Bull named Frosty who weighed around 2,000 pounds. Fess would ride the bull in different parades and work him at fairs and rodeos. He treated the bull as if it was a member of the family. There was a picture that circulated in newspapers around the world with Fess sitting on Frosty in front of President Dwight D. Eisenhower's inauguration ceremony.

He once told me a story about one of his movie stunts. He said it was the one time in his life he was scared and worried about a stunt. It was a lot of money and all he had to do was have Frosty jump out of an airplane and parachute to the ground.

The stunt was possible but Fess did not want Frosty to tumble while parachuting to the ground. To make sure Frosty was safe, Fess worked with the prop people of the movie department. They developed a slide for the bull. When the airplane door was open, Frosty would simply slide out into the sky while he was in a standing position. When the chute opened, Frosty would be in a perfect upright position. He would then float to the ground.

At least that was the plan.

The producer had a camera crew in the plane and on the ground. All this was done in Arizona with a lot of flat ground. The plan was for the landing to be in an irrigated alfalfa field to provide a softer landing for what could possibly be a very confused bull!

Fess would be in the plane trying to keep the bull calm and make sure everything went off as planned. As soon as the bull was airborne, the plane would land and Fess would get in a pickup truck and rush to the landing site.

The plane with Frosty took to the sky. The door was opened and the bull was released. The plane landed and Fess was quickly in a pickup and racing to the scene.

Fess was glad things had gone as planned while in the air but all he could think about was his friend, Frosty. The money was great and because of that money Fess had put the life of his friend in danger and now he was afraid for the well-being and health of Frosty.

As he neared the landing zone, Fess could see the alfalfa and near the edge of the field he could see the white parachute blowing in the breeze. He figured this was Frosty's landing spot because there was no other 'bull' scheduled to be parachuting that day. He drove as fast as he could looking for his pet. Then, off to one side he spotted his beloved Frosty who was now grazing in the alfalfa field.

His biggest fear was the bull would land and break a leg but as he watched, Frosty walked easily as he went through the alfalfa field. Fess finally got to his bull. As he did, Fess said the bull looked at him as if to say, "What, you could not have brought me here in a trailer instead of this?" We all thought this was a lot of 'bull' but Fess swore it was true! I have since seen the movie clip of this jump several times and it still amazes me!

Years later, after Montie's show, I ran across Fess. I was ready for another of his stories.

"What have you been doing with yourself?" I asked him. "I mean, where have you been working?"

His story was amazing and reminded me how unique Fess and his training methods were. A movie producer in California had contacted him. The man had a problem and he thought Fess could help him. The company was filming in the Sonora Desert area of Arizona. There was a scene where about a dozen camels were to come over a desert hill and do a stampede. Two cameras, about 200 feet apart were to film the scene. The camels were to do the stampede between the cameras.

To make the camels run, the studio hired a stunt crew who said they could accomplish the job. Instead of 'camel wranglers' the stunt crew consisted of cowboys and horses. They tried to make the camels stampede by using the same technique as they would use with cattle. Unfortunately, they could not control the camels who became skittish and scattered in all directions!

Fact: A horse can only run full speed at approximately 35 mph before they start to slow down and that is on a racing surface, this was on a desert floor.

Fact: Camels are made to run on desert floors and they can run up to 40 mph for very long distances.

Needless to say, the horses were not going to catch the camels because they were completely outmatched! Their first attempt at wrangling the camels was a disaster.

Fess knew they were in a bind and that was why they came to him. The studio wanted to know how much he would charge to get the camels to do what they wanted them to do. He told them it would take time but the studio said it was costing them a lot of money every day they had to wait so they needed it done quickly.

"How much are you willing to pay if I work overtime on the project?" Fess asked.

"How much will it cost for your workers and helpers?" they asked.

"Put it in my cost and I will hire whatever I need," he told them.

He knew he had them and now it was just a matter of time. The producer made a few phone calls and told Fess the amount of money he would get if he could get the job done in less than eight days. Fess said he could do it in less than eight days and the deal was made.

He said it was the best paying and most satisfying job he ever had! In less than eight days Fess told them the camels were ready.

The producer got his crew and put them in position. When they were ready, Fess gave the signal to get the camels moving. Fess took his hat off and signaled for the camels to stampede. Just a few minutes after he gave the signal, the camels came running over the desert hill and they went straight through the 200-foot area between the cameras.

When they were done and the producer yelled, "Cut," everyone was astonished! The producer starting yelling and jumping up and down. He came over to Fess.

"I don't know how you did it," he yelled, "But it was perfect! *Perfect!*"

Fess was happy, too. When he got paid he did not have to work for a long time!

I was curious so I asked him how he managed to get the camels to stampede between the cameras. To me, it sounded almost impossible. Fess told me they built a corral down past where the cameras were to be placed. It was a shady spot with water and full of alfalfa for the camels to feed. It turned out alfalfa was one of the camel's favorite goodies. Fess said he kept them there for a few days.

He observed them as a group and noticed which one was the dominant, more aggressive camel. This camel was obviously the leader. He knew when you put horses or cows together there is always one who will be the boss of the group. Fess found the camel that showed these traits. It turned out the leader was the oldest of the herd. (These were not 'wild' camels and Fess knew he could ride them if he wanted).

Fess and his crew then built a regular square pen for the camels. They built it over the hill and out of sight from the other pen and the cameras. It had no shade, no water and no alfalfa.

The camels were then hauled from the 'good' pen over the hill to the 'bad' pen and locked inside overnight. The next morning, a rider got on the ring leader. Another worker opened the gate and the rider led the lead camel out of the pen. The rest of the camels were left in the pen. The rider then rode the camel to the top of the hill and toward the 'good' pen! When he was about 100 feet from the food and water, they let the remaining camels out of the pen.

The camels saw their leader trotting away from them and they immediately began to follow him over the hill and down to the corral where they drank and ate to their hearts content. If it was needed, some of the help would use firecrackers to get the camels in the corral moving.

For the next several days they hauled the camels from the good pen to the bad pen. They left them overnight and repeated the 'leader' first project the next day. This went on for several days until Fess was satisfied the camels knew what to do to.

There was a small town about 8 miles from the movie set. Most every night the cast members would go to one of the bars where they could get sandwiches and other food snacks. They could also play pool and drink at the bar. Fess also went there and one night the producer was there.

"Everything going okay with the camel training?" the producer asked.

"Yea, it's going fine," Fess told him.

The producer was nervous about the scene.

"Your time is almost up," the producer told him. "You only have four days left."

"I will try my best to be ready," Fess replied as he noticed the nervous look on the producer's face.

"We want to shoot this scene in four days."

"Fine," Fess told him. "What time?"

The producer thought for a second and then said, "The sun will be in the best position around 5 AM."

"Good," Fess said, "Bring the camera crew and it will be done!"

The producer had his crew ready and waiting for the stampede. He gave the signal to Fess who gave the signal to his crew who let the lead camel out and then the rest of the camels.

As they had been taught, the camels stampeded over the hill and headed straight for their food and water!

When it was over, the production team was ecstatic!

"How did you do that?" the producer asked.

"It's my job," Fess replied, "And if you need me again, just let me know."

I had to laugh. That was Fess!

"It was terrific money, an easy job and like I said, I did not have to work for a long, long time!" Fess repeated.

I marveled at the way Fess thought. It was genius.

CHAPTER 23

ONE SHOW ENDS, ANOTHER ONE BEGINS

Back at the Buffalo Bill's Wild West Show, Montie and I were becoming good friends. We performed for the full three months. It was a busy time. We all worked hard and had a lot of fun doing it.

The office staff put out questionnaires for the people in the grandstand. They wanted to know which acts the fans liked best. The family from Texas (aka, the Warvells!) was their usual preference! Montie never told us this but the office staff always congratulated us about being the favorite act. When the show was over, Montie knew he could depend on us to work with him.

Our next project was the State Fair of New Mexico. Montie folded his Wild West show about this time and decided to go to San Diego and do another show. He wanted us to go with him and work there but he knew we had a previous engagement. Montie said we could miss the first few days and then join the show for the weekends.

We went to New Mexico and the show went off without a hitch. As soon as it was over, we left Albuquerque and headed for San Diego as fast as we could!

Driving straight through the night we got to Montie's Wild West show late in the evening. We unloaded our horses and met George and Kathy Taylor. They had also worked in North Platte with us. George asked us if we wanted to get something to eat.

I looked and suggested we go to the Mexican restaurant across the road.

George was a great guy and he usually was ready to go along with any suggestion. This time, however, he said he did not want to have Mexican food.

The nearest other restaurant was 4 or 5 miles down the road and that was where George wanted to go. Jan and I had been driving all night and day to get here and we were both tired. I told George I understood but we would just like to walk to the Mexican place and eat there. After we had rested we would be willing to eat at the other restaurant. George understood but was not going to eat with us. The conversation ended there and the two of them left.

Jan and I ate dinner and then went to the Airstream to get some sleep. The next morning, I went out to feed the horses and discovered things were not going very good in San Diego. As always, Montie, Jr., had brought several acts with him. He was paying us in cash but everyone else was paid by check. Unfortunately, the banks were not accepting the checks and would not cash them. Montie's excuse was he had some late expenses that just 'had to be paid' and that depleted his funds. This had started while they were working in North Platte.

To alleviate the problem, Montie told them to follow him to San Diego and he would pay for all their meals, no charge to them! It turned out the crew had been eating nothing but beans and rice for breakfast, lunch and dinner and this had been going on for the past several days.

Not only had Montie not come up with the money he owed them but he had also hired new stunt people from the Los Angeles area. The times Jan and I missed were nothing but rehearsals!

The people who were in North Platte and had not been paid in over a month decided to boycott Montie's show if Montie did not pay them. I wanted to talk to my friend but could not find him. Someone said he would be back in an hour as he was having a conversation with the coliseum manager. I stayed close by the building because I wanted to catch him as soon as he was done.

As I stood there waiting, I started to reminisce about the time we were in North Platte. There were always 10-12 people in the office during the first 2-3 weeks. The typewriters and phones were humming away. Everyone was promoting the show and trying to find new and different places to work or advertise the Wild West Show.

Some of the people I easily recognized as they had worked other shows that we had worked. Montie had gone all out and hired everybody he could for North Platte.

I remember standing in the office and listening to a man on the phone as he tried to get someone to invest in the show. Investors were always welcome and they usually received a percentage of the profits from this and future shows. That was standard practice for all shows.

However, standing there gave me a new outlook. All I could see was the amount of money it took to pay all the office staff and the utilities. Montie also had the best performers of the time and they did not come cheap! We were having good crowds and that meant a lot to all of us.

But oh, those expenses!

By the time the show came to the end that summer, the office staff had been whittled down to two secretaries and a good friend of Montie's was acting as manager.

We were now working at the San Diego Coliseum and I wondered if the financial situation had changed. The show was running smoothly and, per our agreement with Montie, we were paid in cash at the end of every week. By now, I was pretty sure the finance part of the show was not going as good as Montie had conveyed and made us to believe.

One day as I stood outside of the coliseum, Montie drove up in his pickup truck.

"Get in," he said.

He seemed to be in a positive mood as I got in the truck.

"Nice to see you," he told me.

"You too and thanks," I replied. "What's going on?"

"When I left North Platte," he began, "I was overextended and had to do some negotiations with the banks and different people to whom I owed some money. We settled everything and now we have to get this show started."

"Do you have the money for the show?" I asked him.

"Well," he said, "We need money for the orchestra, the spotlight men and the coliseum management needs a down payment before we can move in and use the building. I am meeting with them right now and I think everything will be okay."

I knew none of this, but up to now, he had not missed any of my paydays (cash), he was paid up with us.

Montie had a silver tongue. He was a fun person to be around and always the life of the party. I don't know what he told the coliseum people or the people he needed to pay (spotlight, musicians, etc.) but, about three hours later, he came to our Airstream trailer and said everything was okay and ready to go.

Some people have the knack of talking themselves into situations and then being able to talk themselves out of those situations. Montie, Jr., was definitely one of those people.

SAN DIEGO

The Wild West Show started as scheduled in the San Diego Coliseum. The first night we only filled the coliseum to half its capacity. The crowd loved us and people were satisfied they had gotten their money's worth.

We all knew Montie would have to do better in the number of people who came to the show. He did not advertise as much as he should have because he did not have the 'advance' money to spend on the advertisements he needed. He was banking on word of mouth to spread the news about the show. Good compliments saying Buffalo Bill's Wild West Show was in town was all he thought it would take.

After that first night, Montie got some more investment money and he hit the airwaves. He did some radio advertisements and hoped that would help.

The second night did not get any better. The coliseum was only half full just like it was the first night. Thankfully, the crowds began to grow and gradually picked up at the end of our run.

As far as I know, the bills were paid and the performers were satisfied.

I saw Montie after the last show. The word was out that he had already booked another show but the people putting on the show were concerned about money issues and Montie was aware of it. Once more Montie and I had a conversation in his pickup truck.

He told me he had a contract with the Chamber of Commerce at a little town in California. It was just for one day but the contract was worth $5,000 if he could produce a Buffalo Bill's Wild West Show for them.

"Listen," he told me, "It's not far out of your way but there is not enough money to pay all the cast members and that is the problem."

He waited while I digested that information.

"I would like you and Jan to work the show and work as many minutes as possible. I will pay you $1,000 for the day and then I will make a deal with the rest of the performers as to how much they will be paid."

"And what are you going to make in terms of money?" I asked.

"Fulfilling the contract will be my reward," he told me but we both knew his reputation was also at stake.

"Sounds okay to me," I replied, "But I want to talk to the cast members to be sure what they are going to do and how much they are going to be paid. In addition, I want to talk to the head man at the Chamber of Commerce, the man who signed the contract."

Montie thought for a few seconds and then said, "No problem."

True to his word, he made all the arrangements. I visited with the cast to be sure we were on the same page. One of the specialty acts wanted to know why Montie was not there.

I told him I did not know.

They said it was not hard to figure out. Many of them were worried about the financial problems Montie was having. They then told me if we (The Warvells) were going to do this one-day show then they felt more assured they would get paid.

"Since he is using your name then it must be alright," they said.

I had not thought of it in those terms. Montie always stood up to his word with us. In all the years that we had worked with him, he had gotten paid and so had we. He did not owe us a dime. We all went to the one-day Wild West Show and everybody got paid. The town and the Chamber of Commerce Committee were satisfied.

This was the start of many Buffalo Bill's Wild West Shows and a situation we would be involved with for many years to come.

THE WARVELL FAMILY

JIM WARVELL

BOX 144, TELEPHONE (817) 594-7792

WEATHERFORD, TEXAS 76086

1973 RODEO SEASON

Wichita Falls, Texas....June 13, 14, 15, 16
Dallas, Texas................................July 7, 8
San Antonio, Texas........................14, 15
El Paso, Texas...........................20, 21, 22
Los Angeles, Calif. 27, 28, 29
San Francisco, Calif..............August 4, 5
Bakersfield, Calif. 10
Fresno, Calif....................................11, 12
Monterey, Calif..............................14, 15
Phoenix, Ariz. 18, 19
Tucson, Ariz.....................................25, 26
New York (Madison Square
Garden ....September 1, 9
Chicago, Illinois......................14, 15, 16
Houston, Texas..............................22, 23
Porta Rica 27, 28, 29, 30
October 1, 2, 3, 4, 5, 6, 7
Not Confirmed.......................12 thru 21
Albuquerque, N. M. 27, 28
Mexico City, Mex......November 3 thru 25

CHAPTER 24

ANTONIO AGUILAR

We were at one of our last rodeos at the end of the season in Pueblo at Colorado State Fair. It was produced by Harry Knight. While we were there, we were contacted by a man named Oscar Narvez. He was asking about our availability in working with a famous Mexican movie star/singer and horseman named Antonio Aguilar.[9]

I had heard about this particular man and his show from Fess Reynolds. Fess had said it was a great show and first class. I told Mr. Narvez that this was our last rodeo of the season. He said he had heard compliments on our work. He wanted to know if we were able to work a ten-day run at Madison Square Garden for Antonio Aguilar. I told him our price and he said he thought that was good, but the Aguilar office would send the contract.

Mr. Narvez added that he had the power to hire. We settled on a price that we would have to have to work the date he requested. We were now booked to work the Antonio Aguilar concert show and rodeo in New York at Madison Square Garden!

After making some inquiries about the Aguilar show and concert, I had nothing but good reports. In those reports, everyone said it was a good classy show. In a number of days, we were heading to New York

9 Antonio Aguilar, born in 1919, was a Mexican singer, actor, songwriter, equestrian, film producer and screen writer. During his career, he recorded over 150 albums which sold 25 million copies. He acted in over 120 films. He was given the honourable nickname of "El Charro de Mexico" (Mexico's Horseman) because he popularized the Mexican equestrian sport 'la charreria' to international audiences. He starred in *Undefeated* with John Wayne and Rock Hudson in 1969. His concerts and rodeos were internationally famous.

where we would go to the Madison Square Garden Coliseum to meet and join the Aguilar people.

When I met with Mr. Aguilar, he was working out the schedule of events for the show. I told him we had two different spots to work, the Roman Riding Act and the Princess Kachina and White Feather act. He said he wanted us to work both acts together. I told him we had to work both acts separately. He was not too happy about that. After some conversation, he said we could work in two different spots. He had never seen our act before, but talking to him after the first performance, he was happy about the two separate acts and understood why they could not be worked together.

The next night was our opening performance. Antonio Aguilar and his wife, Flor Silvestre, worked their two different presentations. Their performances were GREAT! I could see why the Antonio Aguilar show had sell-out crowds. Every night the grandstand was filled to capacity with 14,000 plus people!

Antonio had two sons that both sang. It was like our family, every member of their family participated. The younger boy was an eight-year old named Pepito. At the age of 8, he was pretty much a polished entertainer already! Today, Pepe Aguilar has followed in his father's footsteps as a famous singer and entertainer.

Antonio Aguilar was satisfied with our work. Before we left New York, he had offered us a contract to work all of his next years' show dates and venues! Over the next 18 years we had numerous engagements with Mr. Aguilar's shows.

Working at Madison Square Garden was Jan's childhood dream—and now she had realized it! It was a very proud moment to see The Warvell Family on the Madison Square Garden's Marquee! The show was GREAT! The reviews in The New York Times were very favorable to The Warvell Family. It was a phenomenal way to end the season. We were excited about the coming year being fully booked with the Antonio Aguilar Show!

We were headed to *Mexico!*

MEXICO

We were hired to go to a big month-long entertainment show at a copper-topped auditorium known as the Palacio de los Deportes (Palace of Sports, capacity of 20,000 spectators). The trip down there was a long one. We had to go through the top half of Mexico, driving through several small towns. Back then, Mexico was a safe country for travel, but there were always exceptions to the rule. We had an ace in our pocket, however! Our Boss! Antonio was so popular in Mexico, that as soon as they knew we were working for him, our safe passage was assured.

On the way, we had to travel over the Sierra Mountains. The road was extremely steep. Our truck and horse trailer with 6 horses made it up the mountain with no problem. However, on top, the view down seemed too steep for our vehicle, so we stopped at the top. Mr. Aguilar had a Recreational Vehicle and several semi-trucks carrying the stock of bulls and horses for the show. Mr. Aguilar's vehicle's brakes burned up on the way down! Luckily, we didn't try it! Les Johnson was in charge of the semi-trucks and tractor trailers. Les noticed we had not made it down the mountain so he unhooked one of the semi-trucks and went back up the mountain to find us.

We put a chain on the back of our trailer and to the front of his semi. This way he could help hold us back from losing control on the steep down-grade.

With Les Johnson's help, we were safe from having a run-away outfit! We made it fine thankfully!

We were told Antonio had a brother named Chino, but his brother did not have the claim to fame and notoriety his brother, Antonio, had. I got to be good friends with Chino when we went to Mexico. Our group traveled in a convoy of trucks, cars, horses and other assorted vehicles. At the Mexican border, Chino took the lead and helped smooth the way.

As we got deeper into Mexico, Chino stopped the convoy at a place to eat. This place might be classified as a truck stop by us but it was more of an upper scale restaurant by Mexican standards. Chino said they had good food so we decided to give it a try.

On our way to the front door, we had to walk by a sidewalk vendor who was in the process of butchering a hog for the restaurant. I could see the food this restaurant had was going to come from this vendor and be fresh, very fresh!

(We did not find out until later that this particular restaurant was not used to having American tourists, especially a convoy of them!)

We went inside. My wife, Jan, and my daughter, Sonna, (my other daughter, Toni, had left the nest), looked at the menu and each got something they recognized from the list. Since my Spanish was little to nonexistent, I had no idea what was on the menu. So, of course, I asked for Chino's suggestion.

He said I should try their tacos. Tacos sounded good. Tacos I knew. I turned and looked at the man in the street who was butchering the pig. I remembered butchering an animal when I was a kid. I also remembered everything we had to do and how good it was when the meat and the cooking were fresh.

Jan and Sonna soon had their kitchen-made tacos and they looked good. I, too, had ordered tacos but from the stand out front and now I was curious as to what part of the pig I might get when my taco arrived.

The man took my food directly off the grill and put it into a taco shell and served it to me. I have to admit, it looked pretty good so I decided to take a bite. Before I could eat it, however, Chino stopped me and recommended I put hot sauce on it, so I did. I took a big bite and began chewing. Then Chino told me it was a "blood" taco made of thick, grilled blood!

"So how do you like it?," he asked me as I struggled with keeping the bite in my mouth. It was then I noticed this first bite of the taco had taken out my taste buds. "It's good," I said reluctantly, forcing the words out through clenched teeth. It took a lot of fist clenching and perseverance, but I got that taco down!

We were close to Mexico City when we made our first stop for the night. As was our custom, we unloaded the horses and took care of them first. The troupe ended up staying in a hotel.

All of us were tired, including me, so we went to bed fairly early. My family and I were on the fourth floor.

It did not take long before it (the taco!) hit me and it (the taco!) hit me hard!

The stomach pains, chills and fever kept getting worse as the night wore on. I doubled over in pain more than once and figured if they got much worse, I would jump off the banister to feel better and remember, I was four stories up!

I struggled, but I made it through the night. The next morning, I was weak, but survived with no sympathy from either Jan or Sonna. They were more particular about their food and they knew it! From then on, I was more careful about my food, too!

Turns out, the biggest "no no" for tourists in Mexico is eating food directly from street vendors. After this episode, however, something changed with my digestive system. Now, I could eat anything I wanted from anywhere I wanted!

For the rest of the trip, if I ever got a little "cocky" about eating anything and not getting sick, Jan would say, "can I get you a taco?" It would always bring me right back to reality!

A few weeks later, we were still working with Antonio when I got the flu. I was coughing, sniffling and just feeling horrible. It was hard for me to work, but I did. Antonio's wife, Flor Silvestre, was a Mexican movie star in her own right. She heard about my problem. I was told she wanted to see me and even though I was feeling horrible, I went to her dressing room in the coliseum. She was, after all, the wife of my boss.

She met me at the door of the dressing room and I introduced myself. "Hi, I'm Jim Warvell." She looked at me, smiled and said, "drop your pants." Hmmm…what do you do when the wife of your boss, who is also a famous singer and star, tells you to drop your pants? What else can you do? You drop your pants and don't ask any questions!

I dropped my pants and, at her request, exposed my rear end to her and about 15 guests who were also in her dressing room! She immediately gave me a shot in my rear and before sending me on my way said, "There, go… Now you are family!" (She always gave the shots to her family!)

PUERTO RICO

One of our next scheduled stops with Antonio Aguilar, was Puerto Rico. We flew our, and Antonio's horses to Puerto Rico from Houston, Texas. We were going to work in one of the most beautiful places in the country, San Juan. Aguilar was a very famous and popular man in Puerto Rico. When we arrived, our horses were quartered in a fenced-in area next to the Roberto Clemente Coliseum.

If the name sounds familiar, it should. Roberto Clemente was a huge baseball star for the Pittsburgh Pirates. He was also one of, if not the most well-known man in Puerto Rico. Roberto was talented enough to sign some big, lucrative contracts and earn a lot of money playing baseball. He was a good man and gave a lot of money back to the Puerto Rican people. His humanitarian acts were known around the world.

One day, he and others loaded food, clothing and other articles onto a small private plane. These items were to be delivered to areas in need. Unfortunately, the plane was overloaded and on takeoff the plane crashed, killing Clemente and all the others on board. This stadium was just one of the many things named for one of the country's most popular and famous man.

We gave two performances every day (Sunday through Friday) and three shows on Saturday starting at 9 o'clock in the morning! Since we worked a night show on Friday, the 9 am Saturday show seemed like it was 2 o'clock in the morning to us!

These shows had one of the best announcers you could find anywhere. He spoke both English and Spanish. When he worked the arena he never missed any question the audience had. He was always ready with information on the acts performing in the show. This may not be a big deal to some people, but I remember how sharp and attentive he was during all of our performances.

The coliseum we were in would hold in the neighborhood of 9,000 to 10,000 people. It was sold out for all of our performances. Every one of them!

During the show, I did a comedy routine. At one point during my act, my team of horses would run around the arena. I would be riding them backwards (the horses faced one way and I was facing the other).

The announcer, I believe his name was George Sandoval, sat in a booth at one end of the arena. When I went past him, I would be riding backwards in a sitting position. I would see him, lay down flat on my back, yawn and pat my mouth as if I was sleepy. As he watched me go by his announcer stand, he said "it's kind of early in the morning for some of these performers." I doubt if any of the audience saw my antics, but it was impressive to me how he picked up on every little thing we did! He would watch us closely and make comments letting us know he was watching. This is what makes an announcer a truly great announcer and he was one of the truly great announcers in my book! After the first time, he saw me lay down and yawn, he told me, "I am glad you made it all the way around the arena because I thought you were going to fall asleep before you got there!"

CHAPTER 25

TIME FOR A CHANGE: INTERNATIONAL SHOWS

Our shows were great! They upped our reputation and before long we decided it was time to take our act international. This was a huge step for us!

In ten years, we had worked our way from Salinas, California on the west coast to Madison Square Garden on the east coast in New York, as well as from Canada to Mexico. We were happy, but now it was time to make yet another change.

After our Mexico City dates were finished, we called my friend Montie Montana, Jr. He was still the promoter and smooth talker we knew and loved. He could talk his way into making a deal that sounded like everyone was going to make a million dollars in no time because of him. He always lived in a dream world and a lot of people would ride that dream with him. Sometimes those dreams would not come true.

JAPAN

Montie Montana Jr. was now booking shows all over the world. He was looking for acts who would be willing to go to Japan, England, South America, Kuwait, Singapore, Canada, and of course, the United States.

We had a lot of fun during our active years in the entertainment business. We had some unusual and quite amusing encounters. Jan and I laughed at them and they still bring a laugh to the family when we talk about them.

He got a big contract in Japan so he called me. He wanted to hire us to do the show. I had to buy 40 horses for the show and then fly with them by plane, in advance to Japan. There was a quarantine for incoming animals and these animals would have to fly early enough so they could pass the Japanese Government's rules and regulations. Montie also wanted me to fly with the horses and stay with them until the rest of the cowboys and Native Americans arrived in Japan for the show.

I was supposed to buy these horses in Texas, take them to my ranch and start training them to be trick riding and team horses. We needed two Roman Riding teams and 4-matched horses to pull the stagecoach, which would go with the horses on the plane.

I needed money in advance to buy these horses. Montie realized this, so he caught a plane and flew to the Dallas-Fort Worth Airport where I met him. The first thing Montie wanted was some Mexican food! He was the boss, so we left the airport and went to one of my favorite Mexican restaurants in North Fort Worth. This area is known as Cowtown.

(Even today, Cowtown still looks much like it did in the cattle drive era. It attracts a lot of 'Northern Tourists' to witness the history of our great state.)

The place I took him looked pretty rough. It still had swinging doors and when you got inside it was a little dark. When I drove the car to the restaurant, Montie stared in disbelief.

"Is this place safe?" he asked me.

"I eat here all the time," I replied. "The food is good and it is authentic, too."

"Yea," he said with some doubt in his voice, "I bet it is!"

I parked the truck and we got out and headed for the restaurant.

"Oh, wait," Montie said after several feet, "I forgot something in the truck."

He went back to the truck while I stopped and waited for him. He came back carrying a paper sack.

"Montie, " I said quietly, "You know you don't have to bring your lunch. They have plenty of food and it's safe to eat." He laughed and we went into the restaurant.

While we ate, the two of us worked out our immediate plans for the trip. We just went over all the plans once more to be sure we had them right. It was a good meal and we both enjoyed it.

Montie had to get back to Los Angeles and his schedule was tight. As we sat there, he seemed to be nervous because he was always looking around. Montie was the kind to always laugh and tell jokes but today he was a little bit different. We were just finishing our food when I had to ask about the money I needed for the horses.

"Did you bring me a check?" I asked him.

He looked around once more and replied, "I know you like to do business in cash. So, I brought you cash." We were sitting at a table and I felt something touch my leg. I looked down and saw the paper bag he had brought in the restaurant with him.

"Your money is here in the sack," he said quietly. "There is $28,000 but I would rather you not count it while we are in here."

Suddenly, it all made sense! I now knew why he went back to the truck and got the paper bag and why he was a little nervous. I took the sack and as soon as it was in my possession, his face started to get more color into it and he began to act like himself.

Later, when I would see him with a paper sack in his hand, I always told him of a good Mexican restaurant where we could go! We would both have a good laugh!

THERE IS ALWAYS ONE

It was time for me to buy the 40 head of horses to use in the show. I had to buy a variety of horses. It was going to be a challenge but Jan and I had been doing this most of our lives.

There were a lot of horse sale barns and horse traders where we could get the horses. We let the word out as to what we needed and were soon buying horses with some of them and we even had horses brought out to our ranch. Sellers were obviously eager for us to buy.

We had a few good cowboys and young horse people who were ready to help us. All of them had hopes of going to Japan with us and working in the Wild West Show.

I kept going to horse auctions in this part of Texas because most of them had a good 150 or more horses for sale at each one. Once I had bought a horse, it was taken back to our training center where we worked with it and tried to find the right job for each horse.

I watched one particular horse go into the 'sale' ring. He was ridden bare back (no saddle) and, at the time, I did not pay attention to him because he had a good stop to him and he could turn on a dime. You could tell this horse had a lot of training in his early years. He was just five years old and showed a lot of promise.

After watching him, I bought him and brought him back to our riding pen. He was tied to the corral fence and left alone. He stood very calm and relaxed at first. Then, when we walked up to him, he became very nervous. When the saddle got close to him he went crazy! No matter how quiet or how careful you were bringing the saddle to him, when he saw it he went crazy! Once, he got so excited he broke the halter rope and ran wild inside the riding pen! There were two or three of us in the pen with him and none of us could catch this crazy horse. If you got him in a corner he would literally run over you to get away.

Something had to be done! I had to think about it but finally came up with a possible solution. We had a horse I had been using for seven years to do the ranch work. He was a very good horse when roping a cow or just about anything else. This horse knew to keep the rope tight and it did not matter if you were riding him at the time or if you were on the ground tending to the animal you had roped.

Most modern-day cowboys don't know the art of roping the front two legs of a horse. When I was young, my tutor Wiley, handled wild horses who were 3-4 years old and had never been touched by human hands. These horses were on big ranches and they would be put into makeshift corrals. The front leg catch was a way to rope these animals and doctor them for whatever problem they might have.

I worked with Wiley on a ranch with over 100 head of wild rodeo horses. Many of them would get 'screw worms' and had to be cured.

The sick horses had to be roped and put on the ground so two men could doctor the horse.

We would rope the front two feet and the horse would have to stop. The rope on the downed horse needed to be kept tight. My job was to get to the opposite side of the horse so the tail could be put between his hind legs and over his flank controlling his movement. With the rope holding the horse's front legs I could pull on the tail and control the horse's hindquarters.

While the horse was down and under control, we would take the medicine and kill the screw worms. Once we were done, the horse would be released.

Wiley was excellent at 'fore-legging' and he taught me the right way to do it. Before long I was the one throwing the rope and other Cowboys were on the ground pulling on the horse's tail.

It became obvious that throwing a rope around the front two legs of my 'crazy' horse was the thing to do. I told my helpers what I wanted them to do once I had roped this crazy horse. We were in a sandy corral and as the horse went by me I threw the rope and had a good catch. Both legs were roped and the horse went to the ground. The helpers were quickly on him and soon had the tail between his legs. My horse knew exactly what to do. He looked down the rope, stepped backwards and kept the rope as tight as he could.

I got off and went to the crazy horse on the ground. He could not get up because my rope was tight around his front legs and my helpers had his rump under control. I took the saddle that was supposed to be on him and laid it next to him but not touching him. Then I bent over and gently rubbed his head while quietly moving the saddle until it was lying on his body. He did not like the saddle on him but began to relax as soon as he stopped being scared.

We let him get up but sidelined him with one hind leg tied up. The hind leg was barely off the ground preventing him from kicking or running away from us. I threw the saddle on his back and then took it off several times. By throwing the saddle on his back a number of times

I was getting him used to having it there. After a few times, I put the saddle on him and pulled the cinch tight to hold the saddle in place.

When I untied the rope on his hind leg, he just stood there. When I got in the saddle he just walked off. He was not nervous or spooky. I could not believe this horse had such a good handle on him and you could even swing a rope over his head as if you were trying to rope a steer. This horse had a lot of training!

You could do almost anything with him including all the things you needed a horse to do while working on a ranch. He would even watch a cow if it needed to be separated from the herd.

The next three or four days I did the same thing with him. I would back him into a corner, tie a rope around his hind leg and repeat the process. He would just stand there like a gentle dog!

Then he would see the saddle! The 'gentle' horse became the 'crazy' horse once again. He would get all spooky and crazy just like before. There was really not much he could do since his butt was in the corner and he had a rope around his hind leg. I could now saddle him once more. After the cinch was tightened and I was on his back, he would change into the quiet and likeable horse he had been before.

On one occasion, the horse was tied to a hitch rail when one of my helpers walked close to him with a paper feed sack. Apparently, the sack reminded the horse of a saddle and he went crazy all over again! The horse jumped away from my helper and then jumped to the side as my helper fell to the ground.

When my helper got to his feet, his face was a little pale!

"I would rather stick my hand into a wasp nest than be around that horse," the helper yelled.

It was at that point the crazy horse got his new name, Wasp!

GETTING READY FOR JAPAN

We needed 40 horses for Japan but I bought 41, including Wasp. I knew Wasp could not go because somebody might get hurt around him, especially if they had a saddle.

I got to liking Wasp and decided to keep him on the ranch. He was good to me and he was really useful when doing ranch work. We were working the other horses and getting them ready for the trip. There were four horses who worked exceptionally good on the stagecoach. They would do other jobs, too, but the stagecoach was their main job in the Wild West Show.

Montie called me and told me when we had to have the horses in San Francisco. Here they would be loaded onto a plane for Japan. Before we could take them, however, we had to test them for an assortment of diseases. We called a veterinarian who came and drew blood from all the horses. These samples were sent to a laboratory and when the tests came back one of the horses did not pass and, therefore, could not make the trip with us.

We were now one horse short. Hmm.

I did not have time to hunt and find one more horse, much less train the horse and see what it was capable of doing. I had no choice. I told Jan, Wasp would have his blood tested and if everything went well, he would be on his way to Japan.

Jan said, "He has such a bad reputation nobody will want him."

"I know," I replied, "So he will be my assigned horse."

When the vet came to get his blood, I told the vet he would have to be very quiet and very careful. I put Wasp in a stall and backed him into a corner and put a twitch on him.

I held the twitch and the vet took his time getting the blood from his vein. There was no problem, thank goodness! His results came back negative and Wasp was cleared for the trip. We now got all of our 40 horses ready for San Francisco.

40 HORSES TO JAPAN

We trucked the horses from Texas to the airport in San Francisco. We also took all the items we needed to keep the horses comfortable as well as the stagecoach.

There were people at the airport who knew what they were doing when it came to loading a plane, so we sat back and watched. At the airport, the handlers put the stagecoach into an open container. I could get to it because we also had the harnesses, blankets and bridles in the container. This was put on the plane first. The horses were loaded next. Then I got on the plane in the same area the horses were located. It would be my job to take care of the animals and make sure everything survived the flight, including me!

The airline was ready for us and did a great job. The horses were put in aluminum 'boxes' with nice stalls inside of each box. My mind relaxed a little because I knew the horses could not kick out the side of the plane! These boxes were on the ground inside a building when we arrived. Each box had five stalls.

One by one the horses were taken off our trucks and put into the stalls. Once a box was full, it was shut and a big fork lift came and picked up the box. It went directly to the plane where it was lifted into the cargo bay. Two men then pushed the box to the rear of the plane and locked it down. I thought there must be a conveyer belt under the box but there was nothing there. I also thought it would be a lot more difficult but they made it look so easy.

Once everything was loaded and the pilots were on the plane, one of the airline men asked me to go with him. He took me to the place where the fork lift was located. We both stepped on a small plate and held on to a set of handrails. Up we went and when we got level to the door, we stepped into the plane.

I saw all the boxes with the horses and one of my questions was soon answered. The floor of the plane was solid with little wheels about the size of roller skates. These wheels were made of steel 'ball bearings' and were all across the floor. Using this method, a man could move the boxes very easily.

It was amazing how my country boy mind worked. If we wanted to move a box with horses in it, the first thing we would do was get a log chain and a tractor. Then we would hook the chain to the box and the tractor and drag the box wherever we wanted it! These city boys were pretty sharp after all!

I was to sit in the 'jump' seat up front next to the pilot and co-pilot. I was a little worried about sitting in this seat but I was strapped in and down the runway we went. In no time at all we had 40 horses, a stagecoach and a cowboy in the air flying over the Pacific Ocean.

I was told if there was a problem with the horses I could work my way back to them and solve the problem. This was my first time flying with horses and I was also told if one of the horses went 'crazy' or uncontrollable (my worst fear!) I was to put the horse down right then and there! Because of this rule I carried a bottle of euthanasia with me. It would be my decision and I hoped there was no decision to be made. This had been one of my biggest worries for weeks before the flight.

I had been working for the past 30 hours and I was getting very tired. I never could sleep in a chair so this jump seat was out of the question. It was not for sleeping anyway. Nevertheless, I tried, but it did not work. I finally got up and worked my way back to the horses. I checked them and found they were relaxed, as though they were in their own stalls at the ranch.

Then I saw the stagecoach. I remembered we had put several horse blankets inside the coach area. I opened the door and made a bed of the blankets. It was a little cold in the back of the plane but I figured with all the blankets I could lay down with some under me and some on top of me and maybe get some sleep.

If the Guinness Book of World Records had been there, I imagine I would be the only man who rode in a stagecoach from California to Japan!

When I awoke, we were about to land. When the plane stopped rolling, it was a great feeling to look out and see the trucks we needed were right on time. They took the horses to the quarantine area. After the trucks were loaded and had left the airport, I took a car to the assigned area.

When we got to Japan, the horses would require a quarantine for 2 weeks. They would stay at the "Agriculture Center" which was about the size of a city block. It had a 10-foot fence around it with only one way in and one way out. This gate was guarded 24 hours a day because Japan was very serious about their quarantine laws. No one was allowed in or out without a clearance badge. I would be in the quarantine area for the entire two weeks taking care of the horses.

When we were in Texas, I had hired a young man who came from a family with a background in horse trading. His family went to horse sales, bought horses, took them home and then got them ready for the next sale. Some of the horses needed work and his family would train them and help improve the horse's image for the average public to ride and have for a pet.

His name was Jimmy Thetford and he helped me train and get the horses ready for the Wild West Show. He knew how to safely get around most any kind of horse and this is a very important skill to have in our line of work. Jimmy was not scared of horses at all! He was there to meet me at the quarantine area when I arrived.

I flew with the horses but Jimmy had to fly on a different plane. He would stay with the horses and me for the full two weeks of the quarantine. We also had a Japanese man who had the job of feeding the horses and cleaning the stalls. Jimmy and I would be the 'overseers' of the quarantine. Once he and I were in the quarantine area with the horses, we were locked in for the next two weeks.

The horses were unloaded and put in their stalls. These stalls were about seven feet wide and the horses had to stand tied but they had enough room to lie down and relax if they wanted.

The Japanese tenants told us they would come in the morning, draw blood and take the temperature of all the horses. They gave Jimmy and I thermometers and we were told to take the horse's temps and write them down in a notebook as a precaution.

The Japanese would only have to draw blood one time (in the morning) and it would solve one part of the quarantine requirements. If the tests came back negative on all the horses, we could move to the location where the Wild West Show was going to be held.

Sure enough, the next morning 6 men showed up to draw blood. I thought they were an unusual sight. They all had white, medical type shirts, white pants, black rubber boots, black rubber gloves and a white mask over their nose and mouth. They carried stainless steel pans with a liquid in them. It might have been alcohol for sterilizing, I don't know.

Jimmy and I thought it was strange. We did not know if they were going to take blood or operate on the horses. None of them spoke much English. I asked if I could help and they made it very clear they did not need any help. Anyway, I was informed, I could not help because I was not wearing the proper clothes!

These men walked in the stall with the first horse and after a few moments they discovered where the big vein was in the horse's neck. They put their 18-gauge into the horse's neck and missed the vein! This was a young horse but he was very gentle and patient.

It looked funny because all of them were in the stall at the same time. They were holding needles and pans waiting for something to happen. They were all pointing at the neck trying to tell the needle holder where to 'stick it.' (I could have told them where…) I could not understand a word they were saying but their gestures said a lot.

After 4 or 5 'exploratory' jabs with the needle, they hit the right spot and drew out 10cc's of blood. They seemed to be happy as they were talking Japanese at a fast pace while they moved to the next stall. Again, it took quite some time for them to get the blood but they were getting it.

Unfortunately, they could not hit the vein without 'exploring' the horse's neck with several jabs. They refused to let me get the blood because I did not have the right clothes and I was not sterilized. Apparently, working on a ranch, doctoring cattle maybe two hundred times a day and using all kinds of medication, vaccinations and doing castrations on a daily basis was not good enough. Anyway, I did not have right clothes.

In this era, when a person entered the world of horses (especially if you worked with 20 or 30 a year), you had to have the knowledge of how to take blood, give shots, etc. It was of the utmost importance for a true horseman to know these skills to maintain his horse's health and well-being.

I have had to inject medicine or vitamins into the main vein of horses on thousands of occasions. It was obvious these Japanese men did not have any experience with horses! They may have had experience with other animals but certainly not with horses.

Drawing a horse's blood is 'maybe' a 2-minute procedure. These men were taking ten to fifteen minutes per horse so the horses had to have patience and so did I! Jimmy and I just stood back and watched the show. We knew there was going to be a big show because these men moved down the line and Wasp was next.

I tried to tell the leader of the Japanese crew about Wasp.

"This next horse is not very gentle," I tried to tell him with slow English and hand gestures. "I can get the blood for you but you might have a problem"

Again, I was turned away. Wrong clothes and their pride was on the line.

Jimmy and I backed up even further and waited. The five Japanese got in the stall with Wasp. The horse stood there like the gentle horse he could be. The man in front had the needle and syringe in his hand. He told the rest of them he was ready to draw blood. He was about to make several *big* mistakes! The first mistake was when he pricked Wasp in the neck with the needle. You could see Wasp roll his eyes and arch his neck. The second mistake was when he touched Wasp for the second time with the needle. Wasp struck the ground with his front foot missing the man but coming close.

As they stood there, you could see Wasp was about to come unglued.

When the man raised his hand to get blood for the third time, Wasp went crazy! The angry horse tried to rear up and get away from these 'crazy' men. In the commotion that ensued, all of the Japanese men were ejected from the stall! Most of them ended up on the ground and their stainless-steel pans holding all the 'sterile' needles and tubes of blood were scattered all over the ground!

Their white pants were now above their shins. Their black boots and white pants had grass stains from being thrown into the grassy patches behind the stalls. Their masks were gone or on the side of their faces. Gloves were torn and did not look like they fit their hands the way they should. It was laughable but we were not in Texas. I now looked more sterile than they did!

Confused, the men stood up and had a conversation about what to do next. They were talking in a very excited manner. Jimmy and I had no knowledge of the language and we had no idea what they were discussing. We started to say something but felt it would be rude so, once more, we continued to stand back and watch. It was definitely a sight to see!

In the United States, if a cowboy got bucked off a horse it was a funny sight and the cowboy was reminded of it for months. Unfortunately, we were not in Texas! The two of us stood there watching and not knowing what the next act would look like.

These men discussed the problem for several minutes before starting back to the stall where Wasp was standing and waiting. When they got close to the horse, Wasp was on the fight and acted up once more.

The Japanese crew stopped. They did not get very close to Wasp. Instead, the leader came over and handed me a needle and syringe. He made hand signs letting me know I was to be the one who was to take the blood from Wasp.

I tried to get across to the leader that I did not have any sterile clothes. He seemed to think it was okay as long as he and his crew did not have to go into the stall again. They did not know his name was Wasp and if you were not careful he could sting you real bad!

The problem now was Wasp himself. He was in 'fight' mode and this job could now become very dangerous to me. I would have had to walk in the very narrow stall beside him with a needle and syringe in my hand where he could see it.

Nope, not me!

I knew we had to unfasten his lead rope so I had Jimmy go around and come in from the other side. He unfastened the rope and tossed it to me. I was now standing at the rear of Wasp with the rope in my hand. I pulled on the rope and Wasp turned around in the stall and came to me. He had a lot of white showing from his eyes meaning he did not trust me.

I backed him up and put his butt in the corner. To calm him, I rubbed his neck until he relaxed. I knew if he saw me with a needle and syringe he would get back to his fighting mode. To fool him, I took a needle without the syringe attached to it and hid the needle in my hand. Jimmy was told to hold the halter and rub his head. We were still trying to relax Wasp.

It was working! He began to relax and I breathed a sigh of relief but the job was not over. Slowly and carefully I worked my way into position. I would have only one good try at hitting the blood vein in his neck with my needle. I had done this hundreds of times and I knew the exact place for the injection. When I thought the time was right, I made a quick move and the needle went into his neck. I was right on target.

The needle stayed in his neck and blood was dripping through the needle, hitting his shoulders and then onto the ground. I knew if I tried to put the syringe on the needle Wasp would go crazy!

I looked at the Japanese man in charge to see if it was okay to take the blood dripping off his shoulder. The man said, "Yes," and nodded.

I got one of the 'sterile' glass tubes and watched as it filled up with his blood. It took several seconds but when it was 2/3 full the leader of the Japanese crew was all smiles. I stopped and gave him the tube. The leader nodded, sealed the tube and handed it off to the official tube holder.

What was so remarkable about this was the start and the finish. In the beginning, everything had to be so sterile I could not even help them. In the end they were happy to accept blood that was dripping off Wasp's shoulder.

The Japanese came back every day to take the official temperatures of the horses. They did not have a volunteer to raise Wasp's tail so Jimmy or I had to do it!

AFTER THE QUARANTINE

When it was all over, we took the horses to the show arena. All the other cast members came by commercial flights. There were 45 members ready to start approximately 500 performances. The Wild West Show began with the grand entry. Jan and I led this entry riding horses and carrying flags. Jan rode one of the horses she would use in her Roman riding act. I rode Wasp.

During the show, we did a 'square dance' on horses. The horses went through different maneuvers at a fast pace. Each team member held hands so the horses stayed close to each other (most of the time). We did figure 8s and when you crossed in the middle it could be dangerous if you were not paying attention. Timing was everything in this business and we did this act during every performance. Wasp was a part of the act and I did not know how much he was a part until one day I realized how smart he really was.

We were about to start the square dance when I put both my hands on the saddle horn. Wasp went through the 6 or 7-minute drill by himself. I never had to ask him to turn, wheel around or tell him where to go. When it was over, he even lined up in the correct spot!

This horse was super! I wished I had left him in Texas because I knew he would make a great all-around horse.

DON'T TRY TO SADDLE MY HORSE

We had finished about 100 performances when I was called to the office for some project they had in the works. Montie was gone and when he was not available I was the man in charge.

Unfortunately, it was about time to start the show and I would not have much time since Jan and I were the first ones into the arena to open the show with the Grand Entry. I immediately headed for the office. The meeting lasted longer than they said it would. I got out as fast as I could and ran to the spot where the entry started. I had to saddle Wasp and I had to saddle him fast! When I got there, Jan told me she had told two cowboys to go down to the barn and saddle Wasp for me.

Okay, this should be fun! About this time, the two cowboys were coming from the barn area. They did not have Wasp with them. Imagine that! I met them and asked, "Where is my horse?"

"That horse is crazy!" one of them shouted at me. "We could not get close to him with the saddle."

I ran down to his stall and backed him into a corner. He stood there like a little puppy and I threw the saddle on him. By now, the two cowboys were outside the stall watching me as I got in the saddle and prepared to go into the arena. I left them standing there with a quizzical look on their faces.

THE END OF THE TRIP

When the show came to an end, it was thought the horses would be coming back to the United States with us. However, it was cheaper for the Japanese to buy the horses and keep them in the country.

Knowing I could bring my horse back to the United States, I had taken my good horse, "Hobo," to Japan. He was 16 and sound. He had also been a loyal and trusted friend for many years working with cattle and doing shows. I had planned to retire him after Japan and let him live out the rest of his life on our ranch.

When I was told the horses would not be coming home, it hit me hard!

I tried to convince myself that Hobo would find a good home as he was so gentle and well trained. Then my thoughts turned to Wasp and his future with his crazy behavior, especially at being saddled.

In all the years since we parted ways, I have lived with a haunting, guilty mind. These horses, especially Hobo and Wasp served me well and I feel I let them down.

SAO PAULO, SOUTH AMERICA

Thinking about all the different places and different situations I have been through in my life, I cannot help but remember Sao Paulo in South America.

I was sent down to buy horses for a show. This time I needed Roman Riding Horses, trick horses and horses just to ride around the arena. I soon met a man who knew about horses and where to get them.

One of the first places he took me was a big ranch with a lot of gauchos working on it. (Gauchos are the name for South American cowboys.) We got there before noon and the owner told one of his men to go and get the horses he wanted to show us.

Pretty soon, out rode four gauchos at a pretty fast pace. They stopped, left the horses, turned and then ran back for more horses. As a cowboy and horseman, I took this time to check out the gauchos and their gear. Their saddles were strapped on to their horses over a thick layer of sheepskin. The stirrups on their saddles were all made of iron rings and when they rode, they put their toes on either side of the ring……… it was an educational day!

During all this commotion, the horses remained calm. These were small, spotted horses and looked just right to me. I figured I could use them for the Native American performers. He brought several horses and I looked at all of them. We soon came to settle on a price for the ones I wanted. It seemed to be a successful trip so far.

I was fixing to leave but the owner said not to go just yet. He wanted us to eat before leaving. We said ok, not feeling we had much of a choice! The ranch house did not have screen doors, much less any other door. The cook was in the house fixing lunch on a brick/stone stove with small logs only 4 inches thick. He kept moving the logs closer and closer to the center of the fire, keeping it going.

The kitchen area looked crude but the living room had a beautiful chandelier and a grand piano in it. I can still see the boss man in his white shirt, white pants and black, up to his knees, riding boots. It is burned into my mind.

He motioned for us to sit down and offered us a drink. We drank and talked about many things. When our deal was finished, and after we had paid for the horses, he wanted us to stay and be his company, so we did.

About 45 minutes later, the cook came in and said it was time to eat. As I said, the kitchen was primitive, but the table was elegant. We had a delicious beef dinner.

After our meal, we thanked him and were ready to leave, but the owner led us to some of the hammocks he had. It was siesta time, so we rested for half an hour. After our "siesta" we wanted to leave, but the owner said, "No"! It was time for another drink. By this time, I was amazed and fascinated by the treatment we had received. This was hospitality!

HOTEL FIRE

Sometimes the habits and natural instincts of people are similar to cattle. When a couple of cattle start walking away from the herd, a few will follow and then the rest of the cows will follow even if they have no idea where they are going. Sometimes the two lead cows don't know where they are going either! It is just a "cow" thing I guess! This reminds me of a situation when we were in Sao Paulo, Brazil. We were staying in a hotel when the incident happened.

I was standing on the sidewalk outside the hotel when the building next to us (it was only 10 feet away) caught on fire. The inside of it suddenly burst into flames and smoke was coming out of the windows. The fire alarm was going off and the fire trucks were arriving. I could see they did not think any of us were in danger. The building on fire was not a threat to the hotel.

As I walked back into the hotel lobby, it was obvious the people and guests heard the fire alarms. Jan and Sonna came up to me and wanted to know what had happened. Before they could hear my story, they learned of the fire. Both of them took off upstairs not knowing what the situation was. I was left standing there alone.

"The fire is not in this hotel," I told myself, "So where are they going?" Still this did not stop Jan and Sonna from running upstairs to their room and getting the things they loved and cherished!

In the meantime, the other guests in the hotel were also running upstairs. If this was a really serious situation, they should not have been running upstairs but running out of the building. I kept telling people, "It is okay. We are safe here. We are safe here."

In just a few minutes, the guests were all rushing down the stairs, throwing suitcases and running out of the hotel. Nobody paid any attention to what I was saying, so, I just sat down in the lobby and did some people-watching!

Before long, Jan and Sonna came down the stairs, dragging their suitcases. "Why are you just sitting in the chair?" She asked me. "I tried to stop you," I explained, "Because the fire is not here. It is in the building next door and it is not a serious fire. We are in no danger." We ended up staying in the hotel even though there was a fire next door.

I guess the moral of the story is how people do not listen. Even my family did not pay any attention to me! If there would have been a problem (a fire in the hotel) these people were willing to save something not as important as their lives!

As I sat there in the lobby, I watched these people and thought about the cattle and how they followed each other and how humans will also do the same thing!

ENGLAND: BUYING HORSES

We got a contract for England and I was sent ahead to buy the horses for the show. My contact in England was a man named Stan and he was well acquainted with the area we would be using. Together, we went to different farmers looking for horses I might like.

Stan was kind of a politician. He got along with people very well. On this particular day, we stopped at a man's house who said he had a horse we needed. It was kind, gentle and anybody could ride it. We walked out to the field and caught it.

I could quickly tell the horse had not been broke well and it spooked very easily as we all were walking back to the barn. They were leading the horse and I was walking behind the horse. The owner was going on and on about how gentle the horse was.

They could not see me as they walked. I took my hat off and threw it under the horse's belly. The horse spooked quickly and kicked the hat with both feet before the hat even hit the ground. The horse then lunged forward and pulled the owner around. I apologized and told him the wind blew my hat off.

We did not buy the horse!

In about two weeks we found around 45 horses for the show. We also found an indoor private arena where we could shut the doors and practice. People could not get in or see us. This way, we would not be disturbed by people who wanted to watch.

The easiest of the horses to find were the wagon or buggy horses because this part of England had a lot of well-trained buggy horses.

One of the things people who came to the arena could not believe was the picket line I had made outside of the arena. I had put posts at each end and one in the middle forming a "picket line." (A "picket line" is simply a rope attached post-to-post drawn tight.) We would tie some of our horses to the picket line while we worked with the other horses inside the building. Sometimes we would have as many as 20 horses tied to the picket line!

I was amazed! People looked at this picket line as if it was something they had never seen before! At home, we always tied the horses to a picket line. There would be 5 or 6 horses tied up and left for some time without a problem. England, however, had different rules.

When they had a truck, trailer or pickup hauling a horse, there had to be someone riding with the horse. When they put shoes on their horses, one person had to hold the horse and one person had to shoe the horse and another person had to be there to keep the horse quiet by gently stroking it!

It was just a lot different than we were used to seeing!

COWBOY FASHION

When we arrived in England for the Wild West Show, the English crew was asked to attend a meeting, so we went. The producer who was backing the Wild West Show was also in charge of what he called the "Appearance and Design" of the show. He said they were going to "suggest" how the crew in the show should dress.

Jan and I looked at each other and said, "Oh, this should be good!"

We waited and the issue was soon answered by a lady who was walking in my direction.

She looked around, pointed at me and said," This is how you are supposed to dress!" Jan looked at me and said, "This is going to be a 'baggy' show, isn't it?" The biggest thing that relieved my mind was when they *did not* ask me to stand up, walk down a model's runway, style and smile!

JONES' TEEPEE

One of the performers working with us was Jones Benally, a very famous Navajo hoop dancing champion and healer. He worked all of the Montie Montana, Jr. shows with us around the world.

Next to the stadium, they had little travel trailers for us to stay in. There were enough of them for the entire cast of the show. It was kind of hot and humid when we were there. Jones (we called him Jonesie) told Montie that he was not staying in one of these trailers. Montie told Jonesie he could do what he wanted.

So Jonesie took those words to heart. He put up a teepee which looked a little odd since he was in line with the rest of the trailers. After the first night, I did not know if Jonesie was comfortable or not. Turned out, he had managed to get an air conditioner! He had put it near the front of the teepee and engineered it so that the air conditioner was kept off the ground. He also had an electrical cord which supplied the power for his a/c unit! It seemed to worked well for Jonesie, but when I think about it, the image seemed odd. Here was an old-fashioned teepee with an air conditioner!

WEMBLEY STADIUM

Here we were at the biggest, most famous stadium in England and it was show time! We were ready for our first performance. We had our Roman Riding horses who turned out to be a really good team for Jan. I had also found a very good team of flashy coach horses for my daughter Sonna.

It did not take very much training as these horses were used to working together. We found Roman Riding teams with very little problem. The trick riding horses were a different story. As you were vaulting from one side to the other and slipping off the rear of the horse and then coming back on it again, you had to have a horse who was willing to accept these strange (to the horse) maneuvers.

At this time Sonna was doing an under the neck trick. This consisted of riding at a run, leaving the saddle on one side, going under the horse's neck, and coming up on the other side ending up on the saddle where she started. The horse I had prepared for Sonna had me a little worried. Sonna, however, seemed to be getting along great with the horse and was comfortable working with it.

Our first three performances went well. The horse ran like it should and Sonna had no problem going from the saddle, passing under the neck, and back into the saddle. During the fourth performance, Sonna was getting into position to go under the horse's neck.

Now, when you get into position to go under the neck, you put your foot in the stirrup on the other side of the saddle. *After* you have your foot in the stirrup, you then twist your body and find the handhold on the saddle. As you get in this position, you have both feet in the stirrups and both hands in the handholds on each side of the horse. For an instant, you are hanging upside down underneath the horse's neck.

This particular night, as Sonna was hanging in this position ready to go to the next movement, the horse stumbled and fell. Sonna lost her handhold on the other side. When she lost this grip, her foot got caught in the stirrup and she had only one hand in the right grip position.

It was at this moment the horse decided to buck. When it did, it jerked her other hand out of the handhold, but her foot was still caught in the stirrup and it stayed there! Because of this, Sonna was suddenly being dragged around the arena. This made the horse even more terrified than it already was! As the horse ran to the other end of the arena, it was kicking and bucking. Sonna was still hooked by her foot. I saw what was happening and I started to run to her. The horse continued to run and when it got to the other end of the arena, it stopped.

Four of the crew in the arena grabbed the horse's head. Sonna was still hanging on and now the horse was really kicking and bucking with both hind feet! I did not have time to think! I went to Sonna to try and get her foot out of the stirrup. In doing so, I was kicked in the upper part of my leg and in the stomach where my belt buckle was located. It did not break my belt buckle, but it sure put a big dent in it!

It took a few long seconds, but I managed to get her leg free and Sonna fell to the ground. I fell on top of her to prevent her from getting kicked. The workers finally got the horse away from us and we were able to get to our feet.

Jan, my wife, had witnessed everything. She ran to us and said she was so scared because she thought she might lose both of us. We were lucky. They took us to the hospital and Sonna got her ankles x-rayed. They were not broken but had been stretched and sprained to the point she would have to use crutches if she wanted to move. Her ankle healed, but to this day, she cannot comfortably wear high heeled shoes!

My injuries were to one leg. It was not broken, but for the next week, it turned blue, green and all the other colors that go with a horse kick. But, I was all right!

In riding horses, one of the biggest fears is falling off and getting a foot caught in the stirrup while the horse is dragging you. This is where the most deaths and broken legs occur. This incident could have been a fatal accident and the thought of a bad outcome has always haunted me because I was the one who told Sonna this was a safe horse to ride. If I did not think it would have been safe, she would have not been on the horse. To this day, I think it was my fault. She could have had a fatal accident. Sometimes it is hard to live with your actions. To make things worse, in talking about it, some of the promoters said to me, "If you can do that every night, it would be a thrilling stunt for the grandstand to see!"

I did not say anything, but I had a lot of thoughts.

ARRESTED FOR ROPING A STEER IN ENGLAND

As we were working with Montie in England, Montie came to me and said the English television studio wanted to film a cowboy roping a steer so they could air it during Christmas week. I had previously found 45 head of horses for the show. To my amazement, it took me only a short time until I got a good handle on them. It did not take very much until these horses started to move around just like our western cow ponies.

Although these horses had originally been broken using a flat, English saddle and many of them were ridden with double reins, they all had a good "mouth" and worked well with the bit. Thankfully, these horses had been trained the same way we trained our young ranch horses, with a broken bit in their mouths. When you want to turn to the right, you pull the rein to the right so the horse goes to the right. Pull to the left, the horse goes to the left. Pull back on the reins and the horse stops.

This was all they needed if they were a jumping horse or a pleasure horse. When I got on these horses, I needed to start riding like I did on our western cow ponies. The difference is we use what we call neck reining. This enables the cowboy to control his horse with one hand and have the rope in the other hand. Simply put, to neck rein, you lay the rein on a horse's neck and he will turn the opposite way of the rein. Also, we (western riders) like for a horse to get back on his hind legs in order to turn smoother and quicker.

I rode with spurs my whole life and used them to help the English horses respond when lightly touched by a spur near the girth on the left to move (turn) to the right and vice versa. I was amazed how fast we got those horses to react like our American cow horses!

"Can you rope a steer off of one of these English horses?" Montie asked me. I thought about it for a few seconds and said, "I think I can, but I would need to practice first just to be sure."

This was a tricky situation. I would need to practice in the middle of the night. There was a simple reason for this. The Humane Society of England was very strict and I did not think they would understand the job I was trying to accomplish or the art of roping a steer. I picked out one of the horses I liked. It was a good horse and handled the way I wanted. Montie found 3 or 4 steers for me to use in training. Every night I would go to the arena and practice. In no time, the horse was following the steer with very little help from me. This horse got the idea very quickly, in fact, it actually got to be fun because the horse was picking up the idea and he liked what we were doing.

On the 3rd or 4th night we made a couple of steer roping chutes. In roping a steer, it is in a confined "chute" with the rider and horse on the outside right next to it. The gate is opened and the steer takes off.

The horse and rider chase the steer. When the horse and rider get close enough, the rider swings his rope forming a loop to catch the horns of the steer. The rope is dallied to the saddle horn and the horse is trained to slow the steer down to a stop. If the steer was out in the pasture and was sick, you would do this and then he could be loaded into a cattle trailer and taken to the barn area to be doctored to get well.

The steers soon got the idea. If they ran to the other end of the chute, they would be safe. Within one week things were looking up. We would turn a steer loose and my horse would break out and lope after it. This horse was usually very quiet and gentle but, to my surprise, it took to this part of the training quickly.

For the next part of the training, we would turn the steer loose and I would follow it to the other end of the arena. I always had my lariat rope in my hand and I would swing it over my head as if I was going to rope the steer. I was getting the horse used to this motion.

Now I had to get the horse used to pressure on the saddle horn. So, I attached one end of the rope firmly to the saddle horn and the other one to a loose gate. We would drag the gate around the arena and this would teach the horse what it felt like to have pressure on his saddle. This is a very important part of roping a steer.

"So, how is your project working out with both the steer and the horse?" Montie wanted to know. "I think I can get the job done," I told him hopefully. "Why don't you go ahead and set it up with the television studios?"

During this time, I became very acquainted with a couple of humane officers. We were soon on a first name basis. They watched what we did and they never saw any animal abuse. It was probably the main reason why we became friends. (They had not seen me do the actual roping up to this point!)

Montie made arrangements with the television station. They came to the arena and set up their cameras. When things were all set up and the time for this particular event arrived, I got a little worried. With all the people in the grandstand and those who would be watching later on television, I wondered if I was going to make a fool of myself. Unfortunately, I had gone too far to back out now!

The show began with the usual acts. Then the announcer said, "The next act is a special act. We will be filming this act and it will be seen at a later date." Our workers were helping me set up the event. They took two of the most "honest" steers. This meant they ran fairly slowly and, more importantly, straight. These steers were put in the chutes and were soon waiting to be let loose.

Now it was my turn. I rode into the arena. No one in the stands knew what was going to happen. I rode my horse into position and told the helpers to turn one of the steers loose just like we had done during our practice sessions. The spotlights came on and they turned the steer loose. We trained at night with minimal lighting and this was what all the animals were used to seeing. Having them run out into bright spotlights and cameras was something we had forgotten to teach them!

This was the first time the steers had seen such bright spotlights. The steer was startled and came out with a slow run across the field. I urged my horse to follow the steer and he did, just as we had practiced. As we got closer, the steer suddenly realized we were there and began to run harder. I got in position and threw my rope, catching the steer just like it was supposed to be done.

At that moment, I thought there was an explosion in the arena! I pulled my horse to a stop and worried about the loud noise I was hearing and how it would affect the animals. In other countries, this type of entertainment deserves applause. In England it, apparently deserved an "explosion" of applause! The people in the stands had never seen anything like this! Their "appreciation" was thunderous and sounded just like an explosion!

After the horse stopped, I stood up in the saddle and began to look around and find what all the commotion was about. Everyone was clapping, standing and staring, at ME! Only then did I realize I was the reason for the "explosion!"

My two humane society friends were soon running towards me. "Jim," one of them said, 'I did not think you would do such a thing!" I took the rope off my saddle horn and handed it to the humane society people. Both of them took hold of the rope which was still attached to the steer. Now this steer knew where the safe place was (at the far end of the arena) and, in the midst of all this excitement, decided to go there. The steer took off at a fast pace and kept going!

My two humane society friends were now trying to hold the rope and keep control of the steer. These men did not want to turn the steer loose so they hung on for dear life. Someone at the other end of the arena opened the back gate. I suspect this was one of Montie's ideas. This gate went to the parking lot. When I looked up, I saw the two men (who were still hanging on to the rope!) taking steps about 20 feet apart as they desperately tried to keep up with the fast running steer which was now headed out to the parking lot!

My deal with Montie was for me to rope two steers. After the steer and his loyal followers were outside of the gate, the workers closed the gate. I rode my horse back to where the other steer was located. After a few seconds, I was ready to rope this second steer. The workers turned the steer loose. I guess I was lucky because I caught this steer about halfway down the arena. Once more the applause was overwhelming! The people in the grandstand were deafening and the applause was thunderous.

So, here I sit, on my horse with a steer on the end of my rope and who do I see coming my way? Yep, it was my two humane society friends and they are not talking to me. "Why don't you guys just relax and stand back for a second?" I asked them.They did and told me "we want to talk to you." I rode my horse outside the arena. There was now another humane society officer waiting and he gave me a piece of paper which I folded and put in my pocket. As I got off my horse, these Humane Society people began asking me a bunch of questions, but I just walked away and ignored them.

Roping a steer is nothing new to me. I have done it all my life. However, it must be something new and exciting to the people of England! I thought nothing about what happened in the arena until the next day when someone brought me a newspaper. I looked at the front page of the paper and there, in huge print, were the words:

TEXAS COWBOY ARRESTED FOR HARRASSING CATTLE

You have got to be kidding me!

My advice to all of you is never throw a rope around a steer if you are in England!

KUWAIT

On another occasion, I got a phone call to buy horses. This deal was for a Wild West Show to be performed in Kuwait. I found out there were no horses available except Arabian race horses and they had to be bought right off the race tracks in Kuwait. It seemed the people in Kuwait loved horse racing and most of their horses were bred for speed and endurance, not for shows and arena acts.

For the show they wanted, I would have to find Roman Riding Teams, trick riding horses, horses capable of being hooked to stagecoaches and some horses we could just use to ride around the arena. It was a tough challenge!

After much work, I gathered about 35 horses and started sorting through them. For the stagecoach, I needed two leaders who had to go against the bit, meaning they wanted to run. I also needed two more for a wheel team (the ones nearest the stagecoach) who were willing to pull.

Finding a wheel team was harder than I imagined! When I said "whoa," they thought I was saying "go"! To make matters worse, I did not have months to train these horses. I only had *days!*

The best way to train a wheel team was to make a sled, attach them to it and train them to pull using the sled instead of a stagecoach. I found some 4x4 pieces of lumber, made a floor to stand on, hooked the wheel team up to the sled and gave it a shot.

I had no choice but to drive these horses in the desert. Contrary to what people think, the desert is not flat! It is more like a bunch of ocean waves. My thinking was, I could let them gallop until they got tired. I found a flat area to start and away we went.

These horses were born and bred to be race horses! They had speed and soon we were going pretty fast. It was then the desert became desert and we hit one of those "waves." The front of the squared-off sled hit the wave and came to an abrupt and sudden STOP! I mean, this sled buried itself in the sand, jerking the horses to a halt. They were almost sitting down!

Needless to say, the driver, ME, went airborne! I flew off the sled landing near the front legs of the horses. I like flying but not this way! When I regained my composure, I discovered the sled was buried so deep, I could not dig it out of the sand. I had to unhitch the horses and ride them back into town. I wish I knew this was going to happen. I could have said, "whoa," and used it as a learning experience for the horses!

The sled was useful and we wanted to keep it so I went back to get it with a few other men. It turned out the sled was buried so deep in the sand that the six of us could not get it out! We got a truck and even the truck had a hard time pulling it out! One good thing did come out of all of this. The next time I hooked the same horses up to the sled, I only had to give a slight tug on the reins, and the horses would stop instantly! A couple more days of driving the sled and they were willing to do whatever I wanted!

My next adventure was hooking them up to the coach. I put the two wheel horses next to the stagecoach (the sled pullers) and the two leaders were attached in front of them. Lo and behold, I had full control of the horses! From then on, I had a good stagecoach team and never had any problems from them.

I often think about the sled in the deep sand and the abrupt stop we made… if only I had said, "Whoa!"

The Wild West Show in Kuwait was a challenge on many fronts! We had a good crowd on the first night. Unfortunately, the next day we had negative reports in their local newspaper. The thing Montie should have thought about, but did not, were the customs of the country where we were performing.

As part of our act, Jan and Sonna rode the Roman Riding teams. The costumes they wore showed bare legs covered only by knit stockings. To the locals, this was more than risqué.

Montie also had a western saloon act consisting of cowboys shooting and fighting. There were also chorus girls dancing arm in arm while doing the can-can. All this was done to a music score which pulled the whole thing together.

During the can-can dance, each girl would "throw" her leg high up in the air because this is what the can-can dance was! The girls all wore long dance hall costumes, but as they kicked up their legs, you could see under their costumes and you could see their legs. I have seen can-can dances in the U.S. hundreds of times and thought nothing of it. The next day, the papers reported the dance and said all of this was too risqué.

Montie never changed the saloon act, but Jan, Sonna and I thought it would be better for their legs not to show. We changed our costumes into a western style outfit.

We had totally underestimated the traditions of another country. Here, the women were not even allowed to drive cars! It seemed to me these women were made to be 2nd class citizens! The show did go on in its usual way, but the crowd soon dropped down to about half of the grandstand capacity. Maybe they decided it was not a family type of entertainment!

I was called into the office since the promoters knew me better than they knew Montie who was now back in California. When I was in the office, they started to quiz me about the entertainers we had in show. They asked me about John and Vi Brady, special entertainers who had worked in Las Vegas and around the world. I was also asked about our group of Bolo dancers from Argentina. I had only seen them one time before, but I knew they had worked everywhere including the main act in Las Vegas. They also asked me if I knew any of the other performers.

I told them, "No, I have not worked with any of them before. Montie put them in the Wild West Show while in California and on the west coast. The only time we were involved was when he would call and we would work out specifics."

They understood about the people we had just discussed, but they were worried about the other people in the show. According to the contract, they had hired 45 professional entertainers. We had just discussed 15 of them. "The only professional entertainers we see," they told me, "are the ones we just talked about. The other 30 people in the contract are the ones who concern us." I quietly told them, "I did not hire them, so I really don't know much of anything about them." They said, "okay," and I was dismissed. The meeting was over.

Later in the day, I spoke to Montie on the phone. I told him there seemed to be a little problem about the performers. They had called me into a meeting and I did not say anything negative about anybody, but they seem to have a beef with you about something!

Montie came back to Kuwait and, when he did, it seemed he was always in a meeting with the new owners. I felt there was a problem on the horizon. One day, when it was time for the performers to arrive and put on the show, the gates were locked!

There was a huge fence around our entertainment area. We could get inside, but the crowd was prevented from entering. "Jan," I told my wife, "This does not look good! We will take all the equipment we have and throw it over the fence because it appears they are not having a show tonight."

We were soon throwing all of our Roman Riding pads, saddles, gear and everything else we owned over the fence. Then, an odd thing happened. A man came up behind me carrying his saddle. I had seen this man on the grounds, but I did not know his name. I learned later he was from the state of Montana. I watched as he threw his saddle and bridle over the fence near our pile of gear. Then he turned and looked at me. "What are you doing?" he asked. I said, "I have a bad feeling here since they have locked the gate up."

"I have been watching," he said, "And I decided I was going to do everything you were going to do. What are you going to do about all the equipment you have thrown on the other side of the fence?"

"I am going to get a taxi and take all of it back to the hotel," I replied. "Do you think there is room for my saddle too?" he wanted to know.

"I don't know, but there should be," I shot back.

Before we left the grounds, there was an announcement. A bus was coming to pick up everyone and take us to the hotel. There was not enough room on the bus for anything except people, so we were to leave everything else behind. The show had been cancelled and all of us were to come back tomorrow.

I knew something was fishy, so I got a taxi just in case. We loaded our gear and headed back to the hotel with everything we had. As we figured, the next day none of the staff was allowed back onto the grounds! The place was locked up and no one could get in. There were several items left behind, including wagons and a $25,000 stagecoach!

John Brady had brought a number of rifles and pistols (six shooters) to use in one of the acts. As a result of the lockout, Brady lost all of these items. Luckily for him, he had all of his whips and boomerangs at the hotel.

This was the end of our shows in Kuwait!

The only good thing was the week before all of us had been paid. Since this happened at the beginning of the work week, we did not really lose any money. Many members of the show lost a lot of their equipment however. We did have the most important thing, we had our prepaid round trip plane tickets back home!

When we got back to the hotel, I immediately found Montie. "What the hell is going on?" I asked bluntly. "I , uh, had some trouble with the promoters," he told me. We just looked at each other. I did not ask him anything else. I needed a cup of coffee, but Montie decided to keep a low profile.

"Can I come back to your room and stay with you for awhile?" Montie asked me. "I am leaving tonight and would rather not see anyone." I had an idea of the problem, but I did not want to pry.

As the evening approached, he asked me to get him a taxi. When it arrived, I stood in front of the walkway and made sure he did not have a problem getting into the vehicle. He got in and as the taxi left and passed by me, Montie rolled down the window and gave me a "thumbs up." I could only look at him.

A couple of days later I called him. He told me "I was so scared! When that plane took off, it felt like a ton of bricks were off of me. I got my feet back in the United States and I felt great!"

That day in Kuwait was the last time I ever saw Montie Montana Jr.

CHAPTER 26

OFF SEASON WORK AT HOME IN WEATHERFORD, TEXAS: BACK TO THE REAL WORLD

When any given year was over for us, we got home with a little money, a lot of memories and great recollections of that past year. Unfortunately, when we got home there was not enough money for us to live on until the next rodeo season. We had to make money the best way we knew how and that was to train horses for the general public. We put the word out to everyone we knew, telling them we would train horses for outdoor and ranch work, general riding horses and barrel racing prospects. In addition to training horses, and sometimes riders as well, I also was a blacksmith.

If I had the time between training horses I would do day work on the ranches in the area. This included taking care of sick cattle, branding and gathering cattle from rough ranch country. By the way, trying to gather cattle into cattle pens is not as easy as it looks on old TV westerns!

Our ranch had 18 stalls. Jan and I usually had them full of young horses that needed to be trained. We worked from sun-up to sundown. It was a good thing neither of us were afraid of work because that is about all we did! We loved our life. It was what we liked to do. As long as we were in the world with horses we were happy. Being home means a lot things change, especially your living quarters and the costs you have.

For instance, when you are traveling, you have a different home every week. The people we worked for would furnish our electricity, water, camping space for our trailers and whatever else we needed. These items were never an expense while we were on the road.

But now we were home! Here we had electric bills, telephone bills, school expenses for two kids, feed for the horses and so much more.

The bills seemed to never end! To pay for these bills, we had to stay busy and earn money until the next rodeo season started. Thankfully, we were young and healthy and willing to work.

It did not take long before we had horses to train for other people. I was getting all the daytime work I could handle on different ranches in the area. Just like Florida, I would take a horse I was training and we would ride through the yearling steers looking for sick or troubled animals. Most of the yearlings, when they are sick, do not move as fast as the healthy ones which is great for training a young horse!

PRICKLY PEARS

I could ride a green horse (who was 'not very knowledgeable about a rope') up to a steer and rope him. When I did this, there was another cowboy alongside of me and he would also rope the steer. With the steer unable to move, the two of us could then doctor the steer with medications. Working with a partner was a lot safer than working alone.

One morning something happened, and I still laugh about it. I was on a young horse who was not familiar with roping a steer. This was his first time so I took all the precautions I could. The steer I chose was so sick he was lying down. As I got close to him, he jumped up, looked at me and my horse then turned and started to walk away, *very slowly!* When I got close enough to rope him, he started to run but it was a very slow run. I spurred my horse close enough to rope the steer but then things went sideways on me!

After you rope a few head of livestock, a horse will learn to brace himself for the 'jerk' you get when the steer hits the end of the rope. Most experienced horses are ready for this but the horse I was on knew nothing about bracing himself! So, when the sick steer hit the end of the rope and the 'jerk' happened (a pull weight of around 700 pounds) my horse was jerked down to the ground. I had chaps on and I was glad I did because the horse and I fell in the middle of a cactus patch! We call them prickly pears but no matter what they are called, they left thorns stuck in my chaps and a few in my Wranglers but I could pull them out with no problem. I still had a little pain when I sat down but it was all part of the job.

My horse had stickers in his side but he was okay. It was winter and he had his winter coat growing which meant he had a lot of hair. I pulled the stickers out of him and we were ready to get back to work.

The cowboy who was with me sat on his horse and doubled up with laughter as he watched this fiasco unfold. He was laughing so hard he could hardly sit up straight in his saddle. I did not know it at the time, but I would get even with him in the near future.

A couple of days later my partner and I started a new day doing the same old thing. At the time, ranch cowboys did not make much money. Most of these ranch cowboys came from families who worked on ranches. They lived in old ranch houses furnished by the ones who owned the ranch. Sometimes food (meat) was also furnished to them but a cowboy never had much money to have a good time or spend on the things they needed or wanted.

NEW SADDLES ARE DANGEROUS?

My partner was in the same shape. His house was old, the doors and windows would not shut tight enough to keep the dust, scorpions and mice from getting into the house. It was always a battle for his wife to keep the house livable.

Even with this low income, one thing a cowboy would always have was a good, stout saddle. This was something he used every day in his work whether it was around his own place or in the pasture working for the rancher.

My partner had been saving his money to buy a new saddle. He finally had enough so he went out and bought one. On this particular morning when we saddled up to go out and doctor the steers, he was using his new saddle for the very first time. When he showed up he was smiles all over! He had been talking about getting a new saddle for a very long time and now it was a reality.

New saddles are usually very stiff until they have been used for a short time. This new saddle was no different. My partner put it on his horse and realized how stiff his new saddle was. The stirrups hung down and were very flat against the horse. When a stirrup lays flat against the horse like these did, it means the leather which attaches the stirrup to the saddle (called a fender) has not shaped to your leg. There are ways you can eliminate the problem but he did not want to take the time to fix the situation. He just put the saddle on the horse exactly the way it came from the saddle maker. Oh, well!

As we rode out in the morning he would have to stop occasionally and tighten his saddle because, being new and not worn in, it would get loose. We soon came upon a young steer who looked sick. This was another of the 700 pound steers who needed medical assistance. I was riding the same horse from a few days before when we had our encounter with the "prickly pear" patch. My partner, who went by the name of "Slim," decided to taunt me a little. "I will rope this sick steer from my horse. It will be easier for me since I do not have to pick any cactus thorns from my ass."

He laughed and headed for the steer. He ran up to the steer and easily roped him. He made a nice throw and catch but when his horse went to stop and get ready for the 'jerk,' his saddle was too loose to stop the steer. The horse stopped but the steer did not.

Instead of staying on the horse, the saddle slipped to one side and Slim went to the ground. One end of the rope was around the steer and the other end of the rope was around the saddle horn of the new saddle, so it kept going. As the horse stopped and the steer kept going, the saddle slipped off the horse and went over the horse's head! Slim watched helplessly as his saddle had no choice but to be dragged behind the steer as the animal ran away at a pretty good clip for a sick steer!

All I could hear was Slim yelling, "The steer is stealing my saddle. The steer is stealing my saddle. Jim, catch that steer, he's stealing my saddle!"

I took off after the steer, but the horse I was on still had a little 'green' in him. We also had a problem getting close to the steer because the saddle was bouncing all over the place both on the ground and in the air and I was worried about a potential wreck. Between the steer, the rope and the saddle bouncing around, it was very confusing to my horse. He did not want any part of the flopping saddle and I don't really blame him.

I knew I could not rope the steer from behind so I decided to get around the steer and get in front of him. We pushed on and finally got there. By now the steer was getting tired and he just came to a stop. I got close enough to rope him and as he tried to get away, my horse braced himself and was soon staring down the rope at the steer. It was a good sign.

Even though I had my rope around the steer, there was not much more I could do without Slim's help. I looked up to see where my partner was but he was still two football fields away! He had his horse by the reins, but he was not riding him. Sometimes he would run, then he would walk, then he would run but he was getting there. All I could do was wait!

Finally, he got to where I was. Slim, I said, trying not to laugh too loud, "Your new saddle is broken in now. It may have scratches, dirt and marks all over it but it don't have any cactus thorns in it!" He stared down and realized I was right. His saddle appeared to be a year old instead of brand new. He shook his head in dismay.

The day was about over so we rode back to the barn and stable area. I had my pickup truck and trailer so I loaded up my bronc. Before I left I walked up to Slim. "I sure do like your saddle," I told him. "It don't look like one of those fancy parade saddles. It looks really good for a ranch saddle." We both laughed for a long time before I got in my truck and drove off. In a couple of weeks my horse was riding pretty good and so was his saddle!

ARABIAN HORSE TRAINING

While I was out taking care of the sick livestock, Jan was at home riding, training and taking care of the other horses. She was soon telling me about some Arabian stallion a doctor in town had purchased. He brought it to us and wanted us to train it.

The horse was very unruly. He would rear up and strike at you with his front feet. Jan told me he did not pay attention to any training process. All this horse wanted to do was look around for other horses and squeal and nicker.

The doctor told us he wanted him trained with a 'flat' or English saddle as they wanted to participate in Arabian horse shows. The doctor would rather not have a cowboy saddle on him. I guess he thought a cowboy saddle was not sophisticated enough for his unruly stallion.

Jan had started working with the stallion but she was having a tough time with him. I told Jan the horse I had been taking to the ranch each morning was riding pretty good and I would trade with her. She would get my horse and I would work with the Arabian.

Before I left my barn the next morning, I found a piece of chain about four feet long. "Just what are you going to do with the chain?" Jan asked as she saw me with it. "I don't want to wear out my rope so I am using this chain," I told her with a smile. She looked at the chain and then at me before letting out a groan. She knew what was in store for the feisty Arabian stallion. I put the horse in my truck and when I got to the big ranch, Slim met me. He took one look at the horse and said, "That horse is as pretty as my saddle used to be!" We laughed but he was absolutely right!

The plan was to load our horses in a trailer and go down to the cow pens where we would continue with our work. The cow pens were down the road about a mile and three quarters but if you drove straight across the pasture to them (as the crow flies) the distance was only one mile. We would do a little work and then load up the horses and go to the pasture.

Slim looked at my Arabian horse and said, "Jim, I don't think your Arabian stallion will ride very good in the trailer, especially with the other ranch horses."

"Slim," I replied, "Don't you worry. My horse is like your new saddle. He will be a lot more comfortable after the first day's big work. This is my horse's first day."

There was a big, old tractor tire laying by the horse barn. It stood about five feet high when upright and it was just right for what I wanted to do. I ran the chain through the tire and fastened the chain together. I then took my rope off the saddle and made a lariat loop at one end. With a short piece of nylon rope, I went through my honda (or loop) at the end of my rope. I then tied the rope to the chain.

I asked Slim to hand me the rope as soon as I got on the Arabian Stallion. I got on the horse and he did his usual stupid stuff just as Jan had said he would. I rode by Slim and he handed me my rope.

"See you at the cow pens!" I told Slim.

I started riding off dragging the tractor tire behind us. Now, instead of being able to look around and do stupid stuff, the Arabian stallion had nothing on his mind but work. He tried to run off a couple of times but I held on to him tightly! With the tire weight dragging behind him he began to get tired and before long I was able to easily control his speed.

He was beginning to understand we could be a team.

I asked him to trot and he slowed down to a trot. Then we went to a walk. Once we were away from everything we stopped for a brief minute of rest. By now the two of us were away from anything the horse could look at or nicker at. It was just the two of us and he knew it.

We got moving again and I repeated the same routine over and over. We loped, trotted, walked and then rested until we were at the cow pens. It was only a mile for us but I am sure it seemed a lot more for the horse! By the time we arrived, the stallion had learned how to brace himself and put pressure on the dragging rope.

Slim was waiting for me. He looked at me and then at my horse who, by now, was standing quiet and looked very tired. "He looks like my saddle after the first day," Slim teased. When the work was done, we loaded the horses to head back to the ranch. After a day's worth of work, there was no kicking, squealing or nickering left in the horse.

I unloaded him off of the trailer at the ranch and loaded him on the trailer for the ride back home. The stallion went straight to his stall. He was quiet and relaxed. Jan said he sure looked better but the doctor who owned him still wanted him to be trained to ride with an English or flat saddle and not a cowboy saddle.

I used this horse for five weeks. We rode in the pasture, through rocky ravines, on steep, narrow paths and whatever else the country threw at us. This horse was very surefooted and when I roped a steer from the back he learned to brace himself so he would not be jerked down. He soon was fun to ride. He clearly began to enjoy the work and was focused.

I always rode a quarter horse who weighed between 1,000 and 1,200 pounds. This stallion was probably only 800 pounds. Regardless of how 'small' this stallion was, I could rope steers as big as he was and he still did the job. He seemed to have a lot of endurance but he did not have the quickness of a quarter horse.

Jan soon began riding him in the arena with the proper saddle so he would get used to the show atmosphere. He was becoming an all-around horse. During the last week of training Jan said the doctor told her he would be there on Sunday to see how much progress his horse had made. "When he comes here," I told her, "you take him to the arena and ride him with whatever saddle he wants. It will work out very well, I promise." It was then Jan and I agreed not to take any more Arabian Horses like this to train. These were more like 'pets' to their owners and we would rather train a working ranch type of horse.

The doctor was satisfied and we turned the horse over to him. We learned that while the doctor may have owned the horse, he had a girl working for him whose job it was to ride the stallion in the arena for the Arabian Horse shows. We wished her luck!

Three weeks after he took his horse home, the doctor drove up to our barn. The first thing that came to my mind was that the stallion had hurt somebody and the doctor was coming to complain. He stopped his car and got out. He had a smile on his face which was nice to see.

He went to Jan and said his horse won both classes he had entered at the Houston Arabian Horse Show! His next statement gave us something to think about.

"I have three more Arabian stallions," he told Jan, "And I want them trained the same way with no cowboy saddle. They have to be ridden with an English saddle, not a cowboy saddle just like the last one. I want you to know that after the last show I was offered a big price in Houston for the Arabian horse you trained."

Needless to say, I was very proud of Jan and the work we did with the horse. I was also very proud of her when she gave him an answer.

"Thank you," she told him, "But I am afraid we have all the horses we can ride and train at the moment. We are also about to leave in the next few months for the show circuit and we do not have room for other horses."

He understood, thanked us and left. We later learned he sold his horse for something in the $30,000 to $40,000 range. Jan and I figured something out really quickly. If his prized horse, a pure Arabian stallion, got hurt while he was out on the big ranch running on land filled with armadillo holes, rocks and snakes while wearing a western saddle and roping steers like the common horses did, then the two of us might be in for a *big* lawsuit. We knew it was better not to ride or train any more the Arabian stallions!

FAST PONY

We were at home with quite a few calf ropers. It was a Sunday and we were having a calf roping "jackpot." It was a common game among us. I had a little Brahma-type calf that would outrun the calf ropers. I got teased by them because they said the calf was too fast for them.

Sensing an opportunity, I made them a bet the calf could not outrun my comedy pony. They laughed and the bet was on! I had a small saddle and it fit the pony perfectly. I caught my pony, saddled him up and went to the calf roping arena. My pony and I backed into the roping chute. I had my rope at the ready. The calf was put into his chute and we were ready to go!

On my signal, the calf was let loose. I took off after him, chased him down and roped him. After the calf was roped, I pulled on the pony and brought him to a stop. While the pony and I stopped, the calf did not. He was still running! The calf was going so hard he jerked my pony upside down and I was soon under him. The saddle horn came down on my chest, right near my stomach.

In the meantime, while I was lying on the ground, in pain, all the cowboys near the chutes were whooping and hollering and laughing and having a "good ole time" at my expense! It may have been funny to them, but I had a bad pain in my chest. Finally, after a few agonizing moments, (they thought I had been playing possum) they eventually walked out to see how I was doing.

The next thing I knew, I was in an ambulance going to the hospital! They took x-rays and it was discovered nothing was broken but somewhere, at the top of my stomach, I had crushed one of the passageways taking food into my stomach. I found I could not swallow any food. The doctor gave me pain pills and relaxation pills. For the next couple of weeks, before I ate, I had to take those relaxation pills.

Even now, 40 years later, I still choke easily.

MEETING THE PAXTONS

When we were at our home in Weatherford, Texas, we had a really good practice area. It was a great place to rope calves and steers. One Sunday we had quite a few ropers come out to our ranch. We were practicing and before too long we started a little $5 jackpot. It was a small but very competitive challenge. I was just happy to have people come out, have fun and practice.

Once, a car turned in and parked in our driveway. I did not recognize the man or the two boys who were with him. The man came to where we were and told me he had been at the local flea market.

"Hi," he began, "I just bought a little donkey at the market and was wondering if I could get you to go and get it for me. I'll pay you for your trouble."

"I'm sorry, but I can't right now," I replied.

"I live close to here," he told me, "So do you know anyone else who could help me?"

I thought about it for a few seconds. "Look," I offered, "Why don't you just take my truck since you live near here? Just bring it back when you are done." He looked at me kind of odd and said, "Do you know me?" "No" I replied, "My name is Jim. What's yours?" "John," he said, "But why are you loaning me your truck when you don't even know me?" I stared at him and laughed. "You came up here wearing a suit and with two little boys," I told him, "And you do not look like a thief to me."

He thanked me, got my truck and trailer and retrieved his donkey. Before the day was over, he returned them to me and handed me his business card. "Are you married?" he asked me. "Yes, I am but my wife, Jan, is not home right now or I would introduce you to her." "Well, listen," he continued, "Why don't you and your wife come to my house? I am having a cookout and it would be really nice if the two of you could join us." He told me when it was, and although it was on a weekend, when Jan and I were usually very busy, we decided to go and see what was happening.

His new place was a rambling ranch style house and a barn. Jan and I were introduced to his wife. She had oodles and oodles of personality and hospitality. We did not know many of the friends and neighbors who were there. We soon discovered they were the owners of one of the *big ranches* in the area! Before we left the cookout, I told Jan we should go up and find out what the last name of our host was. It turned out to be Paxton, Mr. John Paxton. We thanked him for his hospitality and went on our way.

Six or seven months later, John pulled in my driveway and said he needed a good, nice, gentle Shetland pony for his two boys. Ponies are pretty cheap, but good, nice and gentle ones usually cost quite a bit more. A friend of mine was a calf roper and he had a boy about 12 years old who owned a pony. The boy used it to chase and rope calves on their ranch. This pony was outstanding! It worked just as well as the bigger horses. The boy had outgrown this horse and was looking for a larger one to ride.

When I talked to my friends, they told me the cost of a good pony was about $350. This pony was the best I had seen and he was shocked when I told him I wanted to buy it. I thought for sure he would not accept the offer. I guess he knew his son needed a bigger horse because he sold me the pony!

"Mr. Paxton," I said when I called him, "I probably have one of the best ponies in Texas for you." He said, "Okay! It sounds like it is just what I want! Could you bring it to the house?"

I took the pony to his house and he was very happy with it. The boys rode him and got along great with him.

Mr. Paxton and I became pretty good friends. I did not know what his occupation was until he told me he owned a lumber yard in Fort Worth where he sold exotic and special types of wood. He had sales all over the world.

I once asked him how he got into the lumber business. His answer was unexpected! "Many years ago, when they struck oil in Kansas, Oklahoma, and Texas," he explained, "My dad and his dad before him furnished all the lumber for the oil rigs. At the time, these two had a monopoly on the wood market in the area. Back then, all the oil rigs were made of wood, not metal, so business was good, very good!"

You can look at some of the old oil rigs and you will see a tremendous amount of lumber used for the framing and support. "Since the oil boom was lucrative, they stayed in the wood business," he continued. John was a descendent of these men and he took over the company.

In talking to Mr. Paxton, I found out he did his banking in Fort Worth. Something came up and I needed to take a loan out using my ranch as collateral. I went to Mr. Paxton and asked him for advice. "Do you know the best bank in Fort Worth where I can get a loan?" I asked him. He laughed, gave me the name of a bank and said, "When you go in the bank, ask for the president of the bank and talk to him personally." I thanked him and headed for Fort Worth. When I walked into the bank, the receptionist was nice and referred me to a loan officer.

When I saw the loan officer, I told him, "I do not have an appointment, but I was wondering if I could speak to the president of this bank instead. Please tell him Mr. John Paxton recommended this bank." With a "good luck" smile, he left me and was gone for a few minutes. He was nice. At this moment, I appreciated John's advice, but doubted I would get to see the president, especially without an appointment.

When he returned, the loan officer had a smile. "You must know somebody," he said with a laugh, "because he will see you." When I walked into the president's office, he stood up and we introduced ourselves and shook hands.

"Well, Mr. Warvell," he asked politely, "What can I do for you today?" "I need to borrow some money," I explained. "I have a ranch for collateral."

"How much do you need?" he asked.

"If I remember correctly, I need about $50,000."

He sat back and smiled.

"John told me you were coming in" he said quietly, "So just go to the loan officer and he will help you fill out the paperwork."

I was shocked and stunned.

"What paperwork?" I asked.

"The loan papers," he told me. "Just go there, sign the papers and get your loan."

I was even more shocked! In a few minutes, I got my money. I paid them back, every penny of it! Things went extremely well!

Later, when I saw Mr. Paxton, I thanked him for sending me to the bank. He told me they were thinking about moving to California and maybe trying to get into the movie business. He said he had done some acting, liked it and was ready to get out of the lumber business for awhile.

The Paxtons always had a big Christmas party at their ranch and for the last 3 or 4 years we were always invited. I still don't know much about the Paxtons, but we really enjoyed their parties.

As usual, Jan and I had to leave and go on the road. We were usually gone for 6 to 7 months at a time. When we came home, the Paxton family had sold their land and moved to California. We said goodbye to them before we left and it was the last time we ever saw them.

Several years later, a movie came out. It was called "Twister" and starred Bill Paxton. We soon discovered he was one of the little boys who came to our ranch when his daddy borrowed our truck and trailer to get their donkey!

After we learned of this, we did some research and found John was also an actor and a producer in Hollywood. We never realized he enjoyed acting and producing as much as he did! John never talked about his movies to me. Jan and I were in complete shock. To us, he was just our friend, John Paxton!

CHAPTER 27

A Few Fun Short Stories Over the Years

TOMMY AND THE PIE

Back in the day, when we were starting to put our acts together in Florida, we had a nice place to practice. It was an area with a quarter horse race track and on Sunday, they would have match races. There was enough room on the grounds to set up a nice arena for our practices.

During this time, we met a lot of different people. One man I met raced champion well-known quarter horses. His name was Tommy and he seemed to have enough money to be very successful at buying, raising and racing horses. He had several brown mares, and one mare in particular who produced several champions and was known throughout the United States. He also had a young stallion who was just coming on to being 2 years old. This horse was his pride and joy.

Sometimes Tommy would ask me to come to the stable for a chat, advice or help. One day, he told me that he had decided to sell the horse he loved because it was going to be in the All-American Futurity, one of the biggest quarter horse races in the world, and he had several buyers for the horse. It was a chance to make some real money.

One of the buyers offered him $8,000 but Tommy said he wanted $20,000 for the horse and he even told the man he already had an offer for $20,000. He wanted the bigger offer and told me if he did not get $20,000 for the horse, then he would give the horse to me! Something must have worked because he sold the horse!

The horse was a good one! It qualified for the All American Futurity and ended up being one of the favorites to win the race. On the day of the race, things did not go according to plan. He did not do well, but to my understanding, the 6666 Ranch had already bought the horse for $40,000, so they decided to use him for a breeding stallion instead.

After Tommy sold the horse, he came to me driving a brand new Jeep. He was on his way to the race track at the New Orleans fairgrounds. He had a stable of horses he wanted to run at their track. He wanted me to drive the Jeep and he would pay the expenses of the trip. Problem was, I had often heard Tommy was on the "shady" side at times and you had to be careful. This may or may not have been true. Still, I never talked to him about it.

I don't know how, but about every six months, Tommy got himself a new Cadillac. When you saw him, he looked like a movie-type underworld man. He portrayed himself as a serious, no joke type of man.

Tommy and I got along very well, we never had any problems. I told him I would drive his Jeep to New Orleans. I did not expect to have trouble doing this. We drove for several hours when Tommy suggested we stop and get something to eat.

I told the waitress I was not hungry and was just going to have a piece of pie. Tommy said he thought he would have pie, too. I ordered a slice of cream pie with meringue and he ordered a slice of apple pie.

When the waitress brought the pies to our table, my meringue-topped pie looked good and tasted good as well! Tommy's pie looked and tasted bad. He did not say anything, so we had our pie, finished our drinks and left.

After a couple more hours of driving, Tommy again suggested we stop and get something to eat. He was the boss and paying the bills, so we stopped. Once again, I was not hungry. I ordered another slice of cream pie with meringue topping. Tommy ordered a slice of peach pie. Lo and behold, the same thing happened again! My cream pie looked good and tasted delicious and Tommy's piece of pie looked like it was a day old…maybe more.

In a frustrated voice he asked me, "What is it you are doing to the waitress so she gives you a good piece of pie and she gives me a bad piece of pie?"

I just laughed and finished eating. I left it alone and did not say anything. This was no time for joking.

We made it to the track, unloaded the horses and put them in their stalls. Race tracks always have a kitchen and this one was no exception. "They have pretty good food here," Tommy said. "Since we have not eaten all day, why don't we stop in and get some real food?" "Sounds good," I replied.

We had a nice meal and when we were done, Tommy wanted to prove a point. He wanted a piece of pie! We each ordered a slice of pie and waited. The lady brought us our two desserts. I ordered cream pie with meringue and once again it looked and tasted delicious! I will never forget what happened next. Tommy ordered a piece of cherry pie. When it came, it looked like it had been stepped on by an elephant! It was terrible looking!

This was the last straw! Tommy could not take it any longer! He stood up and asked the waitress to come back to the table. When she came, he went ballistic! I was sitting there and did not want to laugh in his presence, but I could hardly hold myself together! Tommy told her to take the pie back, he did not want it anymore. It was just fun to watch and I enjoyed the show!

As I look back, I will always remember the great pieces of pie I had on that trip!

DENVER

We were fortunate to work the Denver National Western Stock Show and Rodeo on our second year in the rodeo business. It was quite an honor, but we soon found out how cold it was around the Rocky Mountains. It was January!

At the time, we had a 20 foot-long house trailer equipped with a kerosene stove. The first night of the rodeo, we went to our trailer and discovered we were all out of kerosene. I got in the pickup and drove to the nearest filling station where I tried to buy 5 gallons of kerosene. I got lucky, found a place and bought it.

During the night, it got down to *35 below zero!* It was the coldest weather I have ever experienced! Our little stove could not put out enough heat for the two of us to be comfortable. To tell you how cold it was, I had snow on my boots when I walked into the trailer. It fell on the floor when I entered the trailer and in the morning, it was still there on the floor!

Jan and I managed to survive the night. Somehow, we thawed out enough to make it through the duration of the rodeo and stock show. Thankfully, our next stop was in the south. What a paradise the south seemed to be with all of its warm weather!

LITTLE RODEO

Jan and I had only been married for a couple of years. The White Horse Troupe was over and we were on our way to a little rodeo out west. Driving down the road, I told Jan I felt, "A little stopped up."

"Well, pull into this truck stop and I will go in and get you something," she told me.

I pulled in and waited while she went inside and came back with something looking a lot like chocolate. I took a little piece of it and it tasted pretty good, sort of like chocolate. It did not take long before I decided it was really good so I ate the whole bar!

A couple of hours later we rolled into the rodeo. I unloaded my horse, saddled it and got ready to do some calf roping. We were soon in the chute and when the time arrived, I rode out and roped my calf. My horse stopped and I was off of it and following the rope to the calf. In less than a heartbeat, I threw the calf to the ground.

Then, everything broke loose! Literally! I stopped, let the calf get up and quickly left the arena.

Jan watched all of this and when she saw me she said, "Is everything okay?" I just went back to the trailer, got out of my clothes, cleaned up and got some new clothes. I had learned a valuable lesson: *I will never, ever eat a whole bar of Ex-Lax again!*

THE REFRIGERATOR

We had an old refrigerator at our house. It did not have a door handle—don't ask, I don't remember! We had to use a straight edge screwdriver whenever we wanted to open it. You took the screwdriver, pushed in the latch and the door would open. Strangely enough, in the early days, our first camping trailer had the same problem with its refrigerator. We also used a screwdriver to open it. In some ways, it was convenient because we could hide things in the refrigerator that we wanted to keep away from the kids!

We finally bought a new refrigerator for the house, and when guests would come over, Sonna, my young daughter (7 or 8 years old at the time), would run over to the refrigerator and was excited to show them how she could open the refrigerator all by herself!

We could do nothing but smile!

WHITE FEATHER

On one occasion, we were on our way to the next rodeo. We had to drive all night and when we finally arrived it was time for the rodeo to begin.

The horses had been in their trailer all night. We stopped to water them at one of the truck stops. Unfortunately, it was a very noisy truck stop with lots of trucks coming and going. This commotion rattled the horses. There was too much on their minds to drink anything because of that.

Since we arrived just as the rodeo was ready to begin, Jan and I quickly unloaded the horses and rushed to get ready for the show. We did not have time to water our horses before the performance since it was close to the time for us to be in the arena.

When Jan and I worked an arena, it was usually a clean show with nothing else in the arena except Jan and I, the horses and our props. The reason for this was because we did not want Jan's horse, White Feather, to be distracted at some foreign object and take his eyes off of Jan while she was working with him.

On this particular day, Jan walked into the middle of the arena. I turned White Feather loose, just as we had done many times before. He would always go to Jan, circle her one time and kneel for her. She would get on his back and ride him bareback (without a saddle or bridle) for her act. This time, when I turned him loose, White Feather ran like he always did, right toward Jan. But, instead of stopping and making a circle around her, he ran right past Jan to the other end of the arena where a big steel water trough had been placed! (The producer of the show had filled the trough with water for the steers and cattle who were used in the show.) White Feather ran straight for the trough! He stuck his head in the water and started to drink. He was thirsty!

I thought to myself, "This is going to be a wreck!"

Then to my surprise, White Feather finished drinking, looked up, saw Jan in the middle of the arena and galloped towards her. When he got close to her, he kneeled for her and the act continued just as if nothing happened.

It was totally amazing that after he got his drink, he was ready to do his performance. He liked his work, but he needed his drink first!

PONY

At one time, I had two white ponies I used in my comedy act. One of the ponies looked like a miniature horse, and boy could he run fast!

My daughter Toni had a good friend, Marcy, whose dad was a calf roper. They were often at the same rodeo as we were. They would ride my horses in the afternoon, including my two ponies. The most fun I think they would have was when we worked at a fairground where they had "starting gates" for the horse races. When the fairgrounds were not having the races, the gates to the starting stalls were always left open. The girls would take my ponies into the starting gates and wait for someone to yell, "Go!" The girls would then take off and begin racing around the track. They showed me their little act one day and I was impressed at how hard and fast the ponies could run.

After they had finished racing once or twice, the girls would go around the fairgrounds to find other kids who had ponies and see if they wanted to match up their ponies and race. (What kind of wagers, if any, were involved we never knew!)

Toni and her friend would beat the competition every time! These girls would "sucker" the competition because they knew their ponies were faster!

There were a few times I was not happy with these races. After the girls finished racing, and it was time for my comedy act, I discovered that my little pony team was worn out from racing all afternoon. It turned out that I could not use the ponies the way I would have liked. I was not going to endanger myself or the ponies.

I just hope their "wagers" were worth it!

CANADA EXPO '67: WORLD'S FAIR, MONTREAL, QUEBEC

One of my best memories was the 1967 International Expo in Montreal, Canada. There were a lot of famous groups invited, including The King's Troop Royal Horse Artillery, The Barbados Artillery Group, The Royal Canadian Mounted Police and The Warvell Family.

Of all these groups, we had the honor of being the only US act (outside of Wayne Newton, that is!) to perform at the World Expo.

For the Expo, the Canadians had built a stadium similar to a football stadium just for the horse entertainment. We were told the stadium was going to be torn down as soon as the Expo was over.

At the one end of the stadium, they built a ramp from the top of the stadium to the floor of the arena. When the show opened, the stadium was dark. The Canadian Mounted Police and other performers were to walk down the ramp as if they were coming out of the heavens above!

One of my greatest memories of this opening ceremony was seeing my 5-year old daughter, Sonna, riding her horse down the ramp and leading the way as she carried a torch! As she came down with those Canadian Mounties behind her, I choked up with pride! Here I was, coming from a small town of 40 people and now I was representing my country at the premier horse show in the world and my daughter was now leading one of the most revered police units in the world at the opening of the World's Fair! It was a sight I never expected to see and one I will never, ever forget!

Another one of those great moments there was when Wayne Newton sang "Happy Birthday" to my other daughter Toni!

When we performed at the Expo, we had to change part of our act. Instead of having Jan ride her horse, White Feather, and jump over a white convertible, they wanted her to jump over a wagon instead. We knew White Feather did not care what he jumped since he never refused to jump anything. It worked, and they were quite happy.

One afternoon, I was sitting at the stables by White Feather's stall when a young lady came by. She told me she was a painter and was there anything I wanted her to paint. It was then I got an idea.

I showed her White Feather and told her as a surprise for Jan, I would like her to paint a picture of White Feather's head. She accepted my offer but little did I know this would create a major problem. I had to find a means to keep Jan away from the stables for two or three hours at a time. To do this, I would send her on a variety of errands so the artist could do her magic. It took at least three sittings before she was done with the portrait. Each time we had to take the horse out and make him stand still.

Thankfully, it was a success. At least it was a success until Jan came back early one day and found her beloved White Feather's stall empty! She was suddenly a mama bear and someone had her cub and she wanted it back! I gave her a good excuse. She refused to believe it. Knowing how a mama bear can be when you stand between her and her cub, I decided it would be better to give up the secret!

To save face, I took her to where White Feather was so she could see the painting. Jan saw it and was very happy. Over the years, I thought she might keep the painting and kick me out!

We both managed to survive and the painting still hangs in our living room.

ANOTHER CANADA STORY

Another time, Jan and I were in Canada working for a Canadian rodeo producer named Harry Vold. He had a rodeo in High Level, Alberta (800 kms north of Edmonton). In order for us to get there, we had to drive 100 miles on paved roads and the rest on a gravel road.

When we got there we pulled into a wooded area. Trees 6 to 8 inches thick were everywhere. They did have electricity for us, but they had no water.

"Where is the rodeo arena?" I asked one of the rodeo workers. He pointed to the woods and walked away. I figured the arena was in there somewhere. After I got settled and had rested, I walked into the woods, but could not find an arena. Thinking I had made a few wrong turns, I asked again. This time he pointed to where I was standing, next to the trees. "What about all these trees?" I asked. "Oh, don't worry," one of the men told me, "They will all be down soon."

The rodeo was Friday, Saturday and Sunday. This was Tuesday! "When are you going to start on it?" I asked. "This afternoon," was the only reply I received. Oh, this was going to be interesting! I wanted to see how these men were going to cut these trees down and build an arena in only 2½ days!

In the afternoon, men were tying ribbons to trees. As I watched them, I could visualize an arena taking shape, but right now, the place was still covered with a lot of trees! Before long, the bulldozer appeared and I realized they were going to push the trees down. In Texas, if you push trees down, it takes a lot of work. After you push the tree over, you will find roots going deep into the ground. Sometimes they break off and you have a hard time getting these roots out of the ground. I wondered what they were going to do!

Now this place was just full of trees. We just stood back and watched the bulldozer. He did not just "creak" along like most bulldozers would do. This bulldozer was in "road" gear mode and he was moving…moving fast! In no time at all he had knocked down lots of trees and simply pushed them out of the way. Before long, he had the area cleared of trees! Now it was beginning to look like an arena. I could not believe it!

One of the locals said they looked like match sticks when they come down fast as they did. He was right, too. I wondered why it was so easy. I learned later, that in this part of the country, the ground is frozen so hard and so deep that the roots of the trees have to grow near and above the ground instead of going deep into the ground. These above-ground roots look like the fingers on a hand. When the bulldozer pushes the trees over, it also pushes the roots out of the way as well.

After the trees were gone, 8 to 10 men showed up and started putting wooden posts into the ground. They put a fence around the outside of the posts and even made some chutes! Much to my amazement, the area went from a forest of trees to an arena in about three quarters of a day. Think about it! They built an arena in less than one day!

We had brought our trailer with us, but since there was no water, we decided to stay in a local hotel so we could shower and have fresh water to drink. This was a small town. In fact, a lot of the sidewalks were nothing but wooden planks. It was still a primitive town to us.

We managed to get a room on the second floor. The first floor had a long wooden bar just like you would see in western movies. The room was also filled with a lot of tables and chairs. It soon became apparent to us that one man seemed to own the whole town from the hotel to the post office to the bank and just about everything else!

Earlier in the day, we were invited to show up for a drink. When I got there, I was shocked at what I saw! There was quite the commotion with men and women everywhere and all of them were shoulder to shoulder in the crowded bar. Their way of life was just so different than what I was used to. I had to go upstairs to our room and tell Jan she had to come down and see what was going on one floor below us!

Everyone in the bar was laughing and they were dancing in a way I had never seen before! We finally found a table with some friends we knew. They were here to work the rodeo too. We sat there and did some people watching. It was very entertaining.

About midnight the bar closed, but we were told everyone was going to the Veterans of Foreign Wars (VFW) hall for an all-night bar and whiskey drinking! The next thing kind of shocked me! Outside of the bar the group was met by five Canadian Mounties. All of these Mounties were riding horses. Two of them led the group and the other three were bringing up the rear as they marched the four blocks to the VFW. When they got there, the crowd went inside and the party picked up right where it had left off. All of them went except for Jan and me. We had our excitement and entertainment for the day. We went upstairs and hit the sack.

The next morning, there was a parade downtown. Once more the Canadian Mounted Police were leading the way. The people lined the sidewalk for one block. They waved and shouted at the parade. As the parade reached the next block, people suddenly appeared and on and on it went. We watched and realized the people lining the sidewalks were the same people we saw at the last block! It seems they were just following the parade and cheering them on block by block! Jan said she had never been in a parade before where she felt like she was waving to the same family the whole time!

The next day was rodeo time. The makeshift grounds were filled with spectators and people were standing all around the rodeo's fenced-in area. The people were very accepting of what we did because there was not a lot happening in this little town. I imagine they could have all gone to the arena, busted balloons and still had a very good time with lots of applause and celebration.

We left the next morning and headed back to civilization. Of course, we had to be sure to fill the gas tank before we left! The only activity I saw was 2 or 3 moose crossing the road. My friend Fred, rode with us. He had partied every night and day we were in the town. Although the road was rough, bumpy and dirty, it did not bother Fred. He slept all the way!

ONE MORE STORY ABOUT A TRIP TO CANADA

One season we worked the Quebec, Canada Shrine Circus. This show had many circus animals. Gene Holder, who entertained people at various fairs and get-togethers, was there with his exotic animals as well.

Gene had a trailer where he transported and kept most of his animals. Usually, he had a lot of room for all his animals, but on this occasion, he ran out of space for his lion. Yes, I said he ran out of room for his *lion!*

At the time, we had our horses in a little barn. At the end of this barn was a small shed. This shed had no windows and only one door, so it made a great place to keep this particular animal!

This lion, like a lot of wild cats, was fed horse meat. As I learned later, the place where Gene normally got his horsemeat was closed. Because of this, Gene would have to wait at least a day before he could feed his lion. In other words, the lion had not been fed for the day!

During the day, one of the attendants came to see how the large cat was doing. He opened the door and the lion managed to get by him and escape! As this was happening, our horses were tied to the wall in the small barn next to the room where the lion was located. (The key words here are "where the lion *was* located!")

When the lion came out of his little room, he ran around a little bit and then ran to where one of our white horses was tied. I do not know what the lion was thinking. It might have been something like, "This particular horse would be pretty tasty to eat!" The name of this white horse was Andy and he was the most docile and gentle horse we had in our entire group.

The lion ran to Andy, reared up on his two hind legs and put his huge lion paws on Andy's withers (shoulders). As he got up there, he had his huge mouth close to Andy's neck. *A lion!* I was not about to try and put my arms around this lion's neck!

There were 3 or 4 animal trainers in the barn area. They were soon in with the lion, as they tried to pull him off and control him enough to get him back in his room. I did not know it at the time, but they told me later that the lion had been declawed! Even if I had known he had been declawed… I still probably would have stood and watched!

I thought it was a scary moment at the time. Then, when I thought about the people who came to the barn, got next to the wild lion not thinking about the danger they were in, and how I watched all of these events unfold, I began to think, "Maybe they thought this was all an act!"

Then I realized how stupid it must be to watch a lion mauling a horse and not realizing you could be next!

Our horse Andy never seemed to get excited. I figured he was probably wondering what all the commotion was about. Guess it was a good thing he was a horse who did not know what a lion could do!

CALIFORNIA, CAMP PENDLETON MARINE BASE: IN TROUBLE WITH THE MILITARY POLICE

One of our trips took us to the Camp Pendleton Marine Base in California. Cotton Rosser, a well-known rodeo producer, hired us to perform.

I noticed the area was being patrolled by the military police. (This was after all, a military base!)

Our Roman Riding act followed the bareback bronc riding event. Before our act came out, I entered the arena 'legitimately' posing as a photographer while the bronc riding event was happening, as I had done before. I appeared to be taking pictures of the bronc riders. Nothing strange about it so far! Usually, to make it even more real, I would set off the camera's flash every now and then. Of course, I would only do it after the horse and rider had gone by.

After the bareback riding event was over, the Roman Riding act entered the arena with Jan and our daughter each standing on their team of two horses. As they galloped by me, as usual, I pretended like I was taking their pictures. While this was happening, the announcer came over the speakers and told me it was too dangerous for me to be in the arena because I could be responsible for an accident if the horses got "spooked."

Again, I pretended not to pay attention to him. The two Roman Riding teams came pretty close to me and I jumped out of the way. Before long, the people in the grandstand started yelling for the "press man" to get out of the arena!

They were yelling, but I ignored them. As the act progressed, the fans got more and more upset as they yelled and screamed for me to get out of the arena. I ignored them and continued to agitate the riders. Soon the announcer came back and asked for the police to come in the arena and escort me out.

On this occasion, things did not go according to plan! I glanced over and saw two military police walking together and coming into the middle of the arena to, obviously, get me!

Unfortunately, I knew what they had in mind. I am sure they did not know or even think this was part of our comedy act! As Jan rode her horses past me, I yelled at her to cut the act short and come to me fast so she could "pull" my pants off because the military police were coming to get me!

Before these military police could grab me, they had to stop and get out of the way of the horses! The Roman Riders rode past me with just enough room for me not to be hit. As they went by, I hooked the loop from my breakaway pants onto the little hook attached to Jan's riding equipment. Jan and her horses kept on going and as they went by me, my pants flew off and the military policemen were now standing there looking at their pant-less victim: me!

I can still see the faces on those men! One was standing at attention and looked very disturbed. The other military policeman took one look at me, realized what had happened and was bent over laughing!

It was a pretty good show, even if we had to cut it short!

JOAN

We made lifelong friends with people all over the world. Here is a story about one of them named Joan. Even though her name was spelled

Joan, everyone called her Jo-Ann, so I will refer to her as Jo-Ann from now on.

The farm where Donny and Jo-Ann lived had a chicken house about 30 feet long. They cleaned it out and made a western store out of it. Jo-Ann was, I am not saying hyper, but she was close to it. Her western store grew and grew for many years. It was called "The Rodeo Shop" and became one of the largest western stores in the state of Ohio. She would go to clothing conventions and western conventions all over the country to buy things for her store.

During her "buying sprees" she would find out where we were and if she could, she would stop and visit with us. This was fun because Jo-Ann and I had this "thing" where we were always playing jokes on each other.

At the time, we had a neighbor who was a rodeo announcer and the main announcer at the Saturday night televised wrestling matches in Fort Worth, Texas. He was a jokester, too. After a couple of times visiting him at his house, I walked in one day to see what I thought was someone standing there. "Excuse me Dan," I told him, "I did not know you had company." He said, 'That's not company. That's Uncle Charlie." As I sat down, I was facing Uncle Charlie and for the first time, I got a good look at him. Uncle Charlie was a "life-sized" dummy. He was an Indian figure stuffed into a pair of jeans and a shirt. He looked pretty real! "Sometimes I get pretty lonely," Dan told me, "so I come in here and talk to Uncle Charlie."

One day, Jo-Ann stopped and visited us at our ranch in Weatherford, Texas. I made her an offer. Dan's house was designed with a western theme and I thought she would enjoy seeing it. "Why don't we hop into the truck and we'll go visit with Dan and you can see his nice, western-style house?"

She agreed, so away we went. I knocked on Dan's door and he told us to come inside. As we walked in the door, Dan told us his Uncle Charlie was tired and had just gone to bed and was asleep. I smiled at Dan and he smiled back. We sat down and visited with him. Then he gave us a tour of the house.

"Let's go visit with Charlie," Dan told us. "He would like to see you. He likes company but he has been feeling a little bad lately."

Jo-Ann and I followed Dan to the bedroom where Uncle Charlie was "sleeping." All of the bedroom lights were off, but we could see fairly well. As we walked into the room, Charlie was on the far side of the bed.

"Charlie, we have visitors," Dan said to the body in the bed. Of course, Charlie just laid there and did not move. Jo-Ann was standing next to me, all 5 feet 4 inches and 110 pounds of her. Dan shook the bed, but Charlie did not respond to it. Dan shook him again. He reached down and looked at his "uncle." "My God, I think he's dead!" Dan shouted. He then picked Charlie up about a foot off the bed, and shook him once more. Dan just stood there and kept on shaking Charlie.

Jo-Ann watched and started screaming! A second later, she jumped on me and her feet were soon wrapped around my waist! This was scaring the wits out of her! While she was clinging to me, Dan let the cat out of the bag. "Oh, don't worry," he said nonchalantly, "Uncle Charlie isn't real. He is just a dummy!" Jo-Ann looked at me, eye to eye and said, "You S… of a B…!"

I love practical jokes!

JOAN AND THE PLASTER HEAD HOAX

Somewhere along the line (don't ask me where!), I had acquired some plaster heads that looked like war criminals. They were left over from one of the shows and I just threw them in the back of my pickup truck and kept them. Jo-Ann was visiting us and she had tickets for the grandstand, about 4 rows up. I just happened to know the drink vendor for this area of the grandstand. He sold his products out of a little red box. I grabbed him and gave him $5 to put one of my plaster heads in his box. When he got next to Jo-Ann, I wanted him to tip his box and let the head roll next to her feet, or close to her.

The vendor and I waited until my act was over and I had my trick horse. This horse would lie on his back with his feet in the air. I would grab his hind legs and steer them like a handlebar. I told the vendor, "When you see me do that, it will be a signal for you to approach her."

He did his job beautifully! The head rolled out of his red container and Jo-Ann jumped and screamed! She knew who was "really" responsible and when she finally settled down, she looked at me. I gave her a little wave and a big smile!

I could easily read her lips and knew exactly what she was calling me! I had been there before!

JOAN AND JONSIE

We were in North Platte, Nebraska and Jo-Ann stopped by to visit Jan and I. We had an airstream trailer which was "home" to us when on the road. On this show, we were lucky enough to have Jones Benally (Jonsie to us, Navajo Hoop Dancing Champion) working on the same show. Jo-Ann visited us in the trailer for a bit, and then we stepped out with her. We turned the corner and Jonsie was getting ready for the show. He had his war paint on and was looking mean and fierce.

He looked right at Jo-Ann and said, "Me no scalp anybody today." Jo-Ann was startled by the comment. It was just an accidental happening, but Jo-Ann thought it was a planned event. I thought it was funny!

GHOST HOTEL

When we went to Japan, I was in the first group to arrive in the country. Our living quarters were at a large hotel. They took me to the floor where all of us would be living. I was surprised at how nice the rooms were but none of the rooms had a bed in them!

In Japan, instead of beds, they used a traditional style of mat called a "futon," which was a padded mattress of woven straw. It was how they did it and what the Japanese were used to using, so we had to use them as well.

After looking around the rooms, we went down to the front desk and asked them why our whole floor of the hotel was empty.

"This is where you are going to stay," they told us. It seemed like a good explanation at the time. As we were about to leave, another interpreter asked about the floor we were assigned to. "Oh" the clerk replied, "That floor of the hotel is empty because it is haunted."

Hmmmmm.

After the work ended for the day, I was escorted back to the hotel. I inquired about the floor where we would be staying and why they said it was haunted. "A lady was found dead from suicide on the floor," they told me.

In addition, they claimed they saw her ghost all the time, but no one would say exactly where.

The next morning, after I had stayed on the floor for the night, the hotel staff was very inquisitive and asked if I had seen the ghost.

"No, I did not see the ghost," I told them. "I left the bedroom door open for her and I am very disappointed she did not come in and visit me."

I stayed in my hotel room for 10 days before the rest of the group arrived. I never saw the ghost once during the entire time. Of course, I did not tell Jan about the ghost when she arrived.

There are some secrets every man should keep from his wife if he wants to stay married!

PEARL DIVING BOAT

Our contract in Japan had us performing 3 shows per day and we worked every day. However, being confined in one spot with so many people was tricky and many of us started to get "cabin fever."

The boss man recognized this and wanted to do something about it. He decided to give us a small "vacation" and take us on a glass bottom boat trip. It was also a fishing trip, and while many of us were fishing, the rest of the cast could look at the ocean's bottom through the glass hull of the boat.

While on the boat, we also got to see one of the main tourist attractions in Japan, pearl diving. It was performed by young, Japanese women wearing rubber diving suits. They hit the water and went under the boat in search of pearls. People would gather round and watch as these girls dove in the water, went under the boat and searched for the elusive pearls.

Our boat was no exception. Most of them watched the pearl diving. However, after a few minutes, those of us fishing on the deck got bored. We went down and began watching the pearl divers with the rest of the passengers.

Why, I will never know, but for some unknown reason, I stood up and said, "For $10, I will dive for pearls!" Before I knew it, the air was filled with Japanese coins and they were all headed in my direction! One of the men with us was a school teacher named John Hosea. This teacher looked at me and said, "For some reason, I knew damn good and well you were going to do something like that!"

He stood up and began gathering all the Japanese Yen and counting them. Back then the Yen was not worth very much and it took a lot of coins *(a lot of coins!)* to reach my $10 request! Suddenly, after gathering coin after coin and doing a lot of counting, he shouted, 'Hey Jim, I got $10 in coins here!"

So, what did I do? You guessed it! I took off my shirt and boots and then took a dive off the side of the boat! Where I am from, a deal was a deal!

As a kid, I was a pretty good swimmer, so I did not think this was going to be a problem for me. Unfortunately, when I hit the water, I discovered why the pearl divers were wearing rubber suits! The water was so cold, it took my breath away! But I had made a deal and they fulfilled their part of the bargain, all $10 of it. Now I had to fulfill my end of the bargain!

I dove about three-fourths of the way under the boat. All of those on the boat were watching and cheering me on. All of them EXCEPT the Japanese pearl divers in their rubber suits! They thought I was committing "Hari Kari" and all of them dove in after me!

They grabbed my legs. My first thought was that I had gotten my legs caught in something on the underbelly of the boat. Those who were watching me through the glass hull said I had a scared look on my face. Truth is, I did!

There was nothing I could do but return to the surface with all the pearl divers by my side. They guided me to the side of the boat where I climbed up the ladder, got a towel and dried off before getting dressed and collecting my $10. After all, a deal is a deal and I had just completed my end of the deal!

The boat soon headed to shore with a lot of good memories for all the passengers. As we headed back, the crew came to me and wanted to know why I would do such a thing. Good question.

When we got to the pier, there was a large group of people lined up and all of them were pointing to me. It seems they had heard about what happened and wanted to see the man who tried to commit suicide!

My wife, Jan, said, "You ______! I thought you were going to die right then and there!"

AMISH STORY

As we had worked Japan many years before, I had developed many friends and contacts there. One day, I got an inquiry from some of the people I knew in Japan who were wanting to buy some draft horses and to see if I could locate and buy this type of horse.

I got in contact with them and said I could get the job done. They wanted to come to the US to see what kind of horses I had in mind before they made a decision, so I made arrangements to meet them in Indianapolis, Indiana. They would fly there and I would negotiate transportation to a big Belgium horse sale.

At this sale, they had all the big size horses that weighed around the 2000 lbs mark. The sale started the next day after their arrival. I took them to the sale to inspect and get an idea of what we were talking about in the type of horse they would want.

There were about 50+ horses sold at the sale, and they sat and discussed the type of horses they were interested in. After the sale, we had a meeting and I assured them I could find these kind of horses at individual farms which would give them a better buying price than the big barn sale would do. The price of the horses in the big barn sale would average in the neighborhood of $5,000-$10,000 a piece. I told them I could buy approximately 30 head of these horses for ½ of that!

I also then told them that, in Canada, I could buy horses called farm chunks. They were smaller, but still weighed between 1300 and 1400 lbs a piece. I never asked what they were going to do with them, but they only wanted mares along with 2 big stallions. I presumed they were going to start raising draft horses in Japan. They wanted 50 head. We came to an agreement on the price. They were to wire me the money to buy the horses.

After our agreement, they returned to Japan. In about 8 or 9 days, the money was deposited in my bank. I was now ready to scour the country looking for the mares to complete my horse purchase. I went to northern Indiana where the counties were nearly 100% Amish where they worked these horses in the fields.

I needed to locate these horses in the Amish community. I could buy these horses better if I had a local Amish man traveling with me. I had a friend that bought and sold draft horses in the Amish community. I called him to see if he could recommend someone to help me locate these horses. My friend told me he knew the perfect person.

Ezra Yoder. Ezra was one of the leading citizens in the Amish community. He helped out in the local sale barn and was a most trusted man. I got in touch with Ezra and explained my situation. He knew my friend as they had done business together and Ezra had a lot of respect for him. After a couple of days, I met Ezra. He had talked to my friend about me and my friend had given him a good character reference of me.

I found a hotel in the community and rented a car so that I could pick up Ezra from his farm and we could ride together looking for horses to buy. The first day was very successful. We had bought 5 or 6 mares. I only had 25 more Belgium mares to buy!

One evening, when I got back to the hotel, I had a message to get in contact with Jan. She told me Bill McDavid wanted me to call him. Bill's family was one of the largest car dealers in the Fort Worth/Dallas area and they had ads about their dealership everyday on TV. They had a dog named Wide Track who was in most of the commercials. Bill told me he wanted to run some ads with a buggy and horse. He wanted the horses to be black and well-trained and not to be scared of TV cameras and floodlights. I told him I thought I could find what he needed. He told me to go ahead and buy one!

The next morning, when I met Ezra, I told him I had an order for a nice black buggy horse and did he know where we could find one? Ezra told me there were some nice black horses around, but he couldn't think of one right now. On the road, the only way the Amish travel was with horse and buggy. You would pass many of them every day. So that day, we went out to find big Belgium mares to fit my order for the Japanese, and while doing so, we kept our eyes open for a black horse attached to a buggy! We saw a lot of buggy horses that day, but these weren't any that I thought could work for my order from Bill.

A couple of days went by, and as Ezra and I were going south of town to his neighbor's farm where he had a couple of mares to sell, we came upon several buggies. We ended up following one of them. The horse was exceptionally black and working nicely. As the horse started slowing down, I saw him pulling into a farmhouse driveway. I told Ezra that there was the horse I needed, right there, if he is gentle and broke pretty well. Ezra told me that he knew that horse and also knew the lady driving the buggy. That was her favorite horse. He told me that she is kind of afraid of horses, but likes this one. It's the horse she goes to town with. He knew for a fact that the horse was not for sale.

We pulled in behind the buggy and I got out and introduced myself. Ezra started to talk to his friend. I asked the man if the horse was for sale, and he told me no, that the horse was his wife's favorite horse and he was not for sale. At that time, you could buy a nice buggy horse for $400–$500. In looking at this horse, I needed to try to buy him. I reached in my pocket and pulled out ten $100 bills: $1,000! I told him to take the $1,000 in to talk to his wife and see if she might sell the horse. He left and went into his house to talk to his wife.

After he was out of earshot, Ezra looked at me and said, "you are being tricky now." I never answered Ezra, just looked ahead. In a few minutes, the man came out of the house. As the man walked up to me, I noticed he did not have the money in his hand. He told me his wife decided to sell the horse! That particular day, we had been driving my pick-up and horse trailer. I told Ezra, let's load the horse in the trailer and leave now, thinking if I came back the next day, they might change their minds! I wanted to get the horse to my own barn area as soon as possible.

Ezra and I turned around and took the horse back to the holding barns I had rented to keep my recently purchased horses. It was getting late and I had something I had to do, so I told Ezra we would start early the next day and go to the south of town as we had planned earlier.

The next day, as we were on our way to the farm where there was supposed to be 2 mares for sale, we had to pass the place where I had just bought the black buggy horse. As we got closer to the house, I saw the Amish woman standing in the yard. As we passed, in her Amish attire with bonnet and dress, she looked straight up at our truck and threw up her hand. She wasn't waving, she had her middle finger sticking up at us! I looked back in the mirror. She was still looking at us with her middle finger in the air!

As we went on, Ezra said we wouldn't want to go back to that house because that woman is pissed off. I told him that we would have to be careful traveling around next time because she may have a stone in her hand! Ezra said that he thought she was just as mad at her husband because he sold the horse whether she liked it or not!

THE BLACK HORSE

I am reminded of the story of the black horse that I purchased from the Amish farmer for the Pontiac dealer, Bill, from Fort Worth, Texas.

One evening, Bill and his girlfriend decided to take his horse and buckboard out for a ride by a dirt tank on his ranch. A dam ran across this tank and they decided to use the top of the dam as a roadway. A dirt tank on a ranch is man-made. It is land that has been dug out with a dam on one side. When it rains the run-off will fill up the tank with water for cattle and other animals to drink out of throughout the year. They can be about 200 feet across or whatever the rancher decides.

As they drove across the top of the dam, Bill got a little too close to the edge of the road and the back wheel of the buckboard dropped off the edge. The buckboard was going over, so Bill and his girlfriend jumped off before it and the horse slid down the dam's wall and into the water below.

They watched as the horse and buckboard floated out a little ways and disappeared under the water. They could see air bubbles coming up where the horse went under and thought he had drowned. The girlfriend was screaming and yelling. After a few minutes, they looked across the tank and saw the horse walking out of the water, buckboard and all! The horse had apparently walked on the bottom of the tank with his head up and managed to reach the shore on the other side. It ended up being a happy ending. It was pretty unbelievable but true!

This was the true story of a horse who went from an Amish buggy horse to doing a television commercial, to walking under water and surviving! Amazing!

CHAPTER 28

OUR NEXT ADVENTURE

We didn't know how it snuck up on us, but Jan and I were getting older. We were now in our fifties and slowing down. Where did the time go? By now, our beloved horse White Feather had passed away. He was 30 years old. We buried him on our ranch in Weatherford, Texas. This was his home and he was going to stay there. We chose his private paddock located next to our front lawn. It was his favorite spot and he deserved nothing less. That was one of the saddest days of our lives. He was gone, but we were so very glad to have had that wonderful horse in our lives!

His memory and legacy will continue to endure for a long time. White Feather was featured in the biggest horse shows and rodeos in countries such as Canada, Mexico, Puerto Rico and, of course, the United States! It was partly because of this beautiful horse that our act became a popular specialty act with the promoters.

We found ourselves at a point in our lives where we had to make a decision. Our daughters had moved out and were on to their own careers. Our oldest daughter Toni, went on to be a competitor in the cutting horse world. She became a dental hygienist. She's continued the family's love of horses by still being involved with them.

Sonna, our youngest daughter's career took her to France to perform the principal role of Annie Oakley in the Disneyland Paris re-creation of Buffalo Bill's Wild West Show. This gave her the opportunity to show not only her riding, but her trick roping skills. As I write this, she has performed over 8,000 live shows for the last 27 years and is still going strong!

There is a little irony to all this. I was born in Darke County, Ohio. This is the birthplace and the resting place of Little Miss Sure Shot, Annie Oakley!

Sonna in Paris, France
Photo courtesy of Jacques Llantia

Sonna performing as Annie Oakley in Paris, France
Photo courtesy of Jacques Llantia

Our expertise was training horses. We had been around them all of our life. We had to think about what profession involving horses, would utilize our knowledge, skills and experience we had gained throughout the years! We decided on the horse racing industry, because as race horse trainers, it did not require us to be as athletic as we were when we were performing.

We both obtained our trainers' licenses for the race track. In no time at all, the pastures on our ranch were filled with thoroughbred mares and foals rather than the performing horses we had in the past.

In the beginning, we needed clients to get us started, but later, decided to go on our own. We found great fulfillment together in taking the race horse through all of the steps; from being bred and born, to training them all the way to the winner's circle!

It was a fulfilling career for us for more than 15 years.

TEXAS COUNTRY DOLL

HOOSIER PARK RACING • CASINO

OWNER: JIM WARVELL
UP: JULIO FELIX
AUGUST 27, 2009
2ND CHAPOLTE

PURSE $27,500
TRAINER: JIM WARVELL
ASSISTANT TRAINER: MARY LEBENS
3RD BELL GOT EVEN

ALLOWANCE 5½ FURLONGS 1:02.3

JACK WARVELL, SHERRY TERHAAR, SONNA WARVELL, ED TERHAAR, JAN WARVELL, NICK TERHAAR, JOE WARVELL, MARY LEBENS, JULIO FELIX AND JIM WARVELL

Jim and Jan at the racetrack

Jim Warvell with his handmade cotton rope (c. 2000s)

THE BEGINNING OF THE END

Unfortunately, it was during this time that we received some horrible news. Jan was diagnosed with Alzheimer's Disease. She could hide her memory loss from her friends, at first, but not from me. There were times the disease reared its ugly head and created problems for both of us.

Once, I was at the race track in Indiana for four weeks, leaving Jan at home with the mares. I hated to leave, but when I left her, she seemed pretty good. We had some mares on the ranch that she had to monitor while I was gone. We had a friend who lived near us and he would check in on her 3 or 4 times a day. When I called him to see how things were going, he said they were good.

One of the things Jan did while I was gone, was to write out the checks for our credit cards. I suddenly received word that our cards had not been paid. I called Jan and asked if she had paid the last month's credit card bill. She said she had. She gave me the date and amount she had paid. I then had the bill sent to me to see if Jan's figures were correct. When the bill was checked against the amount she told me, there was no problem. Yet, something was wrong! There was a problem somewhere!

I called Jan back and said there was an issue with the bill, but I would be home in another week or 10 days and we would try to find the problem when I returned. During the time I was away, a couple of my credit cards were declined. That really worried me, as it would anyone!

When my trip was over, and I arrived home, and after the horses were taken care of, I told Jan we needed to see her records on the payments for our credit cards. Jan pulled out her folder (where she kept the records). I looked at the monthly payments. Her records looked great! All the numbers in her book matched the numbers on the bills. Her items were very precise and I was pleased. "You did a great job, Jan," I told her.

She smiled but I was baffled by the problems we were having with the bills. As I sat there, I rechecked everything and then I saw there was one section in the folder that had a lot more papers in it than the others. Out of curiosity, I opened the section and discovered it was full of checks that Jan had made out for our credit card payments but had never mailed!

"Jan," I asked, "What are these checks doing in here?"

She looked at the papers and then said, "After I make out the checks, I put them in there for our records."

I was stunned! After sorting the checks, I discovered there were three months of checks that had been made out but had never been sent to our creditors!

"What is the trouble?" she asked, with a confused and innocent look on her face. To her, she had done nothing wrong.

It was at that moment I realized that her Alzheimer's was raising its ugly head! Jan was a very intelligent girl in school making the honor roll every year in high school. She was very interested in Civil War history and could tell you all the dates of the major Civil War events.

She even liked to tell tongue twister jokes and she had one that was her all-time favorite! I heard it many times over our 50 years of marriage. She could repeat it, but I never could and neither could many of our friends. (I refuse to even put it down on paper!)

Jan always had a remarkable memory! It was, however, fading fast and always going to the past. I knew now that I could never leave her alone without supervision. I had a lot of horses to take to the race track come next spring and I could not leave her at our ranch by herself. There was only one thing left to do.

I decided to buy a new Airstream so we could be together all of the time. When spring came, we loaded up and headed to the racetracks. She was very happy to be on the road again, but it did not last long. Things were much different from the last time we had been on the road!

While working at the racetrack, I would get up every morning at 4:30 AM to start my busy day. That, in itself, was a major change for both of us. All of our married life we worked shows at night and ate our last meal between 11 and midnight! When we got to bed it was usually around 1 AM. We would sleep until 8:30 or 9 the next morning. Only then would we start our day on the rodeo and show circuit. We did this for over 35 years!

Needless to say, we got into the habit of eating and going to sleep late. We also slept late in the morning. All this went out the window as we left the show circuit and went on the race circuit!

ADJUSTING TO A NEW LIFE

For the first week or so Jan and I would leave the Airstream and head for the track. In most race tracks, there is a 'track kitchen' where you can get coffee and order from their menu. Jan knew this and she would head for the kitchen where she would sit, drink coffee and smoke her cigarettes while telling stories of the Wild West. Everybody liked her! She could fool people with her outgoing personality and ability to spin a tale! Nobody suspected she had dementia or a mental health disorder. After an hour or so I would go to the kitchen and get her. We would then go to our barn where we had our horses stabled. That was our normal routine.

In the last years, I hired a young woman named Mary to help me on the race track. She was eager and quick to learn about race horses. She became very professional and soon obtained an assistant trainer's license. I could be away from the track and the stables and know my horses were in good hands and being well taken care of. Mary was basically doing the work that Jan normally did but was unable to do.

To alleviate the problem, I told Jan the job of racing horses was a lot of work and it was time for her to rest more. That did not go well with Jan as she was used to working all the time.

We had to compromise, so we agreed she would help take care of the "Shed Row" which, in the horse race business, is the area in front of the stable where your horse is located.

There would be stables on each side of the row and this area has to be cleaned, raked and look spotless every day. She would also do some of the work when it came to taking care of the horses, under supervision, of course.

We tried but it did not go so well!

Jan fell into her old routine as she tried to do everything. She would water the horses in the stalls by bringing them full buckets of water. Then, later in the day, she would walk past the stalls and when I checked the buckets they would be empty. She had forgotten to fill them and she had just walked past them! She had forgotten to finish her work.

She would rake the Shed Row area and do a good job of it. Unfortunately, she would forget to put the rake in its proper place and the next time we needed the rake it was like looking for Easter eggs! You had to check everywhere and, if you were lucky, you might find the rake. It could be found anywhere outside the barn and maybe even in somebody else's area. No matter when or where she used it, the rake was never put back. She would start talking to someone and either forget about the rake or take it with her. This was not like her! She used to be so precise in all she did. Details were important to her but not anymore.

Once I watched her go into a horse stall and when she was done she exited the stall and forgot to shut the gate behind her. This could have been disastrous! It was a good thing I was there to shut the door behind her and keep the horse from escaping.

It soon became a full-time job following her around. Things were just not working the way I hoped they would. She did not get up at 4:30 AM for one thing. A couple of times I left her in the Airstream. We were parked about 3½ miles from the track. The trailer park was run by a very nice couple and I would stop and tell them I was going to leave Jan that morning and would return around 10 AM.

They had my phone number and could call if a problem came up. They never called but said Jan would come in their little store three or four times during the morning hours. She would buy cigarettes from them each time she came in the store. That meant she was buying a lot of cigarettes! When I asked her about buying all those cigarettes she would tell me it was because she ran out of them.

It soon became apparent there was more to the story and I soon found out what it was! As I went through the Airstream I was finding packs of cigarettes all over the trailer. Some were half used and some had only one or two missing. I think she would smoke one or two out of a pack then put the pack down and forget where she put them. I did not know what to do!

About this time a woman named Karen, who had worked for us when we had the White Horse Troupe came to the race track to visit with Jan and I. Karen and I talked about Jan's Alzheimer's disease. I told her I was getting worried about leaving her alone. Karen, who lived 25 miles from the track said she could come and be with Jan when I was at work. It sounded like a great idea. She would come over to the Airstream at 4:30 AM every morning. She would stay until I came home from work. After awhile I decided it would be easier on everyone if I rented a nice room for Karen and a room for us at a nearby hotel. Karen was true to her word and never missed a morning. She would visit with Jan for hours and talk about the ol' days during the White Horse Troupe years. How could you have a better friend than that?

A NEW PLAN FOR JAN

It was several years later, I told Sonna how I had my hands full with Jan and her disease. The racing season was just about over and Sonna said she would fly home during the last week of the season and help me get the horses and the trailer back to our ranch in Texas. Jan and I went to the local airport to pick her up.

Jan was excited to see her and hear all about the Wild West Show. Jan was a Leo and since they say Leos are "hams" and make good entertainers it suited her to a 'T.' She loved being in a business that allowed her to ride horses in the rodeo and do the shows we did. She also loved hearing about those in the business, especially when it was a family member.

We had two pickup trucks to go with us when we headed to Texas. One pulled the Airstream and the other pulled the horse trailer. Sonna drove the truck with the Airstream and Jan rode with her. I drove the other truck with the horses.

Jan was very happy to be back on the road again. She loved being with the horses and the family. It was a thousand-mile trip so Jan and Sonna had a lot of time to visit and talk. Apparently, they also made some future plans.

When we arrived at the ranch, I heard all about the new plan. Jan was going to fly back to France with Sonna who said it could be arranged so the two of them would always be together. When it came time to work, due to Sonna's job responsibilities at Disney, she arranged to have Jan taken care of by the Moody Family who are life-long friends of the Warvell Family. Carlton Moody, an internationally known musician from an entertainment family as well, performed with Sonna in the Wild West Show at Disney.

Jan returned with Sonna and seemed to enjoy Paris. She loved the slower pace of life, the beautiful gardens, walking to the bakery with Sonna or just spending time with new friends at a café. She took Sparky, her little dog, with her everywhere.

Sonna would come home from work and share all the wonderful stories from the evening performances. Through their conversations, they would share their memories of show business with all its glamour and excitement.

Unfortunately, as time went on the disease got worse. Jan's memory was such that Sonna now had to keep a constant eye on her. She wanted to go to the show with Sonna, but we knew that wasn't possible. After one night with the Moodys however, Jan was a happy camper! She discovered there were western movies to watch and as long as a movie involved horses, she was going to watch it. Her favorite of course, were John Wayne movies which she could watch in English whenever she wanted.

While with the Moodys, Jan would also help Sonna's friend Margie do the dishes. This was something Jan always liked to do. It was such a routine that when Sonna would leave for work Jan would tell her, "I have to go and help do the dishes." Sonna would return from work eight hours later. Her mother would always tell her about the evening, with special emphasis on the dishes!

I would talk to Jan and Sonna about every other night and sometimes every day. Jan was in France and she was very happy. She would tell me about the Wild West Show and how good Sonna was in the show. I was happy that she was happy.

During her performances as Annie Oakley, Sonna would have somebody from the audience come into the arena to participate in a special shooting contest involving a big target with a bullseye. The audience member would try to hit the target and the one who hit the bullseye would win the contest and the gold medal. It was here the magic of Disney would make its appearance.

One night, a special spectator was chosen. It was Jan! The entire event was planned, but Jan did not know about it. When they took her into the arena Jan was all smiles. For her stunt, Jan was going to have a shootout with Annie Oakley (her daughter!).

Annie Oakley never missed a shot during the act but Jan did not care. Jan took the job seriously and was determined to win. Jan shot the Winchester rifle and *BOOM* right into the bullseye! She had won the contest! With great fanfare Jan received the ribbon with the gold medal attached to it. She loved the applause and the spotlight. She did not want to leave the arena! She was so ecstatic that she had 'outshot' Annie Oakley that it was hard to get her to take the ribbon off her neck!

The next day I talked to her on the phone. Her 'victory' was all she could talk about. I knew how wonderful it was for her to have such a 'victory.' She was once again back in an arena and getting applause from hundreds of fans.

She kept the Disney medallion close by her for a long time. When I would talk to her in the weeks ahead, Jan would always put the medallion by the phone and I would once again listen to the story of how she had outshot Annie Oakley in front of a huge crowd.

It is amazing how some things leave the mind and other things stick to it. For Jan, it was a matter of just trying to survive and remember what she could. Anyone who has had to deal with this horrible disease knows how tough it can be on the person who has it. They also know how tough it is on those who are taking care of an Alzheimer's patient.

REUNION

It was that time of year. The racing season was over so Jan, Sonna and Margie were on their way to Texas. I was going to be home for quite a while and that meant I could look after Jan.

When Jan walked into our ranch house, she looked around and said she would have supper ready in a short time. This was going to be interesting because she had not cooked in probably three years. We had a gas stove and in the past when she was finished using the stove she would leave the burner on with a pan on top of it. After that the kitchen was off limits to her unless she had someone with her. We talked her out of fixing supper but she was not happy about it. It was apparent that taking care of her was going to be a very big job for me.

On about the third day of the visit, Sonna and Margie took me outside so we could talk in private. We left Jan in the house, alone. After a few minutes, Sonna went back into the house. She returned and motioned for Margie and me to come with her. She led us into the bathroom.

On top of the bathroom sink was a roll of toilet paper laying on its side. Across the roll was a cigarette burn. It seemed that Jan had laid a lit cigarette on top of the toilet paper as it had a burn mark all the way across it. We were lucky the paper never caught on fire! It was scary! We were not out of the house for more than five minutes and during that time Jan had almost burnt the house down!

The next day, we were all sitting in the living room and Jan was roaming around the house seeming to enjoy herself. She was back in familiar surroundings and that was a good thing.

Jan was a big coffee drinker. It did not make any difference what kind of coffee it was as long as it was coffee! She could drink 'cowboy coffee,' made over an open flame with water from a nearby stream, or 'truck stop' coffee made with, well, it was coffee! At home Jan would make instant coffee. Unfortunately, when her memory loss kicked in things became scary. We were worried that she would make her coffee but would forget to take the pan off the stove.

To alleviate this problem, I bought her an electric tea pot so she could heat her water without using the stove. The pot would turn off automatically when the water reached a certain temperature so Jan did not have to worry about it. This idea only worked one or two times.

The bottom of the tea pot was plastic. This was where the wires were located as we were soon to learn.

We were all sitting in the living room when we started to smell a strange odor. Then we saw smoke. We got up to find Jan in the kitchen. She had put the electric teapot on the open flame of the stove and the bottom unit of the teapot (the plastic part!) had melted and started to burn! We had a stainless-steel sink and it soon contained a melting teapot and a lot of water as we tried to solve a sticky situation. Thankfully, we had averted another disaster!

Before long, it was time for Sonna and Margie to go back to France. Both of them came to me and said there was more 24 hour-a-day help in France to care for Jan than there was in Texas. I knew they were right. There was certainly more care in Paris than I could provide.

We had tried to find a woman companion for Jan in Texas. It was very difficult and all I got was negative advice. They said it was very difficult to find competent people who could take care of an Alzheimer's patient.

We knew Jan liked France and wanted to go back with Sonna. After some discussion it was decided Jan would go back with our daughter and stay there until other arrangements could be made. We said our goodbyes and soon Jan, Sonna and Margie were headed back to France.

I hated to see them go but knew it was the best thing for Jan since Sonna had already worked out arrangements for the care of her mother.

RECOGNITION

It seemed like no time at all after they left, I received a letter announcing that our entire family would be inducted into the Texas Cowboy Hall of Fame! This was a very high honor that has been bestowed upon some amazing people, including famous athletes, rodeo champions and entertainers. Now the Warvell Family was going to be inducted at the ceremony taking place in the middle of January. This was about two months away!

To make the honor even greater, this was the first time they were inducting an entire family into their prestigious group. Usually, the Hall of Fame just inducted individuals but here we were, the entire family, getting the chance to be recognized for what we had accomplished.

When word got out, we had friends from all over the country calling me and making plans to attend the induction ceremony. People from California, Nebraska, Ohio, Indiana, Texas and Oklahoma were going to be there. In addition, several people from France were also coming to the ceremony. It was going to be a big reunion in the Cowtown of Fort Worth, Texas!

Tommy Lee Jones, Jan, and Jim at the
2010 Texas Cowboy Hall of Fame Induction, Fort Worth, Texas
Photo courtesy of Marsha and Steven Brown

The Hall of Fame is located just 20 miles east of where we live. We would stay at our ranch instead of a hotel. Sonna got two weeks off from work. She and Jan flew home with some of the people who wanted to attend the event. We had people staying at our house and at a local motel.

Jan was full of herself and rightly so. She covered her illness well, hiding it from a lot of people. She was very professional most of the time. Often, after speaking to one of our friends or guests she would come over to me and ask, "Who was that person?"

Jim and Jan at the 2010 Texas Cowboy Hall of Fame Induction, Fort Worth, Texas. Photo courtesy Of Marsha and Steven Brown

Our house became a beehive of activity. We had newspaper and magazine people doing all sorts of interviews. Some of the western magazines wrote stories and took pictures that were to be used at a later date. It was fun but also draining.

The Hall of Fame has a huge banquet room and it would be filled with 500-600 people. This was where we would all sit around and enjoy a delicious meal before the ceremony started.

As in years past, all the inductees were guests at the big hotel across the street from the Texas Cowboy Hall of Fame. It was the place where everybody stayed the night of the ceremony and often before the ceremony. The inductees had special rooms where we would prepare for the ceremony before heading across the street to the main event.

One of the girls who was helping Jan get ready came to me and said I needed to go and see Jan. They said she was very nervous and upset. When I got to her, Jan was sitting in a chair about to cry.

I went to her and we sat down on a couch to discuss the issue. She was shaking and sobbing. She said she did not know what was happening and did not know what to do. She wanted to go home and be around things that were familiar to her.

I put my arms around her and told her everything would be fine. I would be right by her side the whole time. She finally said, "Okay, but don't leave me!" In another 10 minutes, we were walking across the street to the ceremony. She was comfortable greeting people as we went to our table.

THE CEREMONY

That night there were four inductees into the Hall of Fame. A small stage was in front of the room. As the inductees were introduced they would go to the stage, receive their award and make an acceptance speech.

When we were introduced, all of us went to the stage, Jan, our daughters Toni and Sonna, and I. The person in charge of the Texas Cowboy Hall of Fame told the audience of our family's achievements and complimented us. She then introduced us on an individual basis. Jan stood with me as I acknowledged the honor and thanked them. Our two girls, also inductees, each spoke and thanked the many people who had been a part of our lives. Jan stood and smiled the whole time.

After the ceremony was over, we sat in our special inductee chairs as photographers snapped picture after picture. We had Tommy Lee Jones on one side and the Baseball Hall of Fame pitcher and cattle breeder

Nolan Ryan on the other side. Needless to say, we were in excellent company!

The Texas Cowboy Hall of Fame had booths for each of the inductees. Inside were articles, memorabilia and pictures of the inductee showing what they did to receive the honor. We stood as a family while picture after picture was taken. Then Jan and I stood together for more pictures.

Hundreds of flashes went off and it seemed to take forever. Jan withstood the onslaught and took it like the trooper she was. She smiled and nodded. She was the ultimate entertainer she always had been. I was very proud of her!

This scene went on for over two hours. It finally came to an end and the festivities were over. We headed back to our ranch in Weatherford, Texas. Jan and I were in the back seat. She still had on the Hall of Fame gold medallion around her neck.

"I got one of these when I was in France and I beat Annie Oakley in a shootout," she told me with pride. I had my arm around her. All I could do was smile.

"I had fun tonight," she added. "Do we have another performance tomorrow night?"

"No," I gently told her.

It was then I realized that she might never understand that her accomplishments would go down in Texas cowboy history. All she had done as an entertainer would be remembered by millions but might not be remembered by the one person who had earned all the awards.

When we got home, there were still a lot of people in the house. They would leave the next day. For us it had been a very long day and I knew Jan was getting tired. Most of our guests were in the kitchen going over the events of the night. I went into the living room and sat down on the couch.

In a minute Jan came in and snuggled up next to me.

"Are you tired?" I asked her.

"Yea, a little bit," she replied.

I put my arm around her. Her head was turned and on my chest. As I pressed her to me I was surprised to feel her ribs. Jan was 5′ 9″ and had always been a very strong woman. You had to be strong to do some of the things she did when we were on the rodeo circuit. I suddenly realized she had dropped a lot of weight and lost a lot of muscle.

"What are you going to do with me, Daddy?" she asked sadly.

I choked up. I could feel the tears run down my cheeks.

"Don't worry," I said as I tried to hide my emotions, "We have always worked out our problems and we will work out this one, too."

Even though I tried to be upbeat, I knew the facts about Alzheimer's disease. There was really no treatment that had a success rate. Her prognosis was not good and this was always on my mind. Every time I thought about it I got choked up. There was nothing I nor anyone else could do for her.

The next day everyone left our home for their own home. A few days later Jan, Sonna and our European friends returned to France. The ranch was soon empty except for me and my thoughts. My health was not that good. Several years ago, I had received a 5-way heart bypass. I was now limited as to what I could do and that severely affected my ability to train horses the way I wanted. I also got tired very easy.

Jan and Sonna would fly to Texas every three months or so. They would stay for 8-10 days before Sonna would have to return to work. When they visited I could see Jan's memory fading more and more. Her health seemed good but her recollections were few and far between. She loved to stay active and she loved to walk but someone had to be with her all the time. In France, Jan was still staying with the Moodys while Sonna worked. Things worked out great for Sonna, Jan and Sparky.

Around Thanksgiving, Jan and Sonna came home for another visit. Jan was a lot different on this visit. Her memory was worse.

She would go into the kitchen and look around before asking, "What happened to our old refrigerator?"

"That is the same refrigerator we have always had," I answered.

She would stare at it and then walk away. I would watch as she would go in our bedroom and rummage through the dresser drawers on a continual basis.

"What are you looking for?" I asked.

She would never reply. Later, she would come into the living room and stare at me.

"Somebody is stealing my stuff," she announced.

"No, I don't think so," I would tell her.

Whenever we disputed her she would get mad. That was not the real Jan but it was the one we now had.

I could see that Sonna and the caregivers had more problems than ever. Not only did they have to deal with the disease but also with her new attitude.

On this visit Jan did not want to stay in Texas. She wanted to go back to France. When we got to the airport, Jan suddenly turned to me and sighed.

"I am not going back to France unless you go with me," she said flatly.

Then she turned to Sonna and said the same thing.

"I am not going back unless he goes with us."

For international flights, we had to be at the airport at least two hours before the departure time. Here we were, standing outside of the ticket area with a new dilemma on our hands. My pickup truck was in the unloading area and we were taking the luggage off the back portion of the truck. I could not stay parked there forever so we had to solve the problem quickly. Jan was adamant! She was not moving unless I told her I would go with her. Neither Sonna nor I could convince her otherwise.

"I will go with you but I have to pack my bags," I explained to Jan. "I can't go without clothes and I will have to go back to the house to pack."

"Okay," she replied, "Then I will go with you to the house and then come back here."

My idea did not work as I had hoped!

Sonna and I finally convinced her she had to go through the line and get ready for the flight. While she did that, we told her I would return home, pack and then meet her on the plane. Jan thought it over and finally realized it was the thing to do. I stood there watching her and Sonna walk towards the entry door. Jan was waving at me and I was waving at her until the two of them disappeared into the crowded airport. I was feeling very disappointed not only in what I had told Jan but at the whole situation. I had a very odd feeling about this separation and their leaving for France.

The plane took off two hours later. I had driven my truck to the parking garage and was watching as the big plane flew off into the sky. The truck was parked in a good vantage point and I refused to leave until I saw them leave the Dallas-Fort Worth Airport.

Did Jan get on the plane or had she made a fuss and refused to board? I worked my way through a lot of scenarios but just before they boarded I got a phone call from Sonna who told me everything was going great! Needless to say, we were both relieved. It turned out they went through the lines with no problem. They sat down in the airline lounge waiting area. Jan discovered the smoking section and bummed a cigarette off of a man sitting there and struck up a conversation while they waited. Sonna said when it came time to board the aircraft Jan's mind was in another place and she had forgotten about waiting for me.

They called me when they arrived in Paris. The two of them were in bed eating a pizza and watching a John Wayne movie. Sparky was at the foot of the bed.

Jan was happy again and it made me feel better.

CHAPTER 29

THE END OF A LEGEND

We fell into a routine of talking every other day. We talked before Christmas and everything seemed to be great! On Christmas Day, Sonna phoned me. She said Jan had fallen and broken her hip. She was taken to the hospital for the operation. The surgery was a success and Jan was now resting and recuperating.

Unfortunately, there was nothing I could do because Texas was in the middle of a snow and ice storm. Everything, was shut down and that included the airports. There were no flights in or out of the Dallas-Fort Worth Airport.

Sonna said the doctors were satisfied with the operation and they were very optimistic about her recovery. We agreed I could do nothing but wait until the airport opened. The doctors were happy with her recovery and there did not seem to be anything to worry about.

Early the next morning, I got a phone call from Sonna. Sometime during the night Jan had suffered a severe stroke. The doctors thought she might be bedridden or confined to a wheel chair. They did not know the severity of the stroke or the brain damage that had occurred.

Within a day of that call my beloved Jan had passed away. I was in total shock!

Jan died at age 77 on January 1st, 2011. I left for Paris immediately and met Sonna and Margie at the airport. The two of them had been at the hospital from the time of the stroke until Jan had passed away. They looked tired and, like me, in total shock. It was late, we were all exhausted, so I went to Sonna's to rest. We would go to the hospital in the morning.

THE LAST RIDE TOGETHER

Jan and I always had a different view when it came to funerals. She would say, "Don't have a funeral for me. I don't want people looking at me in a casket." Those were her wishes and we, as a family agreed to abide by them.

As for me, I could never understand why people liked to look at other people in a casket and say how nice they looked. I never thought anybody looked good if they were dead. I would rather remember that person when they were alive and not have my last view of them when they were dead and in a casket.

I had reservations about going to the hospital and seeing Jan in that state but I did. She was lying there and I reached down and put a hand around her arm near her wrist. She always had fine features and I knew I was holding a small, delicate arm which was always full of life. I was not ready for the cold touch she offered me. There was no more energy or life in her and I had to leave the room.

Per her wishes, Jan was cremated. We spent the next few days getting the paperwork we needed to get her ashes from France to Texas. These were very sad days in my life.

There were people in the Disney Wild West Show who wanted a remembrance party so they could remember Jan. They all knew her and she knew them. Two nights after her death, there was quite a gathering of cast and crew at our friend Marilyn's house. We all had stories to tell about Jan.

Among the guests were 5 or 6 Native Americans. They felt compelled to chant their native beliefs so Jan could go to the Happy Hunting Grounds. They were very serious and we not only watched them with sincerity but we also acknowledged their beliefs and thanked them for their ceremony. The Native Americans were amazing and I thank them for their support.

It was very moving to see the respect Disney's Wild West Show and their cast, including stage hands, cowboys, Indians and management had for Jan. She would have been proud and thankful. I know I was.

It took more than a month before we got the permission and all the legal papers to take her ashes home. Jan never wanted a funeral for the masses. She only wanted a funeral that was for the family. I told Toni and Sonna, our daughters, when we were going to pay our respects to Jan.

I did not, however, tell them what I had in mind. I just said to wear your Wranglers and gave them the time we needed to get together on the ranch in Texas. We would meet at the outdoor training facility where we worked and practiced all of our skills when it came to riding horses.

Jan always had Mason jars in the house. She would buy them by the case. I found a new box of them. They were the pint-sized jars, just right for what I had in mind. I divided Jan's ashes into three jars and waited. When the girls arrived, I saddled up my horse and asked them to walk with me out to the practice arena. I led my horse and carried the three jars with me.

When we got to the spot I had selected, I gave each girl a jar of ashes.

"We are going to take turns and scatter her ashes. We will ride out and scatter them anywhere on the ranch that has a special meaning to each of us."

They agreed, and when we were ready, I went first. I got on my horse and headed for the track where she and I had ridden so many times that we seemed to know the grains of dirt on a first name basis. As I rode the track, I spread her ashes in the different places where Jan and I had shared some sort of adventure or where we had experienced something personal. One of those places was a turn in the track where we had a horse that would always run through and off the track.

We had riders who rode this particular horse but when they got to this turn the horse always ran off the track. When Jan saw this, she decided to ride the horse. Sure enough, when the horse got to the turn it ran off the track. Jan stayed with it and she pulled hard to the left while the horse was running to the right. The result was a horse running about 200 feet sideways!

Jan refused to give up. She stayed on that horse and kept pulling it to the left even though the horse still wanted to go right. There was an electric pole in the area and Jan was heading right dead center toward it! I saw all this while it was happening but there was nothing I could do!

They kept heading toward the pole and Jan just barely missed the guide wire that ran from the ground to the pole. They missed the guide wire but the horse hit the pole around its shoulder and neck area. The horse was stunned and came to an abrupt halt.

Jan was fine but the horse was a little dazed. After a few minutes she rode the horse back to the track and began to gallop once more around the circle. When they came to the turn the horse went around the turn perfectly. Jan wanted to be sure so she rode a couple more laps. Each time they came to 'the turn' the horse took it perfectly.

The next day the riders arrived. We asked for volunteers to ride the horse but none of them did. Jan, however, did volunteer. She got on the horse and rode that horse around the track with no problems whatsoever. The riders were shocked but from that moment on the horse did not give any rider trouble when it took 'the turn'!

That was how Jan was. If there was a problem with a horse she would stay with it until the problem was solved.

She also practiced Roman Riding on the track. I once asked Jan why she liked to stand up on two horses and what kind of enjoyment it gave her.

"It is the greatest feeling in the world," she happily explained. "You have the freedom of running two horses across a field and letting the wind blow in your face while your hair is blowing in the wind."

I could understand her happiness and I knew this type of riding had always been her first love.

There could be no better place than this track for her final resting place. I scattered some ashes right there on the spot of the curve. When I was done, I rode back and got off my horse.

"This jar," I told them as I pointed to the jar that had just held Jan's ashes, "Will never be used again."

With that I threw the jar up against a concrete structure and watched as it broke into a thousand pieces.

It was now time for our girls to pay their respects to their mother.

Toni got on the horse and was given her jar of ashes. She rode to the arena area where she and Jan had practiced Roman Riding on many occasions. Some of the ashes were spread there. She then went to the round pen where we had trained so many wild horses to be show horses or just riding horses. More of the ashes were scattered there because she and her mother had a special spot in that area. Toni then rode back to Sonna and me.

Toni got off the horse and smashed her jar against the concrete structure.

It was now Sonna's turn. She got on the horse and went across the field to a piece of land we called 'the bottom.' It was very beautiful with a stream running through it. There was also a pecan grove in the area. Jan and Sonna used to ride down and spend hours talking and watching the water run over a little dam I had built in the creek.

When she disappeared over the hill I knew exactly where she was going and why. This was their spot, where mother and daughter spent much of their free time.

After she had said her goodbyes in the bottom, Sonna returned and rode straight to the training track. When she hit the track, she let the horse run very fast and I could see her hair blowing in the wind as she scattered the few ashes she had left. There was a huge smile on her face.

She returned to us, got off the horse and threw her jar against the concrete structure. All three jars would never be used for anything again.

We then had a silent moment in honor of the woman we all loved.

That was our memorial to a wife, a beloved mother and our best friend.

Goodbye, Jan.

We love you.

A SPECIAL THANK YOU

I would like to acknowledge and thank Bill Stevens,
for without his inspiration and encouragement,
this book would not have been written.

COWBOY TERMINOLOGY

So that you can better understand the terms and special language used by cowboys, here is a list of the ones used in this book.

BALLYHOO: When a promoter asks performers to be in costume before the show. He will have them stand in front of the grandstand or box office in order to arouse interest and get the public to come to the show.

BANDANA: A kerchief used for a variety of purposes. They can be used to cover the mouth and nose to keep out dirt and dust. They are often put around the neck for protection and are also used for wiping sweat. The bright, highly decorative bandanas are used as a fashion statement during rodeo events.

BARREL RACER: A cowgirl who competes in the rodeo event called *barrel racing.*

BARREL RACING: A rodeo event for cowgirls. They race their horse in a clover-leaf pattern around three barrels. This is a timed event and the rider with the fastest time is the winner.

BIT: The *bit* is a type of horse tack usually made of metal. It is placed in the mouth of a horse and assists a rider in communicating with the animal.

BLACKSMITH: The individual who takes care of the metal items on a farm or in the city. He will put the horseshoes on the horses. Other names for this job include *farrier,* and if you are an old racing fan, they are called *platers.*

BOZAL: See *Hackamore.*

BREAK A LEG: A term used by show people from the world of the circus and stage. While it may sound like an evil omen, it is actually a way to wish someone good luck.

BRONC: A wild, unbroken horse. Bronc riding is a rodeo event where a cowboy rides a bronc for 8 seconds to gain points and, hopefully, win the event.

BRONC BUSTER: A cowboy that makes the first two or three rides on a wild horse (bronc).

BUCKBOARD: An open horse-drawn carriage with four wheels and seating that is attached to a plank stretching between the front and rear axles.

BUCK REIN: A rope from the bronc's halter, long enough for the rider to hold on to.

BULL DOGGING: Also known as *steer wrestling.* A rodeo event where the steer is put into a chute. The bulldogger/steer wrestler (on horseback) is on the left-hand side of the chute. The *hazer* (another cowboy on horseback) is on the right-hand side of the chute. When the steer is released, the hazer tries to keep the steer running in a straight line while the steer wrestler runs along the left side of the steer. When he feels the time is right, the steer wrestler will slide off his saddle, grab the steer by the horns and try to wrestle the steer to the ground. When the steer is stopped and lands on his side, the time will stop. The fastest time wins.

CALF ROPER: A cowboy who chases a calf in the hopes of roping it.

CALF ROPING: Once the calf is roped, the cowboy jumps off his horse, flips the calf onto its back, ties three of the calf's legs together and then lifts his hands in the air signaling he is through. The cowboy with the fastest time wins.

CAMP FOLLOWER: This is an old-fashioned term for the women who followed the various camps on the circuit. The modern term for this is *buckle bunny.*

CARNIE: A slang term used for carnival workers.

CHAPS: (pronounced "shaps") Leather coverings intended to protect the legs of cowboys from brush and other thorny vegetation.

CHINKS: Short leggings (chaps) that are usually made of leather. They are usually worn with fringes on them.

CHOUSED: A rider who over-works and does not give his horse a rest.

CHUNKS: Smaller, lighter, general purpose draft horse.

CIRCUIT: Rodeos move from city to city and this is called a *circuit.* Each event has its own circuit and this allows cowboys to join these shows at any time since they know where the event will be located during a given time frame.

CONTEST HORSE SHOW RIDERS: Riders who compete in games at events for ribbons, trophies or money.

COWBOY BUCKLE: A belt buckle worn by cowboys during events. Special buckles are given to champions and winners of certain events. These buckles are highly valued and become prized possessions.

CRIBBER: Also known as a *stump sucker,* this is a horse known to use the top part of his mouth to bite onto an object such as a fence, bucket, etc., and then suck in air.

CUTTING: Cowboy term for separating one animal from a herd or group.

CUTTING HORSE: A horse trained for cutting. This horse is trained to separate one, and only one, cow from the herd. This is not as easy as it sounds!

CUTTING HORSE SADDLE: A special saddle designed for events where cutting is required. Originally from the saddles used by bronc riders, these saddles are refined to fit the rider, giving him better control when the horse turns quickly to the right or left while cutting (separating) the animal from the herd.

DALLY: When an animal or object is roped, the cowboy will *dally* by wrapping the rope around the saddle horn two or three times. He will then pull (or drag) the animal or object. The rope can be released quickly in case of trouble.

FEATHER: A spot in a horse's eye caused by an infection or damage to the eye.

FEATHERS: The longer hairs on the front, back, lower leg, and the hoof areas of certain horses such as Clydesdales, Belgians, etc.

FIRST OF MAY: A slang term for a newcomer or someone who is new to the rodeo circuit or to a ranch. These individuals show up around the 1st of May (hence the name) when the spring circuit begins.

FLIPPER: A horse who is under so much pressure that it goes up and falls backwards.

FORELEG: To throw a loop that catches the front two legs.

FREEZING UP: A term applied to a horse that panics and will not move. This may lead the horse to suddenly go over backwards (see *flipper)* or go into a bucking fit.

GOOD HANDS: A compliment given to a rider who has a light touch with his horse.

GOOD LUCK: Most circus and stage performers *never* say this as it is deemed bad luck to the performer.

GUNSEL: A "wannabee" cowboy.

HACKAMORE: Also called a *Bozal.* A rope or nose band used for new horses before they are introduced to the bit that goes into their mouth.

HAND: A term for a laborer on a ranch or at a rodeo.

HAT ON A BED: A term for bad luck, not as you planned, or a bad omen.

HIND LEG HORSE: A horse trained to walk on his hind legs in a rearing position. These horses are usually used for special events and specialty acts.

HOG-BACK: The spine of the horse is higher than the withers. A ridge with a sharp summit and steeply sloping sides.

HOBBLE: A sideline rope or leg rope used in taming or training a young horse.

HOOKS: Another term for spurs.

HORSE SHOE: A U-shaped protective metal plate fitted to the rim of the bottom part of a horse's hoof.

HORSE TRADER: A person whose business it is to buy and sell horses.

JIG'S UP: An expression that signifies the real truth is exposed, i.e., *The jig's up and the monkey is dead!*

JOCKEY: A person who rides horses in a race against other horses.

KHAKI: Another name for a cowboy's saddle.

KICKER: A horse who is dangerous and will kick at the sound of any noise or the sight of strange surroundings.

LARIAT: A rope. The word comes from the Spanish. Most cowboys just say rope!

LASSO: A French word meaning rope. The word lasso is popular in Hollywood as well, but the cowboys just say rope!

LEGGINGS: Tight, long, leather pant-type protection that fits over the front of a cowboy's pants.

LID: Slang term for a hat or sombrero.

LINES: Officially known as *driving lines.* They are the technical term for reins that are used for driving a buggy, wagon, carriage or stagecoach, etc.

MONKEY MOUTH: A horse with a severe under-slung jaw.

MOUTH LIKE VELVET: A horse needing a light touch by its rider.

NIPPERS: Pinchers used to cut and trim a horse's hoof so the horseshoe will fit better.

PARROT MOUTH: A horse with a severe overbite of the upper mouth.

PICKUP MAN: A person on horseback who stays in the rodeo arena waiting to assist with the bucking stock to exit the arena and, if needed, to help a contestant (bronc rider) to dismount safely after the timed ride.

PLEASURE HORSE RIDER: An event where a horse and rider are judged to be in harmony with one another.

PLUG: Piece of compressed tobacco around 2″ wide and 3″ long and about ½″ thick. Cowboys could put these in their pocket and break off some when desired.

POLO MAN: Someone who plays polo.

POWDER IS DAMP: When a person has lost his nerve or is scared. This expression is often used when a person such as a race car driver or stuntman executes a stunt but does not have the "championship edge" while doing it.

RASP: A shoeing tool that files (rasps) the hooves of the horse so the horse shoes will fit better.

REINS: A leather strap, fastened to each end of the bit of a bridle. They are held in the cowboy's hands so that he can control the horse by pulling on one rein or the other to get the horse going in the desired direction.

"RING OF RED AND A LOAF OF BREAD": Expression used to depict having only bologna and bread to eat.

RODEO: A series of contests for cowboys. It is used to show a cowboy's skill at a variety of events. Rodeos may also feature specialty acts.

RODEO ANNOUNCER: The master of ceremony (MC) at a rodeo event. It is the MC's job to keep the crowd excited and aware of what is happening.

RODEO BAREBACK RIDING: The contest where a cowboy rides a wild horse (bronc) with a bareback rigging. The rider must stay on for 8 seconds to gain points. The highest point total wins.

RODEO BAREBACK RIGGIN': This fastens on a horse like a saddle but does not have a seat or stirrups. It only has a suitcase-type handle for the rider to hold onto.

RODEO CLOWN: A person who dresses as a clown (to please the crowd) and then tries to protect a bull rider from the bull after the bull rider has been thrown from the bull. He often uses barrels as his form of protection. The rodeo clown also entertains the audience between events.

ROMAN RIDER: A person who stands on two or more horses while doing stunts or racing them (Roman racing).

ROWEL: A small wheel with radiating points, forming the extremity of a spur.

RUNNING W: A safety rope used on runaways or spoiled "kicking horses." The rope is made into the shape of a "W" when attached to the front legs of a horse. The trainer can then impose the horse to go to a kneeling position and stay there until released by the trainer. Usually, the word "Whoa" is used while training the horse in this manner. Afterwards, the horse will obey and respond to the word "Whoa."

SADDLE BRONC RIDER: A rodeo contestant who competes on a bronc with a saddle. The rider must stay on for 8 seconds to gain points. The highest point total wins.

SADDLE HORN: A part of the saddle that sticks up near the horse's neck.

SADDLE HORSE: A horse suited for or trained for riding.

SADDLE PAD: A blanket or pad that goes under the saddle to protect the back of the horse.

SLIDER: A horse with a good stop; a horse who slides to a stop.

SPINNER: A horse who can turn so tightly that it looks like a spinning top! A compliment would be to say, "That horse could spin on a dime!"

SPURS: Worn on a boot, spurs have two parts. The "U"-shaped part attaches to the rear of the boot. The second part is a small wheel with several points that spin freely. Spurs are a communication between the rider and the horse.

STAMPEDE STRING: Leather strings attached to a hat and fed under the chin to keep a hat on in bad weather or when riding a horse.

STOCK PRODUCER: A man who provides wild stock (horses, bulls, etc.) to a rodeo.

STUMP SUCKER: See *Cribber.*

SWAY BACK: A horse having an abnormally sagging back.

TAPADEROS: These are coverings on a stirrup to protect the cowboy's feet while riding through brush and cactus.

TRICK RIDER: A person who performs stunts on a running horse. This includes drags, vaults or other acrobatic maneuvers.

TWITCH: A *twitch* is commonly used to distract the horse's attention. It is a stick with a rope loop that goes around the end of the horse's nose, twisting the nose softly and gently.

WHITE FOOTED HORSE: A horse with white hooves. These hooves were believed to be hard and brittle.

WILD WEST SHOW: Riders and performers who entertain and depict scenes from the old west. The most famous is probably Buffalo Bill's Wild West Show.

WITHERS: The highest point on a horse which is the ridge between the shoulder bones of a horse. A horse's height is measured from the withers to the ground.

WRANGLER: Someone who herds and cares for livestock of all kinds.

ABOUT THE AUTHOR

JIM WARVELL from Weatherford, Texas, grew up on a farm in Darke County, Ohio. His adventures led to meeting his wife, Jan, who was born in Indiana. Together they traveled all over the world performing specialty acts which included their two daughters.

Jim, as was Jan, is a Gold Card member of the Professional Rodeo Cowboys Association. The Warvell Family was inducted into the Texas Cowboy Hall of Fame in Fort Worth, Texas, in 2010.

INDEX

*The White Horse Troupe, Chapter 17:
Barbara Ames
Della (Townsend) Barrett
Sharon (Egan) Chartier
Karen McGeorge
Helene "Cookie" (Voelkel) O'Rourke
Roxie McIntyre
Dorothy Clark
Kathy Zwechel
Mary Jean "Skeets" Holland
Mary Hawck
Holly (from Quebec)
Doris
Pat
Cindy
Coral (Clark) Hutchens
Sandy (from 1959)

www.ingramcontent.com/pod-product-compliance
Lightning Source LLC
Chambersburg PA
CBHW060419100426
42812CB00030B/3241/J

* 9 7 8 1 6 2 6 6 0 1 4 9 9 *